Leaving and Coming Home

WITHDRAWN

REGIS COLLEGE LIBRARY
100 Wellesley Street West
Toronto, Ontario
Canada M5S 2Z5

D1713343

Leaving and Coming Home

New Wineskins for Catholic Sexual Ethics

Edited by

DAVID CLOUTIER

REGIS COLLEGE LIBRARY
100 Wellesley Street West
Toronto, Ontario
Canada M5S 2Z5

WITHDRAWN

BX
1795
S48
L43
2010

 CASCADE *Books* · Eugene, Oregon

LEAVING AND COMING HOME
New Wineskins for Catholic Sexual Ethics

Copyright © 2010 Wipf and Stock Publishers. All rights reserved. Except for brief quotations in critical publications or reviews, no part of this book may be reproduced in any manner without prior written permission from the publisher. Write: Permissions, Wipf and Stock Publishers, 199 W. 8th Ave., Suite 3, Eugene, OR 97401.

Cascade Books
An Imprint of Wipf and Stock Publishers
199 W. 8th Ave., Suite 3
Eugene, OR 97401

www. wipfandstock.com

ISBN 13: 978-1-60899-091-7

Cataloging-in-Publication data:

Leaving and coming home : new wineskins for Catholic sexual ethics / edited by David Cloutier.

xii + 270 p. ; cm. 23

ISBN 13: 978-1-60899-091-7

1. Sex—Religious aspects—Catholic Church. 2. Sexual ethics. 3. Catholic Church—Doctrines. I. Cloutier, David. II. Title.

BX1795.S48 L35 2010

Manufactured in the U.S.A.

Scripture texts in this work are taken from the following sources, which are hereby acknowledged:

Revised Standard Version of the Bible, copyright © 1952 [2nd edition, 1971] by the Division of Christian Education of the National Council of the Churches of Christ in the United States of America. Used by permission. All rights reserved.

The Catholic Edition of the Revised Standard Version of the Bible, copyright © 1965, 1966 by the Division of Christian Education of the National Council of the Churches of Christ in the United States of America. Used by permission. All rights reserved.

New Revised Standard Version Bible, copyright © 1989, Division of Christian Education of the National Council of the Churches of Christ in the United States of America. Used by permission. All rights reserved.

The New American Bible with Revised New Testament and Revised Psalms © 1991, 1986, 1970 Confraternity of Christian Doctrine, Washington, D.C. and are used by permission of the copyright owner. All Rights Reserved. No part of the New American Bible may be reproduced in any form without permission in writing from the copyright owner.

Contents

Contributors

Rev. Nicanor Pier Giorgio Austriaco, O.P., is an assistant professor of biology and an instructor of theology at Providence College in Providence, Rhode Island. In theology, Fr. Austriaco teaches courses and has research interests in bioethics, sexual ethics, and fundamental moral theology. He is the author of *Biomedicine and Beatitude: An Introduction to Catholic Bioethics* (CUA Press, forthcoming).

Jana Marguerite Bennett is Assistant Professor of Religious Studies at the University of Dayton, where she teaches courses in sexual ethics and Catholic moral theology. She has written more about singleness and the relationship between singleness and marriage in her book *Water is Thicker than Blood: An Augustinian Theology of Marriage and Singleness* (Oxford University Press, 2008).

Florence Caffrey Bourg is the author of *Where Two or Three Are Gathered: Christian Families as Domestic Churches* (University of Notre Dame Press), as well as many articles and reviews on theology of marriage and family. Dr. Bourg taught at the College of Mount St. Joseph in Cincinnati before returning home to New Orleans. She now teaches at the Academy of the Sacred Heart, and has been a visiting professor at Loyola University and Springhill College.

David Cloutier is Associate Professor of Theology at Mount St. Mary's University in Emmitsburg, MD. He is the author of *Love, Reason, and God's Story: An Introduction to Catholic Sexual Ethics* (Anselm Academic/Saint Mary's Press, 2008), as well as a number of essays on Catholic sexual ethics and fundamental moral theology.

Jason King is currently Chair of the theology department at St. Vincent College in Latrobe, PA. His works include *Save the Date: A Spirituality of Dating, Love, Dinner and the Divine* (Crossroad, 2003), *Dating: A Practical Catholic Guide* (Knights of Columbus Supreme Council Veritas Series,

2007), and "Ecumenical Marriage as Leaven for Christian Unity" in the *Journal of Ecumenical Studies*. He has recently done work for the United States Conference of Catholic Bishops website *For Your Marriage*. He is married and has three children.

WILLIAM C. MATTISON III is Assistant Professor of Theology at the Catholic University of America in Washington, DC. His primary area of research is Thomistic moral theology and virtue ethics. He recently completed an introductory book entitled *Introducing Moral Theology: True Happiness and the Virtues* (Brazos, 2008).

DAVID MATZKO MCCARTHY is the Father Forker Professor of Catholic Social Teaching at Mount St. Mary's University in Emmitsburg, MD. He is the author of *Sex and Love in the Home: A Theology of the Household* (SCM, 2001, 2004 revised ed.).

MARIA C. MORROW is a doctoral candidate at the University of Dayton whose interests in Catholic moral theology include the interconnection of virtue and sacrament, with particular interest in penance.

CHRISTOPHER C. ROBERTS is the author of *Creation & Covenant: the significance of sexual difference in the moral theology of marriage* (Continuum, 2008). He is a research fellow in the ethics program at Villanova University. He graduated from Yale, Oxford and King's College London and is a former PBS television reporter.

JULIE HANLON RUBIO is Associate Professor of Christian Ethics at St. Louis University. She is the author of *A Christian Theology of Marriage and Family* (Paulist, 2003) and *Family Ethics: Practices for Christians* (Georgetown University Press, 2010), and co-editor of *Readings in Moral Theology No. 15: Marriage* (Paulist, 2009). She lives in St. Louis with her husband and three sons.

MICHEL THERRIEN is a professor of Fundamental Moral Theology and the Academic Dean at St. Vincent Seminary. He holds a Licentiate in Sacred Theology from the International Theological Institute for Studies on Marriage and the Family in Tramau, Austria, and a Doctorate in Fundamental Moral Theology from the University of Fribourg in Switzerland.

KARI-SHANE DAVIS ZIMMERMAN teaches at the College of Saint Benedict/Saint John's University in Minnesota. She specializes in courses that deal with the intersection of family and church life, as well as issues pertaining to sex and work. She received her PhD in theological ethics from Marquette University in 2007.

Acknowledgments

First and foremost, I would like to acknowledge the funding sources that have allowed New Wine, New Wineskins to provide the space and hospitality for the conference over the past few years. Their generosity has made it possible for us to charge only a nominal registration fee, and provide all meals for the conference. I thank John Cavadini and the Institute for Church Life at Notre Dame, David Solomon at the Notre Dame Center for Ethics and Culture, Tim Scully, CSC, at the Institute for Educational Initiatives, Timothy Matovina and the Cushwa Center for American Catholicism, and John O'Callaghan at the Erasmus Institute. I also thank the staff and residents of Moreau Seminary at the University of Notre Dame, where the group meets, for their hospitality. I owe a debt of gratitude to those with whom I served on the leadership team of New Wine, New Wineskins: Bill Mattison, Dana Dillon, Christopher Vogt, and David Clairmont.

New Wineskins owes a special debt of gratitude to senior scholars, who not only send their graduate students to the conference to keep it fresh, but also have attended our "senior scholar" seminar mornings to discuss their work with us newbies. Over the years, Jean Porter, Paulinus Odozor, Lisa Sowle Cahill, Robert Barron, and Stanley Hauerwas have been with us, and we are grateful for their generosity. Their participation has helped establish the symposium as a place where younger scholars gather.

Obviously, I am in great debt to the authors in the volume for offering their work for this collection, as well as their conversations. The original conversation around early versions of some of these essays was, I think, one of the finest days in Wineskins history, and that was because we were fortunate enough to gather generous and open people to discuss high-quality work. It has been great to see the full scope of this collection validate our initial conversations. I hope it will inspire more, and not just among us! I especially thank Bill Mattison, Julie Rubio, and David

McCarthy for conversations on the introduction, and for encouragement in finding a publisher for these essays.

A couple of the essays in this collection have appeared in different forms elsewhere. We acknowledge and thank: the Loyola Institute for Ministry Extension Program (LIMEX) and Loyola University of New Orleans, whose forthcoming course textbook, *Spirituality, Morality, and Ethics*, includes a different form of Florence Caffrey Bourg's essay, under the title "Marital Spirituality and Sexual Ethics"; INTAMS Review and SPCK, for permission to use a version of Christopher Roberts' essay, which appeared in a slightly different form in *INTAMS Review* 13 (2007), and in a forthcoming collection from SPCK in England edited by Andrew Goddard, *Sexuality and the Church*; and Georgetown University Press and *Josephinum Journal of Theology*, for portions of Julie Hanlon Rubio's essay that have appeared in her article "Practicing Sexual Fidelity," *Josephinum Journal of Theology* 14 (2007), and in chapter 4 of her book, *Family Ethics: Practices for Christians* (Georgetown University Press, 2010).

I am pleased to thank the staff of Wipf and Stock, who have been helpful to this first-time editor. I especially thank editor Charlie Collier for his interest in the collection. I and many others are grateful for Wipf and Stock's unique and growing place in the theological publishing world. I also thank my colleagues here at Mount Saint Mary's University for their help, and especially our secretary, Gloria Balsley, on whose work we rely. Finally, we are all indebted to the Vatican II generation of Catholic moral theologians. All of us stand on your shoulders, one way or another.

Introduction

The Trajectories of Catholic Sexual Ethics

David Cloutier

F AMILY RESEARCHER ANDREW CHERLIN'S recent book called *The Marriage-Go-Round* is one in a long line of studies seeking to understand, as its subtitle states, "the state of marriage and family in America today." The many tomes indicate a great deal of puzzlement. In Cherlin's case, it is based on the observation that Americans place an unusually high and positive value on both "marriage" and on "individual freedom," and consequently value marriage more highly than most other developed countries, but at the same time, deal with marital failure at a much higher rate.[1] Cherlin's book is a study of how members of the society juggle both scripts over time, despite their contradictions.

This fundamental puzzlement extends "downward" into the basic attitudes about sex and courtship encountered by adolescents long before they reach the altar (or justice of the peace, or Vegas). Recent literature has focused more and more on what has come to be called "the hook-up culture." Such a culture is characterized by short-term encounters with no strings. But the rise of the hook-up culture has not meant the death of what is usually called "the relationship." Hook-up studies are often filled with commentary from students for whom the hook-up culture is an ambiguous but seemingly inevitable pathway into "something more." They comment that a relationship is not "official" until it is "Facebook official"—that is, the partners change their relationship status to "in a

---

1. Cherlin, *Marriage-Go-Round*, 4–11.

relationship." (However, in between "single" and "in a relationship" is a new category: "it's complicated.")

As with marriage, such confusion results from the presence of two simultaneous scripts, scripts that one will encounter every hour on any popular radio station. One song may talk about a new conquest every night of the week, while the next sings passionately about finding love that will last forever. As with marriage, a script that exalts romantic love is culturally available right alongside one that values, above all, individual choice and freedom from "strings."

One of the more interesting connections that Cherlin's study makes is the critical role that "mobility" (he calls it "the M-word") plays in shaping American marriage. Cherlin notes that, even today, Americans are twice as likely to move in a given year than are citizens of Europe or Japan.[2] This sense of "restlessness" is one that is both a national character trait, perhaps dependent on ours being a nation of immigrants (yesterday and today), and a practical matter of living in a large, quite diverse country where opportunities for well-being are often located elsewhere. As researcher Bill Bishop notes in *The Big Sort*, Americans are more and more able and willing to sort themselves into quite large "lifestyle regions," especially driven by Richard Florida's "creative class," whose education and job prospects often give them the freedom to relocate in desirable locales of like-minded people, with cultural amenities aimed at their demographic niche.[3]

Why is mobility important in understanding sex and marriage? Cherlin highlights two points, which (after the fact!) give some justification to the title of this collection. First, he notes that "in the past half century, young adults have become much more likely to leave home before they marry."[4] Prior to the 1950s, fewer than five percent of twentysomethings headed their own households. Today nearly a third do, and such statistics do not also account for the higher and higher prevalence of "going away to college." Jeffrey Jensen Arnett has called this phenomenon "emerging adulthood," describing it as something of a "new life stage."[5] This stage, Cherlin writes, "makes it more likely that they will have a series of intimate partners during their adult lives."

2. Cherlin, *Marriage-Go-Round*, 147.

3. Bishop, *Big Sort*; Florida, *Creative Class*.

4. Cherlin, *Marriage-Go-Round*, 152.

5. Arnett, *Emerging Adulthood*.

But the significance of "leaving home" stretches further than this observation that it will increase the number of partnerships. Such movement often means not merely heading one's own household, but moving out of the immediate geographical area of one's own family. This is a further "leaving home," in the sense that choices about sexual partners and marriage often come about with extremely limited parental involvement. Beyond this geographical fact, it is also important to note the "meaning" or purpose often attached to this period. In the wake of rising divorce rates, many young adults want the chance to "try out" relationships, to see what "works for them," as well as assuming that they need to "establish their own identity" (and financial status) before "settling down." Culturally, this period is seen as a major one for forming one's own idea of self, and significantly, such a formation is thought best to happen "away from home." Authors have written about the increasing significance of "urban tribes" as stand-in family-like networks of support for young adults in this cohort.[6] In all these ways, marriage and sex in our culture appear on a journey away from home.

Yet most yearn to come back home, if not in a geographical sense, at least in the sense of having a spouse, raising children, and building a household. The path home may be, as Arnett puts it, "meandering," but most people are searching down this path. As we noted above, in the face of divorce, most Americans continue to hope for marital permanence. Yet, as the old saying wonders, perhaps "you can never go home again." If "leaving home" begins the trajectory that presents challenging and complex choices about sex and marriage, "coming home" continues to present challenges related to a culture of mobility.

Cherlin argues that data indicates strong regional variations of divorce rates correlate very well with migration rates. That is, areas where many people are from elsewhere show higher divorce rates, while areas that show little in-migration—especially the upper Midwest—have lower divorce rates. Cherlin suggests that this phenomenon may have to do with what sociologist Emile Durkheim called "social integration." As the recent spate of "happiness studies" have also shown, human individuals are happier and more successful insofar as they feel well-integrated into networks of relationships.[7] Places with low in-migration tend to have

6. Watters, *Urban Tribes*.

7. See, for example, Layard, *Happiness*, and McKibben, *Deep Economy*, both of whom summarize and popularize scientific studies that have gone on for decades by econo-

strongly knit networks of belonging (just ask anyone who has lived in rural Minnesota!) in which individuals "have others who care about them and will watch out for them, draw them into social groups, provide them with models of how to live one's life, and express disapproval if they deviate from accepted behavior."[8] Suicide patterns mimic migration patterns as well, suggesting that the lack of belonging leads to a risk of "anomie."

Cherlin's idea does not purport to explain everything about divorce, but it does raise interesting questions about what it means to "come home" and "build a home" in a mobile culture. Especially in white-collar fields, couples often come from different areas, and then end up residing in a third area, near neither set of parents. Their strongest geographical affinity may be to their college. One or the other may have to make career sacrifices in order to stay in the same place. While earlier generations experienced migrations (obviously), these often involved large familial moves within ethnic enclaves. Today, mobility may be the greatest mark of having "made it" in America. Such a culture presents unique challenges for "coming home" in the face of social dis-integration.

THE SHAPE OF CATHOLIC DISCUSSION

"Leaving home" and "coming home" have not been typical categories for discussion in Catholic moral theology. Usually, this area is comprised of debates about "sex" and about "marriage"—and specifically, what these two acts do and do not mean, in terms of their "purposes." So in this section I hope to sketch a brief history of the shift from an act-centered "physicalism" to a person-centered "personalism" in Catholicism. Such a shift sets the stage for the essays in this collection, which, I will contend, display a further shift toward a practice-based analysis of this area of ethics.

As most historians of moral theology have noted, Catholic sexual ethics spent centuries in a "juridical" or "legalistic" mode, focusing squarely on acts and norms.[9] Given the focus on sexual acts that were

---

mists and psychologists. In an excellent article, Joshua Wolf Shenk interviews a leading happiness researcher, who sums up the findings of the biggest longitudinal study on the subject as "the only thing that really matters in life are your relationships to other people" (Shenk, "What Makes Us Happy?" 46).

8. Cherlin, *Marriage-Go-Round*, 149.

9. Standard histories include Mahoney, *Making*, and Pinckaers, *Sources*.

acceptable or not acceptable, the cultural backdrop for such acts was almost invisible. Such theology, as many have noted, was not conscious of history or historical context.

However, the twentieth-century development of Catholic sexual and marriage ethics displayed a significant shift.[10] The dominant shift, again characteristic of moral theology as a whole, was the shift from acts to persons, from an act-centered moral theology to a person-centered moral theology, usually premised on a theological anthropology. Theologians as disparate as Charles Curran and Germain Grisez fled from the "biologism" or "physicalism" that clearly marked pre-Vatican II reflection in this area. "Physicalism" was a term applied to a moral argument that claimed to read a moral judgment off of physical or biological realities. For example, barrier methods of contraception were wrong because they physically impeded the (God-willed) "finality" of the act. The remarkable dominance of physicalism can be seen in the single most significant debate of the era, which arose so strongly in the early 1960s because of the development of the birth control pill by a Catholic physician, John Rock. Rock believed quite sincerely that this sort of non-barrier method of birth control would not violate traditional Catholic morality. The fact that methods of periodic abstinence, however unsuccessful, were also now meeting with papal approval also correlated with the apparent physicalism of identifying the real problem with contraception as the "unnatural barrier" introduced into the act.[11]

The shift to a personalist approach was, like other changes of the period, rapid. The Second Vatican Council's *Gaudium et Spes* included a rich and remarkably positive account of marriage and married sex.[12]

10. An excellent, quite broad survey of key articles and chapters is now available in Curran and Rubio, *Marriage*. This collection fills out and completes the earlier collection, Curran and McCormick, *Readings*, which has significant crossover theoretically, but which collects more articles from the debates over sexual norms that dominated the 1970s and early 1980s.

11. Pope Pius XII's famous "Address to Midwives" (1951), which gave papal approval to such natural methods of birth planning, offered the following statement in favor of it: "they do not hinder or jeopardize in any way the consummation of the natural act and its ulterior natural consequences," whereas other methods consist in "a perversion of the act itself." Here, the object of the act and the physical structure of the act seem equated. The development represented by the Pope's address is seen in two chapters of Ford and Kelly, *Contemporary Moral Theology*, 378–430. The first is entitled "Periodic Continence Before 1951"!

12. *Gaudium et Spes*, nos. 48–53. The document, as with many Vatican II develop-

Notoriously, language about "primary and secondary ends" of sex and of marriage was nowhere to be found. The positive account of marriage was placed within a document that developed a Christian humanism (nos. 12–22), which was intended as the means by which the Church could be responsive to the "joys" and "anguish" of the modern world.[13] This theological anthropology of the person's basic dignity and freedom, and of the perils that accompany it, depicts "man" as possessing a set of potentials, of capacities, which could be developed well or used for great evil and self-destruction. By focusing on potentials and capacities of the *person*, the document avoided a depiction of the person's good and evil merely as a set of *acts* that did or did not conform to given rules and principles, or to any preset teleology. Rather, the section culminated in a rendering of Christ as "the new man," as the response to "the mystery of man," and as the way in which "the whole man is renewed from within."[14] A personalist account of the human condition then received the response of a person (Christ). As Richard McCormick wrote in 1967, "A moral theology which does not reflect out of and talk in terms of the centrality of the person is going to die on the vine very quickly."[15]

However, the greatest riddle of the era in Catholic moral theology came when, in the wake of this theological shift, Pope Paul VI issued the encyclical *Humanae Vitae* on July 25, 1968. All this personalism, and yet the rule against all use of contraception remained. It is not necessary here to go over the well-rehearsed ground of the response to the encyclical. A great deal of anticipation had built up, because of the Council and because of Paul VI's novel use of "commissions" to investigate the question. All of these moves seemed to many to indicate that a change

---

ments, was preceded by certain pioneering theologians. In the case of personalism, Herbert Doms and Dietrich von Hildebrand are the most frequently cited.

13. On the novelty and evolution of "Schema 13," see the recent, very balanced account from O'Malley, *What Happened*. Notably, the whole idea of a "church in the modern world" text was not in the original agenda for the Council, and so the text was controversial. For an early, rather critical analysis of paragraphs 12–22, see none other than Joseph Ratzinger, "Dignity," 115–63. Ratzinger's view exemplifies what O'Malley terms the "German" view of the text, which saw the "French" view as too optimistic in its reading of modern developments.

14. *Gaudium et Spes*, no. 22. This was John Paul II's favorite Vatican II passage to cite.

15. McCormick, "Moral Theology of Vatican II," 7.

was coming. When it did not come, the field of Catholic moral theology essentially split in two.

Yet personalism proved to be a quite flexible foundation from which to do sexual ethics, whether one dissented from the encyclical or not. Many examples might be cited, but two will be noted here.[16] The 1977 CTSA report on human sexuality argued from a "biblical anthropology" of male–female relationality, in order to establish "the wholistic view of person expressed in the documents of Vatican II," a view that should lead to understanding human sexuality "more broadly . . . than it was in much of our earlier tradition."[17] "We are our bodies," the report explains, in our fundamental human "being-with-another."[18] Our sexuality aims at such "creative growth toward integration," which forms the basic criterion against which sexual acts should be judged.[19] Such an anthropology was meant to expand the traditional terms: "creativity" was a broader version of procreation, while "integration" represented a psychologized version of unitive love. Since the movement was "toward" integration, the full union of the couple was something that did not happen immediately. As is well known, on this basis the report suggested many changes to traditional norms. Only a few years later, Pope John Paul II's "theology of the body" built on a "biblical anthropology" to give a view of humanity seeking "original unity" in the fullness of mutual self-giving. Such self-giving was not merely spiritual, but bodily, since the body itself has a "language" oriented toward mutual relationship.[20] Our sexuality not only brings us into intimacy with another, but teaches us the truth about God. John Paul used the same stories—yet the conclusion was a vigorous defense of traditional norms, rather than a "broadening" of them. Traditional norms, especially *Humanae Vitae*, defend "the language of the body," insofar as a

16. For a fine summary of key texts in this era, at least in the U.S., see Curran, *Catholic Moral Theology*, 204–10.

17. Kosnik et al., *Human Sexuality*, 102. The Congregation for the Doctrine of the Faith responded to the text, criticizing its "manipulation" of the definition of sexuality and the subsequent "broad and vague" redefinition of its purpose, which "yield no manageable or helpful rules for conscience formation in matters of sexuality." See CDF, "Human Sexuality."

18. Kosnik et al., *Human Sexuality*, 103–4.

19. Ibid., 106.

20. Several essays in this collection describe and engage the theology of the body in detail. For an excellent summary, which brings out the personalist foundations and language, see Anderson and Granados, *Called to Love*, especially chapters 1 and 2.

contraceptive "bodily union . . . does not correspond to the interior truth and to the dignity of personal communion-communion of persons."[21] In short, sexual acts prohibited by the norms in fact contradict the fully *personal* character of the mutual gift of human sexuality.

The flexibility of personalism sometimes meant that proponents of one side or the other relied on a caricatured picture of their opponents. On one side, many "liberal" personalists continued to rehearse the Church's "anti-sex" history and its legalism (maintained by celibate men) as evidence for the urgency of change. Yet many laypeople (including women) were now writing in defense of traditional norms, and on the basis of personalism, not some "dislike" of sex. On the other side, "conservative" personalists often persisted in depicting any variation on traditional norms as evidence of "relativism," of just letting people "decide for themselves" in this sensitive area. Any "exceptions" on contraception or premarital sex or masturbation would quickly erupt into the "anything goes" hedonism of the culture. Such accusations came despite clear assertions of normativity and rejections of hedonism by revisionists.[22] It was as if (as some liberals charged) Catholic social teaching, which followed this exact model of broad principles subject to varying applications, was itself "relativist," simply because much of the teaching was not in the form of absolute norms. After all, "liberal" personalists offered quite substantial pictures of human flourishing that were meant to provide clear, if not exact, guidance. Thus, the debate was plagued by mutual mischaracterizations.

But it would be impossible to avoid another sneaking suspicion: that the plasticity of personalism was useful precisely because it could be deployed in ways amenable to one's already-determined positions on the significant normative questions. In the "theology of the body," the Pope used a personalist presentation of human sexuality that justified the traditional norms, even to the extent of criticizing contraception on unitive grounds, not just procreative grounds. Many "conservative" personalists, following the pope, maintained that contraceptive sex was "a lie" because it purported to meet the personalist criterion of complete

---

21. John Paul II, *Theology of the Body*, 398.

22. For example, see Guindon, *Sexual Language*, 30–31. More extensively, Moore, *Body in Context*, offers the most extended discussion of the normative limits of sexuality understood as a language, limits that nevertheless differ from the traditional list of exceptionless norms.

mutual self-giving, but in fact "held something back."[23] The body did not signify the total giving of the person in love.

On the other hand, there was no doubt that on issues like contraception and divorce (and later, homosexuality), "liberal" personalists found it pastorally impossible to maintain absolute norms in the face of their experiences in a culture where divorce was common and contraception almost universal, as well as in light of what was considered substantial development of psychological, scientific knowledge.[24] After all, what made the norms against divorce and contraception (as examples) so difficult was that, unlike adultery or theft, these norms seemed to prohibit actions that were not only not harmful, but in fact produced real *good* in many people's experiences (in the form of good marriages or good second marriages). As Lisa Cahill wonders, referencing the prominent use of experience in the pope's theology, "Whose experience is to be examined?" After all, "one can hardly avoid the impression that the experience of married persons and of women in general has not been heard with real openness, if references to their experience are used by celibate, male theologians, clergy, and Church authorities to support conclusions which are in all essential points unvarying."[25]

Whether through overdrawn caricatures or falsely clear conclusions, personalist "foundations" often served to obscure, rather than clarify, what was actually driving the disagreements. Yet the prevalence of personalism continues today (even if certain authors attempt to move beyond this approach).[26] Recent books continue to develop it on the "liberal" side, and "conservatives" offer popularized versions of the Pope, as well as a few sophisticated works.[27] But what impact has this forty years

23. See *Familiaris Consortio*, no. 32, in which Pope John Paul II contends that the "innate language that expresses total reciprocal self-giving of husband and wife is overlaid, through contraception, by an objectively contradictory language, namely, that of not giving oneself totally to the other." Contraception is thus not only not open to procreation, but is also "a falsification of the inner truth of conjugal love." There is some precedent for this argument that contraception contradicts the unitive end of sex, briefly noted by Ford and Kelly, *Contemporary Moral Theology*, 290.

24. As I note later in the introduction, Charles Curran points out that revisionist moralists wrote first on particular issues, and only later began to develop systematic approaches. See *Catholic Moral Theology*, 192.

25. Cahill, "Current Teaching," 531.

26. Books such as Cahill, *Sex, Gender*, and Grabowski, *Sex and Virtue*, can be seen moving beyond personalism from either "side."

27. Most importantly, on the liberal side, Farley, *Just Love*, and Salzman and Lawler, *Sexual Person*. Much work on the conservative side aims at a more popular audience,

of debate had on the wider life of the Church? Sadly, it has had very little. Opinion polls suggest that, by and large, Catholics are no longer taking their cues on these matters from the Church—but not because they have suddenly developed a sophisticated personalism. Rather, their voices sound remarkably like the tides of the culture, especially among young people who have grown up after Vatican II.[28] (Cahill is still right: there is no "credible witness.") Stories have discussed the vocal minority, a minority that probably is increasing somewhat, which has tried to popularize discussion of magisterial teachings, especially via the theology of the body.[29] And surely there is influence here, especially in their increasing presence in the diocesan priesthood and lay ministerial ranks (not to mention among academic theologians). But it would be excessive to think the impact is "sweeping the Church."

BEYOND PERSONALISM: NEW WINESKINS FOR CATHOLIC SEXUAL ETHICS

Thinking about "home" doesn't fit personalist categories, because "home" is a set of persons (and, distinctively, a set of persons one may not be able to pick and choose) *and* a place, not to mention a material good. Home, we might say, is a setting for shared *practice*, one in which identity and meaning are established and carried out through ongoing shared activity. Certain canonical traditions of marriage define it specifically in terms of "bed and board," traditions that Robert Farrar Capon in 1965 names and uses to outline "a geography of matrimony."[30] Similarly, Wendell Berry's 1977 essay maintains that "without the household . . . husband and wife find it less and less possible to imagine and enact their marriage."[31] Instead, the "isolation" of sexuality from concepts and

most prominently the work of Christopher West. But also note less-studied texts such as Scola, *Nuptial Mystery*, and Asci, *Conjugal Act.*

28. See, for example, Wuthnow, *Baby Boomers*, 140–41. His surveys indicate that the percentage of young adult Catholics who think premarital sex is "always wrong" has dropped by half over the last twenty years, to near 10%, and that more young Catholics have had premarital sex (over 80 percent) than groups of "unaffiliated" or mainline Protestant young adults. These numbers are largely confirmed by the oft-cited study, Davidson et al., *Common Ground.*

29. See Carroll, *New Faithful*, and Navarro, "Spreading." For more on the appeal and limits of this revival, see Cloutier, "Heaven is a Place."

30. Capon, *Bed and Board.*

31. Berry, "Body and Earth," 117.

practices of the home reduces it either to "the lore of sexual romance" or "capitalist economics." That is to say, sex is placed in the context of idealizations of romantic love or markets of hedonistic consumption.

But it is significant that neither author here cited is a Catholic moral theologian! Their reflections on love, sex, and marriage simply fall outside the definitions and debates characterized in the above history. However, in this collection, the authors move in such a direction. Strikingly, the essays here build on a common literature that both engages and appreciates the work of the personalist era. Yet, in moving beyond personalist categories, we are able to discern two shifts, which are displayed in the essays of this collection, and which offer indications about the future development of reflection in Catholic sexual ethics. One is a shift from persons to practices, the other a shift from a crisis of personal freedom to a crisis of shared meanings.

From Persons to Practices

In the earlier collection of New Wine, New Wineskins essays, William Mattison and I suggested that a key distinctive feature of young Catholic moral theologians was their post-subculture historical location.[32] Unlike the previous generation, of whatever "side," the current generation never experienced the changes of Vatican II, the "decision" of *Humanae Vitae*'s teaching—but more important than all this, the formation in a clear community of Catholic scripts. Rather, our experience is growing up amidst cultural pluralism, taking for granted the availability of multiple cultural possibilities. And multiple sexual possibilities, too.

Post-subculture sexual ethics, then, displays a shift from personalist analysis toward an analysis of sexuality in terms of competing cultural practices. As I noted in the initial survey of the landscape, the contemporary world presents young adults and young married couples with a wide variety of cultural scripts and possibilities. The essays in this collection all seek to provide ways of negotiating one's way through these various practices. The essays engage in much description and re-description of practices in an attempt to gain clarity about "what is really going on"—both in various non-marital practices, such as cohabitation and prolonged singleness, and in marriage itself.

---

32. Cloutier and Mattison, "Introduction," 4–5.

I want to suggest here that the strategy of practical description and re-description can be understood as a reaction against the limitations of both "personalisms" above. As mentioned, the essays here all build on the personalist turn. However, such personalisms rely on general, abstract claims of what is now usually dubbed "theological anthropology." Moreover, almost unanimously, these claims position human persons as abstract individuals, and develop a sexual ethic focused on what is supposed to be happening between two people, and especially their interiorities. In both their abstract descriptions and their focus on private interiority, personalisms neglect the complexities of contexts. True, most start off with some sort of survey of the current sexual landscape, but this is mere prelude to the normative work done by conceptions about abstract individuals. Personalisms even offer an account of intimacy that neglects longstanding claims about the importance of family background in attraction and commitment. A colleague of mine always showed her students a scene from the movie *The Story of Us*, in which the spouses are having an argument in bed, and their parents are shown (like ghosts) in the bed with them, saying things to each one, which they then "respond" to in responding to the spouse. The lesson is that the argument is going on as much with and through the parents as with the spouse.

And, of course, even at this elementary level, one notes that in our society couples often come from quite different households. "Every couple is different"—on a whole variety of levels, not least their relationship histories—is true, even if its status as universal undergraduate conversation-stopper is not! Post-subculture theologians are wary of a simple imposition of ideals, of whatever sort, and pay much more attention to analyzing and evaluating practices. They seek specifics in such an analysis—whether of marital sexual acts, of cohabiting couples, or of dating. And because practices, by definition, are social practices, the analysis here almost inevitably contains what would normally be seen as "social ethics."

While such a sensitivity to context and wider practices might be thought to tend in a "liberal" direction, the collection here contradicts that oversimplification. Why? Another point Mattison and I made in the earlier collection is relevant here: post-subculture Catholics are less concerned about "fitting into" the culture and more concerned about "standing out" and establishing their identity, sometimes against the culture.[33]

---

33. Cloutier and Mattison, "Introduction," 5. This "high-tension" identity should not be seen as simply "liberal" or "conservative."

Actual analysis of today's sexual culture, far from yielding a welcoming embrace of the contemporary world, presents many features that are not only "puzzling" but remarkably destructive. From disturbing reports of tween-age oral sex to the continuing of a 40 percent divorce rate, it seems far less clear to us that "the culture" has all the answers than it might have seemed in the 1960s. Not that it is necessarily the case that "the Church" has all the answers, either—but nevertheless, attention to the ambiguity of the culture and the desire to intentionally form a Catholic identity combine to make it easier to recognize the Church's practices and norms as genuinely liberatory. Some, though not all, essays in this collection quite clearly wish to claim practices (such as the sacrament of reconciliation and the use of Natural Family Planning) as liberatory and prophetic "answers"—or counter-practices—to destructive practices in contemporary sexual culture. Is this the case or not? Others argue that a more thorough development of the tradition in new ways offers a better response to the weaknesses of the culture. Either way, what's important is to recognize that the ground has shifted, to identifying Catholic practices as liberatory alternatives to cultural practices.

Such a shift, furthermore, opens up a way of understanding sexuality "theologically" that has often been neglected in the past. Some personalist theology began moving in this direction, for example, in attempts to narrate the experience of sex as sacred.[34] However, a practice-based account "thinks theologically" about sexuality not necessarily by theologizing sex itself, but by placing the practices of sex and marriage *within larger accounts of the Christian life as a whole.* In this way, particular acts take on their meanings and significance contextually, rather than directly. This sort of shift also opens up Christianity as potentially liberatory, because it moves beyond the impasse that beset the personalist age: whether the tradition has viewed sex as somehow "evil" or not. Instead, it is a question of the context—or as I have put it elsewhere, the "story"—within which sex and marriage are going on.[35] Such attention to the context of sexuality within the Christian life as a whole then also must attend to the living out of that story within particular cultural "stories."

34. See, for example, numerous essays in Nelson and Longfellow, *Sexuality and the Sacred.*

35. See Cloutier, *God's Story.*

From Seeking Freedom to Finding Meaning

The difficulty of understanding this shift has a lot to do with a second key shift (displayed in this collection): a move from a crisis over *individual freedom* to a crisis over *shared meaning.* Without doubt, everything from the Vatican II conciliar debates through *Veritatis Splendor* highlighted the fact that "freedom" was the great contested reality. A history of the theology of this period specifically in terms of the use and contestation of the term "freedom" is waiting to be written. And of course, this period coincided with immense cultural shifts, like civil rights movements and the end of colonialism, which in a world church evoked a constant wrestling with what "liberation" was all about.

But for our topic, it is crucial to recognize how very real this crisis was in on-the-ground terms. Though none of the authors here experienced it directly, there seems little doubt that those who grew up Catholic prior to Vatican II experienced the church as a powerful force pervading their everyday lives and choices. It wasn't just a set of institutional politics, of "liberals" and "conservatives" facing off at academic meetings or in the press. Church authority was a *reality*, and its presence was especially pronounced in terms of sexuality, where the Church's teachings were constantly present (even if not followed), marking off boundaries in relationships, in bedrooms, and even in one's own mind. Even now, Bishop Geoffrey Robinson evokes the power of such a presence by reminding us that all these boundaries were enforced under the threat of "direct offense against God"—that is, "mortal sin."[36]

And then what happened? Well, as Garry Wills put it in his historical reflection, the dirty little secret that came out of Vatican II was "the Church can change."[37] Sure, theologians engaged in much hair-splitting about "development," and, on the books, not a single sexual norm today is different from the ones taught in 1960. But the experience of change, above all in the liturgy, provoked a clear recognition that the Church's boundaries were not fixed. "Change" of itself is a morally neutral word, though, so what happens after Vatican II is a struggle between an apparent new freedom and a continued attempt to limit and criticize

36. See Robinson, *Confronting Power and Sex*, 202–4. By citing Robinson, I do not mean to endorse his view. In fact, his chapters on sex construct exactly the debate between freedom and condemnation which I argue is *not* the central concern of the present generation.

37. Wills, *Bare Ruined Choirs*.

such freedom. And it happened in souls who remembered what it was like to live under the previous rigid regime of mortal condemnation for sexual sins.

But there is no longer a crisis over freedom. Freedom has won. Consider Donna Freitas's recent extensive interview-study of Catholic undergraduates, many at Catholic colleges.[38] When questioned about how the Church's teaching affected their attitudes about sex, almost all *laughed*, she reports. Few had much detailed knowledge at all (or accurate knowledge—many stated that the Catholic teaching is simply, sex is for procreation, period). And almost to a person, their response was simply that Catholic teaching was "outdated" and/or "unrealistic." The Church's teaching is not an oppressive, scary force to them—it's a *joke*. What's important about this response is not that it dismisses the Church's teachings, but that it dismisses them with a shrug, like something that has never had any relevance. This is what it means to say "freedom won"—these students do not experience a struggle to be liberated from the Church's teachings. The teachings have always been irrelevant to them. Sex for them really has no theological context at all. It is thoroughly secularized.[39]

However, as Freitas also makes clear, these students experience a different crisis: a crisis of shared meaning. Like the culture at large, students value sexuality (and marriage) as crucial areas of their lives, as meaningful, but there is a remarkable difficulty is articulating what these meanings are. One female student at a Catholic college, who holds typically vague and dismissive views about Catholic teachings on sex, nevertheless describes her recent relationships in generally "spiritual" terms, trying to "cobble together" her own understanding of how "something clicked" in this relationship, as well as a fear that sex could "destroy

---

38. Freitas, *Sex and the Soul*, 194–202.

39. Freitas's specific chapter on Catholic institutions suggest that such perceptions are only reinforced at most Catholic schools, which students view as providing a surface-level set of "Catholic" things (e.g., crucifixes in classrooms, required theology classes) wrapped around a generalized ethos and conduct no different than non-religious colleges and universities. See ibid., 43–56. She notes that the sole exceptions were very small cliques of "evangelical Catholics," who exhibited interest in and language for issues of faith, spirituality, and sexuality. Similarly, her entire study shows conclusively that the only campuses able to handle this at all are evangelical Protestant colleges, which at least offer a known, shared language within which to come to understandings.

something."[40] Freitas uses the story to illustrate how, when Catholicism is communicated in vague or apparently "unrealistic" terms, students then simply try to make up meanings as they go along.

The crisis of shared meaning is certainly part of why some young Catholics come to experience Church practices as liberatory: they are liberatory because they provide a meaning, and not a purely private one, through which to understand this important area of life. Freitas, in her study, suggests four things that students seek: a sense of boundaries, a sense of some sort of right and wrong not dependent on fleeting emotions (or the will of others, which ends up being the tyranny in a consent culture), a framework for discernment, and a place for forgiveness and redemption after failure.[41] If Freitas is right, then most of these students are *not* "relativists," in the sense that they think "there's no right and wrong choices." Rather, they are deeply confused, because they don't have plausible ways to name, identify, and practice "the sexual game." Many of the essays in the first part of this collection should be seen as attempts to address the crisis of meaning in various non-marital contexts. Most notably, authors are less quick to impose norms and more interested in understanding both the meaningfulness and meaninglessness that drives practices like cohabitation and pornography.

But the crisis of shared meaning extends to marriage, as well. Marriage has become ever more individualized—"every couple is different"—not least with the rise of what has been called "companionate marriage." As Judith Wallerstein notes in describing how these marriage work well, she notes that they involve "the belief that both partners have equal responsibilities in all domains of the marriage."[42] Such a relationship "requires high levels of self-confidence, trust, and self awareness and the ability to postpone gratification."[43] Moreover, since partners are continually changing and facing new circumstances, the friendship/partnership requires ongoing negotiation, which in turn "requires unwavering attentiveness and empathy."[44] This sort of marriage can of course be very rewarding, but exactly what makes it rewarding is also "what makes it so hard." As Wallerstein notes, she was "stunned by the contrasts" with her

40. Ibid., 200–201.
41. Ibid., 227.
42. Wallerstein and Blakeslee, *Good Marriage*, 155.
43. Ibid., 155–56.
44. Ibid., 157.

own life, insofar as "all of the major steps that my generation took for granted are now open-ended questions."[45]

As Wallerstein's examples show, companionate marriages are positive in many ways, but highly fragile. What happens if or when the couple starts to lose what they share? What is the point of staying? And where is the breaking point when the ongoing negotiations break down into impasse? As this ideal is more and more commonly held, some (increasing) number of folks simply eschew marriage altogether, regarding it as "meaningless"—or "just a piece of paper." Friends never march down to the courthouse to register their friendship (or end it), and these marriages ultimately rest on continued friendship. Of course, it is also "more"—but how? Just like young adults away from home face uncertainty of meaning, married couples are more and more challenged to identify where the meaning lies in their relationship.

The *shared* meanings associated with marriage face challenges not only from those who eschew marriage and cannot identify the purpose of lifelong vows, but also from those who demand social and ecclesial sanction of same-sex unions. This issue is an unusually complex one, but it is surely a contest over meanings. Typically, defenders of various forms of same-sex unions express bewilderment at the idea that gay marriage will somehow "harm" others' marriages precisely because they already assume *either* that marriage has no shared meaning *or* that the shared meaning is simply a partnership of sexual affection, whose parameters are defined such that this affection (or the disappearance of it) constitutes the basis for marrying or divorcing. Yet same-sex couples desire civil recognition precisely because they desire their union to have *public* meaning. However, this meaning is evidently different from the shared meaning defended by the other side of the issue.

However these civil conflicts turn out, Catholic Christians assume that marriage is a relationship that is part of a larger whole, most especially the whole shared sacramental life of the Church. Thus, instead of focusing on marriage as a practice in isolation, our authors increasingly place marriage within a larger life of Christian vocation and discipleship. The shared meaning for the marriage comes not simply from the partners' mutual love, but how their marriage is to be understood in the context of career, of church, of society, and (of course) of parenting. Notably, such reflections build on two chapters of John Paul II's most

45. Ibid., 164.

authoritative writing on marriage, *Familiaris Consortio*, which go beyond the traditional "internal" goods that define marriage and discuss
how marriage serves (and in turn is served by) the common good of the
society and the upbuilding of the Church.[46] The move to link the sexual
ethics of the Catholic tradition with its social teachings was immeasur-
ably strengthened by Pope Benedict XVI's *Caritas in Veritate*, in which
he makes these connections explicit, connections that go back to a recognition that the Paul VI of *Populorum Progressio* and of *Humanae Vitae*
are not two separate figures.[47] In the encyclical, Benedict in particular
makes the connection by providing the strongest papal endorsement to
date for environmentalism, while also noting that "it is contradictory
to insist that future generations respect the natural environment when
our educational systems and laws do not help them to respect themselves. The book of nature is one and indivisible: it takes in not only
the environment but also life, sexuality, marriage, the family, social relations; in a word, integral human development."[48] This is not meant as a
swipe against environmentalism, but rather a strong claim that what the
Pope calls the "grammar" of nature provides a blueprint for proper and
improper human relations, one that includes the "wise use" of human
sexuality and (more broadly) all technology.[49] Moreover, by insisting in
the encyclical on the centrality of love, and not simply justice, in the
economic sphere of society, the Pope breaks down the illusory private/
public barrier that sometimes separates sexual and social ethics. In this
collection, the attention to practices and shared meanings point to a "so-
cialized" sexual ethics.

Other essays in this collection also begin reflection on the partners'
mutual love and intimacy itself, recognizing that real intimacy is a task
requiring discipline, quite different from the faux intimacy that tends to
dominate cultural representations of interpersonal love.[50] These reflections on the practice of the traditional "unitive end" make clear that a
love specified as exclusive and life-long requires a richer understand-

46. The sections entitled "Participating in the Development of Society" (nos. 42–48)
and "Sharing in the Life and Mission of the Church" (nos. 49–64).

47. For a full defense of this claim, see McCarthy, "Procreation."

48. *Caritas in Veritate*, no. 51.

49. Ibid., no. 48.

50. An excellent and accessible work moving in this direction, by an ecclesiologist
able to avoid some of the ethics debates, is Gaillardetz, *Daring Promise*.

ing of love than is provided by the dominant cultural account ("feelings") and an underdeveloped theological account ("self-giving"). Thus, whether "inside" the home or "outside," married couples face the task of developing shared meaning for this relationship in a culture that gives less and less guidance. By conceiving of marriage as a practice and by placing that practice within a larger life narrative, Christian resources are found to name the meanings lived out in the relationship.

What does this mean for the ethical "methods" employed here? First, most of the essays here seek to cultivate and enrich the *Catholic identity* of the agents, both leaving and coming home. One participant in the conference asked a telling question: "Is the fundamental issue wrong acts or a lack of a sense of vocation?" There is a ongoing sense that the problems to be addressed are not simply issues of sex and marriage, and that debates over norms are incomprehensible without sustained attention to an overall vision of living the Christian life. Second, the essays engage in a lot of *description and re-description.* Such a description ordinarily tries to find a way to name experiences that slip between the Scylla of pre-conciliar legalism and the Charybdis of the dominant culture. One participant wondered that day, "Is there a *nature* underneath all this description?" Certainly some of the essays here want to argue that there is; others are less interested in this question, not least because identifying such "nature" seems impossible in any "pure" form. However, it is noteworthy that even those who defend a clear position on the "nature" question nevertheless go on to engage in description—indeed, theology of the body is precisely such a description. By highlighting the importance of thicker descriptions, Catholic sexual ethics moves away from simply-applied formulae that are supposed to "solve" ethical problems.

THE PRACTICE OF NEW WINE, NEW WINESKINS

I've summarized the movement beyond personalism here with reference to the development of *practices* and *meanings*. While anthropological principles are certainly more flexible than legalistic rules, the principles of personalism still retain a convenient ability to "translate" into norms (or exceptions, usually by making norms broader). Such does not seem to be the case with practices and meanings. And it is true that, to use an example, a description of the "contraceptive mentality" isn't going to get you an *airtight* argument for or against *Humanae Vitae*'s norm. Since this is an introduction to a diverse collection, all I should do here is state that. If Freitas is right, then the present collection is simply a reflection that no straightforward presentation of norms (or exceptions) is sufficient in a time when practices are diverse and meanings are thin and individualized.

The priority of normative debates was characteristic of the personalist era. Charles Curran, in his history of moral theology, actually treats debates over specific norms *before* outlining broader approaches to sexual ethics as a whole, commenting that writers "working in the 1960s and 1970s were so busy dealing with particular issues that they wrote primarily essays rather than monographs."[51] It is only more recently that more fundamental debates have come to the forefront. Some authors in this collection clearly support traditional norms; others pretty clearly question them. But all share a sense that Catholic discussion about sex and marriage cannot begin and end with debates over the standard norms. That is to put the cart before the horse—or, to change the metaphor slightly, to close the barn door when the horse has already left the barn! By focusing on the practical rationality embedded within practices, and the correlative narratives, they follow Alasdair MacIntyre's hope to move moral conversation beyond an impasse between "moral relativism" and "moral dogmatism."[52] Again, that is not to make an argument one way or the other on particular norms—but only to place such debates about norms within a context where one can "make sense" of them. Thus, the collection (happily) mirrors many a late-night conversation in Notre Dame's Moreau Seminary, where a dozen young moral theologians sat around and discovered that yet another conversation had come back to a debate about *Humanae Vitae*. It's not that the norms don't matter. It's that the conversation about the norms appears unfruitful if it is not contextualized by reflection and description of these larger frameworks.

It has been a gift of the New Wine New Wineskins symposium to offer so many of us, from different backgrounds and with different views, the opportunity to have such conversations, at length, in the context of friendship. The original conference invitation in 2002 "hoped that the incipient friendships nourished at the conference will contribute to greater collegiality in our field and engender further scholarly projects."[53]

51. Curran, *Catholic Moral Theology*, 192.
52. MacIntyre, "Recovery," 115.
53. Cloutier and Mattison, "Introduction," 12.

Surely such friendship remains quite needed in the area of sexual ethics specifically, where issues have sometimes become "litmus tests" (on both sides). Just as our meetings strive to do, Wineskins publications seek to collect scholarly work arising from these conversations, which would highlight both convergences and areas of debate, without any pre-set agenda. Thus, this collection of essays.

Some of the essays appearing here were first drafted for a daylong pre-conference that preceded the 2007 symposium. The discussions of the pre-conference participants, a selected group, all of whom had published on or were teaching sexual ethics, were extraordinarily fruitful, not least because of the obvious diversity of perspectives. It is impossible, in a collection like this, to recreate the best interchanges, but two things should be noted about them. First, participants were remarkably generous in seeking common ground—that is, seeking common concerns and ideas that would bring together a shared perspective, despite a difference on this or that norm. Such a common perspective is sorely needed if the Church is to develop any effective catechesis and formation of present and future generations of Catholics. Second, even in the midst of such generosity, participants were exposed to pointed, challenging questions from other views. One of the great potential (perhaps actual?) dangers of present-day Catholic theology is that it is so easy for us to give papers and be in discussion with *only those people who already agree with us.* If anything, "we" simply read a text or two from "the other side," and we rack up the arguments against "them." The pre-conference offered an extended, close gathering where questions could be discussed and hashed out—it was not like typical conference sessions. Part of the hope I have for this collection is that its diversity can engender more possibilities where this kind of exchange can take place, where real "pushing" (not literal, of course!) happens. A number of other papers in this collection were solicited from other Wineskins participants, as well as appearing in the regular conference line-up of papers for the past several years. Like the first collection, but more specifically themed, it is hoped that the volume offers some indication of future pathways for the field.

The two parts of our collection mirror the title. The collection begins with three essays, by Jason King, Kari-Shane Davis Zimmerman, and Maria Morrow, which offer narrations of certain contemporary phenomena that don't fit well into typical theological categories. King explains how theology can identify and respond to dating violence. Zimmerman sets out the contemporary "hook-up" culture, and offers comment on how it might be understood. Morrow engages the phenomenal increase in pornography, and in images inspired by pornography, and offers a complex response through a particular understanding of the sacrament of penance. Next, Jana Bennett's essay engages the problem of singleness in general, particularly singleness after college, indicating that Christians need to develop an understanding where all are single and all are married, in terms of ecclesiology. The final two essays take up particular contested phenomena that edge closer to "coming home"—but in new and different ways. David McCarthy outlines the rise of cohabitation, arguing that its advocates (including theological voices) misunderstand marriage as a "personal capstone" rather than an "institutional practice," thereby making it an institution increasingly sustainable only for the socially privileged. Fr. Nicanor Austriaco, a Dominican biologist, offers an extensive inquiry into scientific data about homosexuality, arguing that such data offers more support for the magisterium's position than is imagined.

In reflecting on marriage, the first two essays look deceptively familiar: they are about *Humanae Vitae* and birth control! Florence Caffrey Bourg, besides offering a helpful summary of the development of the tradition, argues that contemporary understandings of vocation and discipleship call into question Paul VI's teachings. On the other hand, Michel Therrien defends the teaching by paying attention to "responsible parenthood" as a practice, placing it within a particular reading of biblical covenant theology. Notice that, for both essays, NFP as a practice is crucial. The next two essays speak more broadly on contemporary understandings of marital love. William Mattison and I argue that while John Paul II's theology of the body improves on some earlier post-conciliar theologies of marital love, it still proves insufficiently prophetic in a culture devoted to a privatized ideal of marriage. Julie Hanlon Rubio responds to such arguments, indicating that sexual love does need to be a central component of marriage theology, but understood in a much deeper way than in earlier work. Finally, Christopher Roberts takes on the ever-vexing issue of male-female complementarity, recovering Augustine and Barth to help offer a description of why gender difference matters for contemporary marriage.

JUST A START

Of course, the collection has no pretensions of being exhaustive. Nor do the papers, for that matter. The collection aims at making the debates accessible, and especially at (as many of the original pre-conference participants stated) saying something about various issues that educated laity and pastors might find useful. As one participant in the original symposium commented that day, "We all get passionate about being pastoral!" Because of the format, authors have been asked to focus more on offering a constructive position, and less on displaying exhaustive knowledge of the scholarly literature. Most authors in the collection have amply demonstrated their scholarly facility elsewhere. Given especially the scarcity of good material on some of the topics in the first section, the collection also may be useful in the undergraduate classroom.

Finally, while the collection has tried to cast a wide net topically, there are a few omissions that should be noted. First, while the collection displays a diversity of positions, as well as a diversity of gender, the collection does not do justice to various ethnic and class differences. Many, perhaps all, the essays depict the context and preoccupations of middle- and upper-class Americans. While it's hard to deny that this is the "dominant culture" or "cultural mainstream" at present in America, it would be equally foolish to assume that it represents everyone. As almost all sociological studies show, different ethnic and class subcultures are dealing with different (though not entirely unrelated) dynamics in terms of both "leaving home" and "coming home."

Secondly, while the collection includes authors with different views, I have not tried to achieve a "balance" on any particular issue. In some cases, there are diverse views—see, for example, the competing takes of Florence Bourg and Michel Therrien on NFP in contemporary marriage. In others, a particular essay stands alone; the essay on science and homosexuality presented by Fr. Nicanor Austriaco occasioned a great deal of intense debate when it was presented at the 2008 Wineskins conference, so its presence in this collection should not indicate any sort of "group consensus" on the issue. As an ongoing group of theologians drawn from a very diverse range of graduate programs, Wineskins has always welcomed a wide variety of papers, and looks forward to future work that might treat a topic differently.

Finally, while Jana Bennett's essay does address the state of single-ness, the collection does not include any essays directly on celibacy.[54] Indeed, perhaps the most notable limitation of its title is the presumption of an itinerary that involves "coming home." Lifelong vowed celibacy lurks as the most striking counter-practice to the culture in the Church's tradition—as it in some sense always has. Today, in the American context (and elsewhere), discussions of celibacy are inevitably tangled up in arguments over mandatory celibacy for priests, which is itself entangled, in contested ways, with both the sexual abuse scandals and homosexuality in the ministry. Thus, any attempt to deal with it in a single essay is even more treacherous than many other sexual topics. Nevertheless, the practice of celibacy remains a seemingly necessary companion to the tradition's reflection on sex and marriage, and so its absence here leaves a certain incompleteness that is perhaps fitting for a collection that hopes to start conversation, not end it.

BIBLIOGRAPHY

Anderson, Carl, and Jose Granados. *Called to Love: Approaching John Paul II's Theology of the Body.* New York: Doubleday, 2009.

Arnett, Jeffrey Jensen. *Emerging Adulthood: The Winding Road from the Late Teens through the Twenties.* New York: Oxford, 2006.

Asci, Donald P. *The Conjugal Act as a Personal Act: A Study of the Catholic Concept of the Conjugal Act in the light of Christian Anthropology.* San Francisco: Ignatius, 2002.

Berry, Wendell. "The Body and the Earth." In *The Unsettling of America*, 97–142. San Francisco: Sierra Club, 1977.

Bishop, Bill. *The Big Sort: Why The Clustering of Like-Minded America is Tearing Us Apart.* New York: Houghton Mifflin, 2008.

Cahill, Lisa Sowle. "Current Teaching on Sexual Ethics." In *Readings in Moral Theology, no. 8: Dialogue About Catholic Sexual Teaching*, edited by Charles E. Curran and Richard A. McCormick, S.J., 525–35. New York: Paulist, 1993.

———. *Sex, Gender, and Christian Ethics.* New York: Cambridge University Press, 1996.

Cahill, Lisa Sowle, et al., editors. *Sexuality and the U.S. Catholic Church: Crisis and Renewal.* New York: Crossroad, 2006.

Capon, Robert Farrar. *Bed and Board: Plain Talk About Marriage.* New York: Simon & Schuster, 1965.

Carroll, Colleen. *The New Faithful.* Chicago: Loyola, 2002.

Cherlin, Andrew J. *The Marriage-Go-Round: The State of Marriage and the Family in America Today.* New York: Knopf, 2009.

---

54. Four essays address historical and contemporary issues involving celibacy in Cahill et al., *Sexuality and the U.S. Catholic Church*, 94–143.

Cloutier, David. "Heaven is a Place on Earth? Analyzing the Popularity of Pope John Paul II's Theology of the Body." In *Sexuality and the U.S. Catholic Church: Crisis and Renewal*, edited by Lisa Sowle Cahill et al., 18–31. New York: Crossroad, 2006.

———. *Love, Reason, and God's Story: An Introduction to Catholic Sexual Ethics.* Winona, MN: Anselm Academic/St. Mary's Press, 2008.

Cloutier, David, and William C. Mattison III. "Introduction." In *New Wine, New Wineskins: A Next Generation Reflects on Key Issues in Catholic Moral Theology*, edited by William C. Mattison III, 1–24. Lanham, MD: Sheed & Ward, 2005.

Congregation for the Doctrine of the Faith. "Human Sexuality." In *Vatican Council II: Volume 2: More Postconciliar Documents*, rev. ed., edited by Austin Flannery, O.P., 505–9. Northport, NY: Costello, 1998.

Curran, Charles E. *Catholic Moral Theology in the United States: A History*. Washington, DC: Georgetown University Press, 2008

Curran, Charles E., and Richard A. McCormick, S.J., editors. *Readings in Moral Theology, no. 8: Dialogue About Catholic Sexual Teaching*. New York: Paulist, 1993.

Curran, Charles E., and Julie Hanlon Rubio, editors. *Marriage (Readings in Moral Theology, no. 15)*. New York: Paulist, 2009

Davidson, James D., et al. *The Search for Common Ground: What Unites and Divides Catholic Americans*. Huntington, IN: Our Sunday Visitor, 1997.

Farley, Margaret. *Just Love: A Framework for Christian Sexual Ethics*. New York: Continuum, 2006.

Florida, Richard. *The Rise of the Creative Class*. New York: Basic, 2002.

Ford, John, and Gerald Kelly. *Contemporary Moral Theology*, vol. 2: *Marriage Questions*. Westminster, MD: Newman, 1963.

Freitas, Donna. *Sex and the Soul: Juggling Sexuality, Spirituality, Romance, and Religion on America's College Campuses*. New York: Oxford, 2008.

Gaillardetz, Richard. *A Daring Promise: A Spirituality of Christian Marriage*. New York: Crossroad, 2002.

Grabowski, John. *Sex and Virtue*. Washington, DC: Catholic University of America Press, 2003.

Guindon, Andre. *The Sexual Language: An Essay in Moral Theology*. Toronto: University of Ottawa Press, 1977.

John Paul II, Pope. *The Theology of the Body*. Boston: Pauline, 1997.

Kosnik, Anthony, et al. *Human Sexuality: New Directions in American Catholic Thought*. Garden City, NY: Doubleday, 1979; orig, 1977.

Layard, Richard. *Happiness: Lessons from a New Science*. New York: Penguin, 2005.

MacIntyre, Alasdair. "The Recovery of Moral Agency?" In *The Best Christian Writing 2000*, edited by John Wilson, 111–36. San Francisco: HarperSanFrancisco, 2000.

Mahoney, John, S.J. *The Making of Moral Theology*. New York: Oxford University Press, 1987.

McCarthy, David Matzko. "Procreation, the Development of Peoples, and the Final Destiny of Humanity." *Communio* 26 (1999) 698–721.

McCormick, Richard, S.J. "The Moral Theology of Vatican II." In *The Future of Ethics and Moral Theology*, edited by Don Brezine, S.J. and James V. McGlynn, S.J., 7–18. Chicago: Argus Communications, 1968.

McKibben, Bill. *Deep Economy*. New York: Times Books/Henry Holt, 2007.

Moore, Gareth, O.P. *The Body in Context*. London: SCM, 1992.

Navarro, Mireya. "Spreading the Pope's Message of Sexuality and a Willing Spirit." *New York Times* (June 7, 2004), 1(B).

Nelson, James B., and Sandra P. Longfellow, editors. *Sexuality and the Sacred: Sources for Theological Reflection.* Louisville: Westminster John Knox, 1994.

O'Malley, John W. *What Happened at Vatican II.* Cambridge: Harvard University Press, 2008.

Pinckaers, Servais, O.P. *The Sources of Christian Ethics.* Translated by Sr. Mary Thomas Noble, O.P. Washington, DC: Catholic University of America Press, 1995.

Pius XII, Pope, "Address to Midwives." Online: http://www.papalencyclicals.net/Pius12/P12midwives.htm.

Ratzinger, Joseph. "The Dignity of the Human Person." In *Commentary on the Documents of Vatican II, volume V,* edited by Herbert Vorgrimler, 115–63. New York: Herder & Herder, 1969.

Robinson, Geoffrey. *Confronting Power and Sex in the Catholic Church.* Collegeville, MN: Liturgical, 2008.

Salzman, Todd, and Michael Lawler. *The Sexual Person: Toward a Renewed Catholic Anthropology.* Washington, DC: Georgetown University Press, 2008.

Scola, Angelo. *The Nuptial Mystery.* Grand Rapids: Eerdmans, 2005.

Shenk, Joshua Wolf. "What Makes Us Happy?" *The Atlantic* 303.5 (2009) 36–53.

Wallerstein, Judith S., and Sandra Blakeslee. *The Good Marriage: How and Why Love Lasts.* Boston: Houghton Mifflin, 1995.

Watters, Ethan. *Urban Tribes: A Generation Redefines Friendship, Family, and Commitment.* New York: Bloomsbury, 2003.

Wills, Gary. *Bare Ruined Choirs: Doubt, Prophecy, and Radical Religion.* Garden City, NY: Doubleday, 1972.

Wuthnow, Robert. *After the Baby Boomers: How Twenty- and Thirty-Somethings Are Shaping the Future of American Religion.* Princeton, NJ: Princeton University Press, 2007.

Leaving

1

A Theology of Dating for a Culture of Abuse

B Y AGE SIXTEEN, 80 percent of people in the United States have been on at least one date. Of these, 25 percent will experience non-sexual violence and almost 20 percent will experience sexual violence.[1] Yet, theological reflection on this time period (16–25) is almost non-existent. What little thought there is about dating barely addresses the violence these relationships often entail.[2]

To be sure, the term dating itself is almost anachronistic. The amorphous and fluidity of relationships during this time period is hard to understand much less reflect upon. Yet, something that is not marriage and is sexual is going on for most people in this country for almost ten years, and it is potentially dangerous.

I have set out two tasks in this paper. First, I outline the dating scripts from the pre-1920s era to today. "Script" is a sociological term meaning "a repertoire of acts and statuses that are recognized by a social group, together with the rules, expectations and sanctions governing theses acts and statuses."[3] In other words, scripts are cultural narratives that people rely on to make sense of and direct specific and recurring social encounters.

1. See Center for Disease Control and Prevention, "Dating Violence Fact Sheet."
2. For Christian reflection on sex and dating, see Bonacci, *Real Love*; Cloutier, *God's Story*; Freitas, *Sex and the Soul*; Harris, *Kissed Dating Goodbye*; King and Freitas, *Save the Date*; West, *Good News*; and Winner, *Real Sex*. Of these, only Freitas's *Sex and the Soul* touches on some of the violence that is occurring in dating relationships.
3. Laws and Schwartz, *Sexual Scripts*.

As I am applying it to dating, scripts are the cultural assumptions for how people should date. Thus, scripts do not tell us how people actually behave on dates but rather what society expects of them. Obviously, behaviors will vary but they will vary in relationship to the script. If people deviate from a script, they are thrust into an area without understanding and thus must explain to themselves or to each other what is going on. While obviously there are several factors at play that lead to violence, I intend to explore one of these important factors: how we arrive at dating scripts that, while they do not advocate violence, provide ready legitimatization for it.

The second task of this paper is to respond to the cultural dating scripts with a theological dating script. Since the Church must labor to stop violence and since so many people in the United States experience violence in their dating relationships, there is a great need to offer an understanding of dating in light of the Christian call to love God and neighbor. While a theological dating script will not stop violence in and of itself, it is a valuable resource for the Church to confront this rampant problem.

A HISTORY OF DATING SCRIPTS

The scripts for dating up to the 1920s were "calling" and "keeping company."[4] During this time, life was mostly rural and travel was limited. So, potential suitors most likely lived close by and were known by the family. A man would come "calling" at a female's house, occasionally of his own initiative, most often at the prompting of the woman's mother. The parents would welcome the potential suitor into their house and carry the announcement of his arrival to their daughter.

The daughter would then make the decision to see or not to see the visitor. If the woman chose not to see him, the man could come back, but if the woman declined several "calls," the man was expected to stop his visits. An acceptance of a "call" usually entailed a conversation in the woman's living room. It implied no commitment to see the caller again or to stop seeing other callers. It was mainly an opportunity for the man and woman to get to know each other.

---

4. In the following section, I am reading the standard history of dating practices in the United States through the category of scripts. For examples of the standard history, see Whyte, "Choosing Mates," and Cloutier, *God's Story*, chapter 5.

If, however, the woman repeatedly saw only one suitor and stopped seeing others, the relationship had moved to a new level: "keeping company." "Keeping company" was not an engagement but rather a recognition that the relationship was quickly moving toward it. If a woman was "keeping company" with a man, both were expected to be exclusive in the relationship. "Keeping company" was a formal relationship. The relationship was usually public knowledge, the expectations were clear, and the movement toward engagement and marriage was assumed.

There are two important aspects to notice about this early script. First, the roles within it were clear. Both the female and the male knew the actions that they needed to take for the relationship to start, stop, and grow. The man was to come "calling" and the female was to make the decision about the suitor and the relationship. In many ways, there was an equality in these roles. Since the woman decided whom she will see and with whom she would keep company, as well as carried out the relationship in her home, this script gave her a real equality with the suitor. (Of course this equality with the suitor is circumscribed by her subordination to her father and, when she married, to her husband.)

Second, the script was primarily enacted in the home and people were formed in their roles by the family. "Calling" and "keeping company" were understood and acceptable relationships. Families taught people how to understand and act the roles in the relationship. The result was that relationships were forced to develop through conversation first, before sexual activity, and, because of the supervision, protection from violence from the suitor was provided.

1920s–1930s

This dating script changed in the 1920s as dating moved outside of women's homes and into men's cars. The familial context and influence began to wane. The terms "calling" and "keeping company" were replaced by "dating" and "going steady." Where the man used to "call" on the woman, he now scheduled a particular day and time, a date, to get together. Where the serious couple "kept company" in the woman's house, the couple now consistently and steadily went places together. While dating was still a form of courtship, it was understood not in terms of companionship but rather in getting or going somewhere. The script changed from forming a relationship to achieving a relationship, from becoming to doing.

The movement outside of women's homes to men's cars, created a power imbalance in the relationship in favor of men. Women were in men's cars, under men's steering, dependent (at least for the extent of the date) on men's money. Given that this new script of dating temporarily removed the couple from the home and the oversight of family, gender roles became more pronounced in dating relationships to help govern and direct dating behavior. Men were in charge, and women were subordinate. Men were aggressive, and women were passive. These scripts attempted to carry the weight of defining expectations that used to be sustained by families and society.

1940s–1950s

The 1920s and 1930s script was expanded in time to include college years. More and more people were going to college (in part because of the GI Bill), so they were more and more removed from homes and more and more "going" on dates and "going" steady. The script for dating expanded accordingly, providing expectations pinned not to the home or car but schools. In junior high, people would casually date, in high school, date a number of people, in college, go steady, and, at the end of college, get engaged and marry.

Gender roles were also intensified. Women, it was assumed, should be more passive, more concerned about marriage. Men were to be more aggressive by pursuing women, even if they said no. The oft-repeated example of these scripts was the widespread belief that men were trying to get "as far" as they could with women, and women were trying to get men to propose and marry. The result was that women's power consisted in manipulating men to marry by giving or withhold sex. Of course, her decisions were usually in the man's car, at the destination of his choosing, with his money. Consequently, the "absence of parental control and pressure to respond to man's initiative put women in a weaker position than they had been under the earlier system of 'calling.'"[5]

There are two trends to notice in the dating scripts of this time period. First, the dating scripts (especially their connection to marriage and permissible sexual activity) are significantly elaborated, pinned to different phases of schooling, and supported by an intensification of gender roles all in the hopes of communicating appropriate expecta-

---

5. Schwartz and Scott, *Marriages and Families*, 131.

tions without the guidance or safety of home and family life. An effect of this connection to progress through school is that people were expected to date for longer periods of their lives. The road to marriage could be preceded by upwards of ten years of dating. While dating was still considered the route to marriage, this end was not taken seriously until the later college years. For the first six or seven years of dating, marriage was a remote end having little impact on dating. Thus begins a decoupling of dating scripts from marriage, even while the "later" scripts (i.e., high school or college) still maintained this connection.

Second, the motion metaphors for dating are clarified. Before people were doing something or going somewhere; now, with the greater influence of gender roles in dating, men were trying to get sex and women were trying to get married. The script was not only refined to clarify the ends of dating but also set up different ends between the genders. The understanding of dating had built into it conflict between men and women.

1960s–1970s

The 1960s and 1970s usher in another radical shift in dating practices as the culture of the era challenged many conventional scripts, including gender roles. Not only should women not be chained to particular careers (e.g., secretarial work), not only should they not just stay at home with the kids, but, in dating, they should not have to wait for men to ask them out, ride in their cars to places of their choosing, and rely on them to pay for the date. Moreover, it was not just men who wanted sex but women did too. Women could be as aggressive about it as men could, so the script went. While the pill did not cause all of these movements and ideas, it did enable many of them to be a real possibility to be chosen by women because, in theory, it negated the possibility of pregnancy. Without becoming pregnant, women could act sexually like men.

This challenge to the problematic gender roles was also a challenge to the traditions that had produced and sustained them. Thus, what society or Christianity or the 1950s or the United States sanctioned were unreliable because they had for so long been complicit in the oppression of women. If these traditions and their taboos cannot be trusted, then it is the negotiation and consent between the individuals that matters. The script of dating that moved from the home to schools had now moved to individuals.

The problem here is not the movement to redress the wrongs against women perpetuated by gender stereotypes. This movement was too long in coming and has still not advanced far enough. The problem, at least as far as dating goes, is that the changes in the dating script contributed to the violence found in dating today. The replacement of the submissive female script with the male aggressive script implied that both genders wanted sex and wanted it without any necessary connection to families, schools, gender roles, or serious relationships. The only requirement became that the two people consent to what was happening.

A consequence of this challenge is a further decoupling of dating from marriage. Marriage was already delayed for some because of college, but now it was also looked upon suspiciously as another institution oppressing women. If marriage is postponed or opposed, the historical understanding of the role and purpose of dating is lost. Dating is replaced by any number of alternatives. Cohabitation and casual sex are two stereotypical examples of this time period. Even the terms "dating" and "going steady" become passé as they are tied to an earlier, problematic time period.

The problem here is not so much a *distinguishing* of dating from marriage. "Calling" and "going on a date" were already social practices several steps removed from marriage. The problem is an absence of the meaning and expectations in dating relationships. Despite their obvious weaknesses, the earlier scripts had a formality that helped couples in relationships to understand them. With the challenge to and, for the most part, rejection of these past practices, there was no reliable way of understanding the status of the relationship. Pair this loss of formal steps with the dominant script of individual choice, and confusion about what dating was could not help but grow.

1980s–2000s

The cultural script of "whatever people consent to is legitimate" that emerged in the 1960s and 1970s intensifies from then until today. While dating is ubiquitous, there is little agreement on what dating is. People can date who they want, when they want, and do what they want, but dating has no accepted meaning, end, categories for communicating commitment levels, and norms. People who decide to wait until marriage to have sex and those who believe sex is nothing more than casual entertainment may differ in what they do on dates but they both view these practices as their own choosing and do not want to impose them upon others.

The only common assumption, other than consent should be gotten, is that men and women both want sex, often desperately. While the 1960s and 1970s dating script initiated the idea that women wanted sex just as men do, since the 1980s this assumption has only been magnified. Our hypersexualized culture inculcates the belief that men and women do not just desire sex but need it. Lack of sex and even a lack of desire for sex is a serious malady. Like the consent piece, the sex piece has changed from the earlier period only by way of being amplified. It is no wonder that what one finds today is not a "dating scene" where people meet, get to know one another, and then go out on dates, but a "hook-up culture" where people regularly engage in "anything 'ranging from kissing to having sex,' and that [they do this] outside the context of commitment."[6]

These two aspects of the consent dating script replace the formality of previous relationships with casual, informal relationships. The result is that "dating" or "hooking up" or any other term for these types of relationships is relatively vacuous because they imply no single and specific set of actions. The categories mean whatever people decide they mean. There are no common terms for what is going on, no markers to determine the status of the relationship, no lines distinguishing what should and should not be done, and the cultural script that people can consent to whatever they want does not help people to negotiate any of these ambiguities. If a relationship gets serious, it has to be talked about, negotiated, and come to be understood as serious between the individuals involved.[7]

This script has only intensified with the rise of the pornography industry. In her article "Love your Enemy: Sex, Power, and Christian Ethics," Karen Lebacqz describes what I term the pornography script as follows:

6. Glenn and Marquardt, *Hooking Up*, 13, as cited in Freitas, *Sex and the Soul*, 261.

7. When I made this argument to an undergraduate class, asking them how they knew they were in a serious relationship, instead of the expected silence I got "you post it on Facebook." Facebook has categories to define relationships, including marriage, in a relationship, and it's complicated. While theses categories do provide some public way to understanding relationships, I am still not sure if they are "thick" enough to provide a common "script."

> Pornography would suggest that men are socialized to find both male power and female powerlessness sexually arousing. In pornography, domination of women by men is portrayed as sexy. It is the power of the man or men to make the woman do what she does not want to do—to make her do something humiliating, degrading, or antithetical to her character—that creates the sexual tension and excitement. . . . In pornography, women are raped, tied up, beaten, humiliated—*and* are portrayed as initially resisting and ultimately enjoying their degradation.[8]

This pornography script does not do away with the standard consent script so much as offer a particular version of it: the *enjoyment* of sexual violence is functionally equivalent to consent. If a woman turns a man down initially, he can force himself on her and she will acquiesce because she really wants sex. Of course, it does not necessarily have to be a man doing the forcing. As Ariel Levy argues in her *Female Chauvinist Pigs*, women can take control either by playing the submissive role or taking the assertive role.[9] This result should not be unexpected as the consent script assumes that women, in the end, want sex as much and as violently as men do. What matters for my argument is that violence becomes just another way, acceptable to some but not others, to get consent.

It should be no surprise that this is the time period when studies of dating violence and date rape emerge. Not that violence in dating never occurred before, but not until a consent script emerges could people study how a consent could go wrong. It would be hard to imagine many opportunities for dating violence before the 1920s; violence would have been perpetuated primarily by spouses and parents. Afterwards, violence in the age of the automobile would have been possible, but the cultural scripts would have explained it (and occasionally still does explain it) not as a failure in the consent but as a failure of people (usually women) to adhere to the gender roles of the cultural script. Women should know men want sex and should carefully guard themselves against men, or so the script went. Violence was often mistakenly read as the result of the woman's failure to adhere to the gender role by dressing in a particular way or making herself too available to men or putting herself into a compromising position.

8. Lebacqz, "Love your Enemy," 8.
9. See Levy, *Female Chauvinist Pigs*.

What the studies find is that violence is rampant during the dating years (16–25). 25 percent of dating relationships have non-sexual violence. 40 percent of domestic violence is between non-married (i.e., cohabitating, courting, dating) couples. 85 percent of the victims are women. 20 percent of the women in college experience non-sexual violence. 70 percent of pregnant teens are beaten by their boyfriends.[10]

Sexual assault statistics are even more staggering. Date rape accounts for 67 percent of the reported sexual assaults on campus. In fact, rape is the most commonly reported crime on campus, with the lowest estimate being one in five women experiences completed or attempted rape. 85 percent of these assaults are perpetrated by parties known to the victim, usually boyfriends, ex-boyfriends, or classmates.[11]

WHY DATING VIOLENCE?

While multiple causes factor into an explanation of such high incidents of sexual and non-sexual dating violence, what is it about the current script and its development that contributes to or exacerbates the problem? I want to argue that the consent script is too dominant. All norms, practices, advice, qualifications are subordinated to individual choice and, thereby, rendered at best ineffective and at worst non-existent. The result is an isolated individual with no way to evaluate a relationship or with rational grounds for saying "no," thus enabling people to legitimate violence.

Here is how it plays out. The consent script emerged as the result of an isolation of the dating couple. People are no longer in a home. While the car left couples more isolated, the date was still monitored by that fact that it was to occur at a publicly known place and time. The emergences of the consent script marginalized these former scripts as well as the corresponding public dimensions. People are not just called to make up their own minds but are thought of as regressive and irresponsible to return to those institutions (e.g., family and church) that created oppressive gender roles.

Since dating is no longer bound by familial practice, grade level, connection to marriage but only by consent, dating has no non-negotiable meaning. The closest one gets to meaning is that people want sex, and

---

10. Schwartz and Scott, *Marriages and Families*, 374–75.
11. Ibid., 379–80.

dating is an opportunity to have sex. The meaning of a dating relationship is stipulated by each discrete couple. Without meaning, there are no
negative norms and no substantive positive practices other than having
sex. People may set their own limits and choose to act in certain ways,
but all of that is personal preference and thus negotiable.

Obviously, even with the earlier, more social scripts, each relationship negotiated the boundaries of the relationship. The difference between these social scripts and the consent script is that the social scripts
gave reasons for adhering to them—this is how people get to know each
other, how we learn about suitable partners, how we prepare for marriage, how we distinguish that status of the relationship, how we know
what relationships to take serious—and thereby demanded reasons for
deviating from it. Once choice is personal and should not be restricted
by others, the reasons for behaving one way as oppose to another, or doing one thing but refusing another, are also personal. Thus, the reasons
are merely *preferences*, and while others might agree with one's preferences and the reasons for them, it is merely their preference to do so. In
short, there is no ability to give a compelling reason for dating in one
way as opposed to another.

An implication of this script for dating violence is that while there
is a reason to say "yes" to sex according to the script (i.e., we all want it),
there is no reason to say "no" to sexual activity other than personal preference. People are at liberty to try and convince people to say "yes" after
they have said "no" as they are just trying to change their individual preferences. Some people might attempt to use verbal persuasion, but others
might "legitimately" use more coercive methods. Any limitation to these
methods is also a personal preference and thus arbitrary. Moreover, the
pornography script provides justification for those who force themselves
on others: while they may not give their consent initially, the pleasure
will, in the end, be functionally equivalent to a consent. In short, the current script gives you reasons to say "yes," no reason to say "no," and justification for using force to change the mind of those who do say "no."

Examples of this implication of the dating script are pervasive.
Convicted rapists believe that their actions are culturally acceptable.
The convicted rapists that admit that they did something wrong (slightly
above 40 percent) blame their failure to recognize a lack of consent but
have little problem with the violence used.[12] Those convicted rapists

12. Mann and Hollin, "Sexual Offenders' Explanation," 3–9

who believe they did nothing wrong explain their action by saying the women wanted sex that way or that the women deserved it because they were thought to be promiscuous. In this case, the women either consent because of their enjoyment or because deep down they want it as witnessed by their willingness to have sex with multiple people.[13]

People have difficulty distinguishing "between sexual violence and ordinary heterosexual sexuality."[14] Roughly 50 percent of teenagers believe it is acceptable for a boy to sexually force himself on a girl if they were dating or if she had previously consented to the act, even if she later changed her mind.[15] While roughly 15 percent of college males admit to behavior that meets the legal definition of rape and 30 percent admit trying to coerce women into having sex after they have said "no," 84 percent of these same college males stated that they did nothing wrong, insisting that they neither raped or attempted to rape the women.[16]

A THEOLOGICAL SCRIPT FOR DATING

The problem facing dating is that the consent script isolates people in their decision making, thereby undermining any meaning to the dating relationship and any concomitant practices or prohibitions. This isolation does not cause violence but makes it possible and even allows for it to be justified. Some might see returning to the 1920s family living room as a solution since it provides a community to regulate behavior. Others might pine for the reemergence of the 1950s gender stereotypes that provided a clear dating script. The 1920s option fails because we cannot return to a bygone era. Family dynamics, expanded educations, protracted adolescences, urbanization, and mobility are just some of the changes that keep us from returning even if we wanted to do so. The 1950s gender roles fail because of its explicit and immoral subordination of women. Moreover, neither of these scripts provides a theological understanding of dating, an understanding rooted in the call to love God and love neighbor.

Yet, what is needed to labor against violence is a script that can communicate a meaning for dating that supports communal involvement as

13. Ibid.

14. Lebacqz, "Love your Enemy," 6.

15. Ibid.

16. Schwartz and Scott, *Marriages and Families*, 161.

well as provides guidelines for behavior. These two dimensions actually reflect two strong themes within the Catholic tradition: the importance of the Church for the life of faith and the expectation arising from the fact that we are all called to be disciples of Christ. These two dimensions can provide a substantive grounding for a theological script for dating.

First, as Douglas Schuurman has argued in *Vocation*, every Christian has two vocations.[17] The first is a general one: everyone is called to love God and love neighbor. This call is the call to discipleship. The second vocation is specific and derived from the first. Human beings are not all-knowing, all-powerful, and all-present. They are finite creatures, inhabiting time and space. Thus, Christians must find specific ways in which they are called to live out this general call of discipleship. These specific ways may be lifelong commitments like religious vows or marriage, long-term commitments like raising children or work, or even short-term commitments like a year of volunteer work or helping out a neighbor's pressing need.

If dating is to be thought about theologically, it is specific and short-term. Dating was not called for by Christ and so is not necessary to being a disciple. Dating, though, can be a way to learn how to love God and neighbor. Moreover, dating tends to be a short-term practice, typically lasting at most a few years. How can dating be a way to learn love? If God is love, love itself, then in loving others, people actually experience God. And since God is love and love is relational, it is only in and through relationships people come to know God as God truly is. Since dating is a relationship with another person, it can be an experience of God, God's love, and loving another.

"Can be" is the verb above because relationships, as is painfully obvious from the discussions earlier, can be also abusive and sinful. If dating is to lead to God, it must be able to foster Christian love. I would argue that it can do so insofar as dating is paschal. It follows a pattern of life–death–new life. The best example is the fact that every dating relationship "dies." People drift apart or break up. Even if the couple weds, the relationship is so different that it is given a new name, "marriage," signifying that one way of relating has been replaced by another. In all of these cases, the dating relationship has ended and people must figure out

17. Schuurman, *Vocation*.

how to redeem it "like the saints and the poets . . . [who] . . . do something creative with the idea of death," to quote Dorothy Sayers.[18]

Dating also witnesses an incarnate love. Dating is amphibious, half friendship, half marriage. Two people are getting to know each other, hanging out together, discussing what happened and what matters. They are friends, even if nascent friends, but they are also more. Everyone knows that dating involves some element of *eros*, some sexuality. The questions surrounding sex and dating are never "is it there" but rather "why, when, and how far." Dating then becomes a practice in trying to balance the friendship and the sexuality, of respecting both spiritual and physical aspects of a relationship. Neglecting either friendship or the realities of sexual desire leads one into a distortion about the relationship and the world, akin to classical heresies. Sexuality without friendship is akin to being an Ebionite and denying the divinity of Christ. Not recognizing sexual tension in a friendship is akin to being Gnostic and denying the goodness and importance of the body.

If dating is to lead to love, it must open people up to others. Bernard Lonergan talks about how falling in love changes people: "falling in love is something disproportionate to its causes, conditions, occasions, antecedents. For falling in love is a new beginning, an exercise of vertical liberty in which one's world undergoes a new organization."[19] Lonergan categorizes the effect of falling in love as a horizon shift. This shift might not be complete and need refinement, but it opens people up to new ways of understanding the world, an opening to someone who is not the self.

This discussion of dating as teaching Christian love is not meant to say that dating automatically does this or that these are the only characteristics of dating. Rather, this discussion is the first step in developing a theology dating script. Since dating can be understood as a short-term and specific vocation, as a way to learn about and how to love, dating can be thought about as a way to learn the requirements of discipleship.

Earlier scripts thought of dating primarily as a relationship leading to marriage or as an opportunity for sex or as doing whatever one chooses to do. Whatever one thinks of these meanings, they are not a Christian framework. Some might argue of these three, dating as leading to marriage is Christian. Yet Christians should try to process their

18. Sayers, *Whimsical Christian*, 133.
19. Lonergan, *Method in Theology*, 122.

experiences first through their faith in God. The New Testament and the early Christians tended to marginalize marriage because the way it was practiced was often unjust (e.g., its treatment of women and children, its orientation toward the state, loyalty to it over and against the neighbor and the stranger) and thereby inimical to the gospel. Thus, simply linking dating to marriage does not make dating Christian.

Moreover, so many of the dating relationships people have do not end in marriage. When people start dating at sixteen, they are not (and, we generally think, should not be) thinking about marriage. If marriage is the only redeeming end in dating, all of these relationships that end are at best useless and at worst sinful. The implication of this position is that people should not date anyone unless they know they intend to marry them. Of course, how do people know they want to marry someone unless they go out with them? And how do people figure out how to have relationships if they are not supposed to have relationships?

Thinking of dating as a specific and short-term form of discipleship takes dating relationships and the people in them seriously. It also accounts for the reality that Christians learn how to love by loving. This theological script of dating thus states that the meaning of dating is to learn about discipleship, to learn about loving God and loving neighbor. As with the Christian belief about love in general, this theology script of dating implies both the necessity of the community and guidelines for behavior.

The Necessity of Community for Dating

Catholicism has always insisted that the Church is necessary for salvation. Whatever one's opinion about how to interpret the ecclesiological and soteriological assumptions in this statement, it is true that Christians need other people in order to learn to be Christians. Only by relating to others do we learn to love, do we learn to imitate that Trinity that is a community of love, and do we acquire the habits necessary to sustain a life of discipleship.

If community in general is necessary to learn to love, it is true for a specific and short-term vocation like dating. Dating is about how to relate to another person where *eros* is present. To learn to love another *genuinely*, genuinely choose what is good for the other, without being clouded (at least too much) by one's own biases, people can benefit greatly from those that do it by imitating them. Through their own relationship, parents can model a love that is respectful of the whole person, and thus people can have a model for balancing or integrating *eros* with the broader relationship.

Good, substantive friendships can also model good relationships. I am not here talking about "having a friend in need," as helpful as this might be. Rather, friendship, if practiced well and reflected upon, can guide people in their dating relationships. Good friendships express, support, and encourage common commitments. Dating relationships can thus learn how to engage these deeper commitments and use them to integrate the experience of *eros* without letting *eros* come to dominate or control the relationship.

Even parishes can model good relationships. It is easy to think of a parish having opportunities for dating couples to come together to talk about their relationship in light of their faith in Christ. But parishes could also help couples focus on others instead of themselves by inviting and calling them to opportunities of service.

Whatever the kind of community, the community is an inextricable part of thinking about a theological script for dating. The community connects the couples to others and helps them to frame their relationship—however brief or extended it might be—in light of the gospel.

This communal dimension is crucial in opposing the legitimization of violence. Violence becomes more pervasive and more acceptable as people become more disconnected from their communities, from people who care about them and watch out for their good. The community provides models on how to behave (and by implication) not behave, not in terms of control or manners, but in light of the call to love God and neighbor. Moreover, in keeping the person from being isolated, the community can stand against abuse or violence. Friends, family, and parishioners can help people discern if the dating relationship is good or bad, violent or loving.

I am not advocating a return to the family living room of the pre-1920s "calling" script. Rather, I am advocating a more substantive communal connection. It is similar to what Lauren Winner advocates in her book, *Real Sex*. In this book, she discusses the cultural and religious misconceptions about sex, its need to be ordered by the spiritual practice of chastity, and the necessity of community for engaging in and sustaining such an enterprise. For example, she says what should guide sexual behavior in dating is the Rotunda Rule: "Don't do anything sexual that you wouldn't be comfortable doing on the steps of the Rotunda [of the University of Virginia]."[20] Winner understands this rule not as some abstract norm but rather as a way to connect her dating relationship to the community. It did so first as the rule itself came from an older campus minister whom she had consulted for guidance in her dating life, and, second, as the public setting of the aphorism reminds the couple that they are always accountable to the community. The Rotunda Rule exemplifies the kind of communal dynamic I am calling for in dating.

Guidelines for Dating

The second implication of the theological dating script is that it comes with norms. I am thinking of norms here primarily as the cumulated wisdom of the community about how to love. Most often when discussing dating, people gravitate to the norms surrounding sexual behavior. But since the theological dating script is about how to love as disciples, the primary norms regard the kinds of behavior consistent with love are found more broadly in the teachings and life of Jesus. Among these are the tasks called for in Matt 25:35: feed the hungry, give drink to the thirsty, welcome the stranger, cloth the naked, care for the sick, and visit the prisoners.

For the purposes of dating violence, the negative norms about love (i.e., what is not consistent with love) are crucial. Do not kill, do not commit adultery, and do not lie are all norms that if violated indicate a failure in or even lack of love. Jesus's expanded norms about not even being angry and not looking lustfully at another are also indicators of behavior militating against love and could lead to violence. Hence, these norms get imbedded in the theology dating script so that people have guides about good and bad relationships, good and bad behaviors.

At a basic level, these norms do two things: they provide people categories to name some actions as wrong and sinful and, in doing so, provide a reason for avoiding their occurrence or reoccurrence. Three examples will suffice. First, the prohibition on murder and angry thoughts enables a person in a dating relationship to identify physical violence as evil and thereby end the relationship. Second, the command not to lie militates against manipulation. The false stereotypes about men and women and the exploitation of low self-esteem, two characteristics that make people

20. Winner, *Real Sex*, 106.

vulnerable to abuse, depend upon deceit and half-truths.[21] While the physical abuse is easier to identify, addressing these contributing factors is more difficult. It is much easier to realize one has been struck than realizing one has been manipulated. The community becomes essential here. Discussing the relationship with others helps one to identify such a problem better and respond in a way to avoid future manipulation. It is no wonder that abusers try to isolate the abused from others.[22] Third, the commandment against adultery and Jesus' admonition against lustful thoughts at the very least reminds people in relationships of potential exploitation and abuse through sexual activity. Reflection and discernment might be needed to name this or that act as exploitative, but the norms not only enable people to be aware of the danger but also to perform the requisite reflection and discernment.

In short, the norms embedded in the dating script stand against dating violence. They are meant to foster love and steer people away from situations that damage or destroy them. They can recognize what is wrong and oppose it. The norms force people to think about what they are doing and, as embedded in a theological dating script, prod people to think about why they are doing it. As opposed to the consent script, these norms not only stand against violence, they also provide a legitimate reason for saying "no". The wisdom of friends, family, and Church, and even one's acceptance of this wisdom are legitimate enough grounds to stand against abuse and violence. With this foundation, dating hopefully has a better chance of fostering a greater love of self, others, and God.

BIBLIOGRAPHY

Bonacci, Mary Beth. *Real Love: Answers to Your Questions on Dating, Marriage and the Real Meaning of Sex*. San Francisco: Ignatius, 1996.

Center for Disease Control and Prevention. "Dating Violence Fact Sheet." No Pages. Online: http://www.cdc.gov/ViolencePrevention/intimatepartnerviolence/dating violence.html

Cloutier, David. *Love, Reason, and God's Story: An Introduction to Catholic Sexual Ethics*. Winona, MN: St Mary's, 2008.

Freitas, Donna. *Sex and the Soul: Juggling Sexuality, Spirituality, Romance, and Religion on America's College Campuses*. New York: Oxford University Press, 2008.

Glenn, Norval, and Elizabeth Marquardt. *Hooking Up, Hanging Out, and Hoping for Mr. Right: College Women on Dating and Mating Today*. New York: Institute for American Values, 2001.

21. Walker, "Battered Woman," 286–89.

22. Ibid., 276, 290.

Harris, Joshua. *I Kissed Dating Goodbye*. Colorado Springs, CO: Multnomah, 1999.

King, Jason, and Donna Freitas. *Save the Date: A Spirituality of Dating, Love, Dinner, and the Divine*. New York: Crossroad, 2003.

Laws, J., and P. Schwartz. *Sexual Scripts: The Social Construction of Female Sexuality*. Hinsdale, IL: Dryden, 1977.

Lebacqz, Karen. "Love Your Enemy: Sex, Power, and Christian Ethics." *Annual of the Society of Christian Ethics* 10 (1990) 3–23.

Levy, Ariel. *Female Chauvinist Pigs: Women and the Rise of Raunch Culture*. New York: Free, 2005.

Lonergan, Bernard. *Method in Theology*. Toronto: University of Toronto Press, 1994.

Mann, Ruth, and Clive Hollin. "Sexual Offenders' Explanation for their offending." *Journal of Sexual Aggression* 13 (2007) 3–9.

Sayers, Dorothy. *The Whimsical Christian*. New York: Collier, 1987.

Schwartz, Mary Ann, and BarBara Marliene Scott. *Marriages and Families: Diversity and Change*. Upper Saddle River, NJ: Pearson Prentice Hall, 2007.

Schuurman, Douglas. *Vocation: Discerning Our Callings in Life*. Grand Rapids: Eerdmans, 2004

Walker, Lenore. "The Battered Woman: Myths and Reality." In *Perspectives on Marriage: A Reader, Third Edition*, edited by Kieran Scott and Michael Warren, 276–92. New York: Oxford University Press, 2007.

West, Christopher. *The Good News about Sex and Marriage*. Cincinnati, OH: Servant Publications, 2000.

Whyte, Martin King. "Choosing Mates—The American Way." In *Shifting the Center: Understanding Contemporary Families, Second Edition*, edited by Susan Ferguson, 129–39. New York: McGraw Hill, 2001

Winner, Lauren. *Real Sex: The Naked Truth about Chastity*. Grand Rapids: Brazos, 2005.

2

In Control? The Hookup Culture and the Practice of Relationships

KARI-SHANE DAVIS ZIMMERMAN

FOR MANY COLLEGE-BOUND YOUNG adults today, the arrival onto a college campus can be filled with a significant amount of anxiety and a rather large dose of uncertainty about what exactly the future holds now that they have left home. In this essay, I will explore one particular slice of the college living environment that in recent times has received a growing amount of attention, that is, the "hookup" culture.

In 2007, Washington Post columnist Laura Sessions Stepp penned *Unhooked: How Young Women Pursue Sex, Delay Love and Lose at Both*. Shortly thereafter came two more texts addressing the "phenomenon" of hooking up: Kathleen Bogle's *Hooking Up: Sex, Dating, and Relationships on Campus*, and Donna Freitas's *Sex and the Soul*. Each has found throughout the course of their research that a new kind of "dating" model is operating on today's college campuses in which some (certainly not all) participate.[1] Moreover, the effects of participating in what Bogle dubs a "subculture with a complex set of rules and expectations," is wreaking havoc on some college-aged men and women's lives.

---

1. The hookup culture is not limited to college campuses; high school students are hooking up as well. However, the definition of hooking up used in high school does not always match the definition used by college-age men and women. As a result, one cannot always be sure what someone means when he or she reports they have "hooked up." According to Kathleen Bogle, it is oftentimes the case that one needs to ask the follow-up question, "How much sexual activity took place?" For a helpful resource on what hooking up looks like at the high school level, see Stepp, *Unhooked*, especially section two.

47

In addition to these writers' work, I want to offer an additional way to think about hooking up. That is, I want to reflect on the following question: What kind of skills does the practice of hooking up promote and how does this influence one's character? This question is pertinent because hooking up involves practicing certain skills that encourage persons to think, feel, and act in a certain manner when it comes to intimate relationships with another individual. Many of these skills work directly against the kinds of practices needed to sustain a marriage (a relationship goal many practitioners of hooking up admit to desiring at some point in their future adult life).[2] For example, I will argue that hooking up works against fostering any sense of *mutual trust* between two partners, even though most hookups take place between friends or at least semi-acquaintances rather than mere strangers. In addition, it is difficult for hookup partners to establish any sense of real physical, emotional, psychological, and spiritual *intimacy* with each other. And yet for a marriage to succeed, one needs not only the encouragement of his/her own community, but more importantly these skills of mutual trust and intimacy to be developed. Hooking up works against the cultivation of such skills, perhaps especially for women who participate in the activity reluctantly as a means to search for relationships.

This essay will begin by first offering a description of the practice of hooking up. Next, I will compare the skills one learns through the practice of hooking up versus those learned through the practice of dating and argue that the latter practice of dating more easily fosters the skills of mutual trust and intimacy necessary for the practice of marriage. Following this, I also will include some brief comments about the role gender plays in the practice of hooking up and why there is additional cause for concern when it comes to women and the practice of hooking up.

---

2. For example, Bogle, *Hooking Up*, notes that beyond psychology and personal biography, many of the women she interviewed wanted to be married by the age of 25 (102). However, the men in her study oftentimes indicated they wanted to wait longer to get married. This conflict in marriage timetables also places men and women's timetables for having serious relationships at odds. Bogle writes, "For this reason, several women indicated that they would like to have a relationship with marriage potential" (102). Women's noted interest in finding a potential marriage partner during college matches the findings of Glenn and Marquardt, *Hooking Up, Hanging Out*. In that study, 63 percent of college women claim they would like to meet their future spouse in college.

SECTION 1: A THICKER DESCRIPTION OF HOOKING UP

When it comes to understanding hooking up, most scholars agree it is difficult to define for several reasons. As Laura Sessions Stepp explains in her work, hooking up can involve an array of physical activity with another individual (from something as simple as kissing to genital intercourse) who might be a friend, an acquaintance, or in what appear to be rare cases, a complete stranger.[3] Hooking up also can happen virtually anywhere on a college campus: a bedroom, dance floor, bar, bathroom, auditorium, or any deserted room on a college campus. More importantly, most hookups are unplanned (although this does not always have to be the case); that is, they are spur-of-the-moment get-togethers that seem to happen most often following the end of some sort of group social gathering like a party. In addition, contributing to the ambiguity of the practice is that a hookup between two consenting individuals may lead to the start of something like an exclusive dating relationship or nothing at all. Thus, in her view, Stepp argues that "hooking up" is really all about the ability to "*unhook*" from a partner at any given time, as well as from the social expectations that coincide with many young adult's views of what it means to date a person of the opposite-sex.[4]

In a slightly different vein, Kathleen Bogle attempts to locate the practice of hooking up in its historical context. She begins by noting that hooking up is not a new word on college campuses; the terminology has been in use since the early to mid-1980s.[5] In addition, studies of college students from the 1960s indicated there was a growing shift away from a more traditional dating script to a group "partying" script where it was common for men and women to "pair off" at the end of an evening.[6] However, Bogle also warns that in the case of "hooking up" today, what might appear as "normal behavior" on the part of a small minority is not necessarily the case for everyone. Students oftentimes misperceive what their peers are doing and therefore falsely assume a mentality of "everyone is doing it." Despite Bogle's cautionary approach, her interviewees consistently indentified hooking up as the "dominant way for men and

---

3. Stepp, *Unhooked*, 24.

4. Ibid., 5.

5. Bogle notes, however, that because "hooking up" is a slang term and slang by definition is an informal and nonstandard language subject to arbitrary change, one should not be surprised that there is confusion and disagreement over the term (7).

6. Bogle, *Hooking Up*, 20.

women to get together and form potential relationships on campus."[7] Given this, the question at hand is how does a hookup happen?

Most of Bogle's interviewees noted that either a hookup happened because of alcohol consumption or they simply did not know how it came about because it is a normal, taken-for-granted aspect of their current social lives on a college campus. Stepp writes that the "unspoken rules" of the hooking up culture are as follows: "Girls get drunk with girls, guys with guys, and the sexes then come together to drink more, flirt, dance and hook up."[8] In other words, alcohol is the "social lubricant that fuels the unhooked culture, beginning in high school and particularly in college, where intercourse becomes more common"[9] When pressed further, however, students agreed the most common first step involves identifying a particular hookup partner, of which initial attraction plays an important role.[10] Following hookup partner identification, a second more critical step is finding a way to bridge the divide between never having been sexually intimate to suddenly becoming sexual intimate. According to Bogle, at this stage much of what takes place between the two partners is done in an indirect manner, e.g., by giving certain kinds of nonverbal clues like eye-contact or perhaps by engaging in a one-on-one conversation, or sensing an overall "vibe" from the potential partner.[11] It appears this kind of nonverbal communication oftentimes continues in the search for a hookup location. Some, but not all, of the factors influencing location choice include: who lives closer to where the two met? Who has the better set up for staying over? Where does the

---

7. Ibid., 25.

8. Stepp, *Unhooked*, 113.

9. Ibid., 115. When it comes to hooking up and alcohol, Stepp argues, however, that one cannot blame hookups solely on alcohol because that misses a larger point, and that is, the alcohol does not cause college students to jump into bed with each other. Rather, alcohol simply makes it easier for them to do something they think they want to do even though they may know it is not good for them (113–20).

10. According to Bogle, how much physical attraction mattered differed for men and women. On the one hand, her male participants claimed a striking physical appearance was the most valued quality a woman could posses. On the other hand, the women also recognized the important role physical appearance played in their decision of who to hookup with, but fraternity or athletic team membership was also a valued quality. For further reading, see Bogle, *Hooking Up*, 32ff.

11. Ibid., 34.

woman feel most safe? Does one partner have a preference for sleeping overnight or not?[12]

In addition to the above-mentioned list of decisions that must be made, a third step involves determining how far to take things sexually. Here Bogle's research suggests more is at stake than simply consulting one's own moral beliefs and sense of self. She writes, "Perception of what peers do sexually also affects the level of sexual interaction."[13] That is, even though the term "hooking up" appears intentionally vague and ambiguous, what students believe is "normal" within the context of the hookup culture also affects how men and women conduct themselves during a hookup. For example, if there is one norm specific to the hookup culture, Bogle notes, it is that some students admit they would go further sexually in a hookup if they did *not* really like the person or think there was any chance for a relationship. On the surface this rationale appears illogical because why would students be more sexually intimate with someone they did not really like? The irony, according to Bogle, is that many college students in her study admitted it was not a smart idea to become overly sexual with a hookup partner if one actually wanted to begin a relationship with the partner. In other words, if someone really likes another person, the operating (and dominant) social consensus is to "take it slow." Thus, it appears socially acceptable to do "whatever" with someone sexually who is "just a hookup," but the situation changes if one is potentially interested in forming a relationship post-hooking up.

This latter point is extremely interesting not only because it demonstrates an anti-hooking up logic within the actual hookup culture, but because it also gives credence to Bogle's findings that there appear to be *rules* attached to the hooking up script.[14] Case in point: if the two hookup partners are friends (or even acquaintances) before the encounter, chances remain high that their status will remain unchanged post-hooking up. However, one can never be sure both parties involved are on the same page concerning what should or should not happen

12. This latter decision is especially important if one wants to avoid the "walk of shame," i.e., walking home the day after a hookup in the same clothes one wore before (ibid., 35).

13. Ibid., 37.

14. One of Stepp's interviewees makes a similar point in that hookups are scripted, i.e., one is supposed to know what to do and how to do it and how to feel both during and after a hookup. Everything gets turned off except the body in order to become "emotionally invulnerable" (Stepp, *Unhooked*, 243).

next. Perhaps the one-time hookup will lead to a repeat hookup or even to what is deemed "going out," being "together," or "seeing each other."[15] When the latter happens, exclusivity is one of the defining features of the relationship and hooking up with someone else is considered cheating. Nonetheless, becoming exclusive with a partner is oftentimes socially shunned, especially early on in one's college experience. Yet, older students in Bogle's study, primarily women, repeatedly acknowledged wanting (and thus looking for) an exclusive relationship.[16] This desire to have a relationship form from a hookup may be what actually keeps the hooking up script intact. She writes, "One can hope that a hookup is going to lead to something more (i.e., some version of a relationship). Although college students generally realized that there are no guarantees, promises, or 'strings attached,' the hope of a hookup leading to a relationship may loom large in the minds of some who decide to take part in hooking up."[17]

Given this brief analysis of what constitutes hooking up, Bogle contends it is obvious the script for how college-aged men and women form intimate relationships with each other has significantly changed from the more traditional dating script previously operative on most college campuses.[18] In the past there clearly was a socially acceptable limit as to how much sexual interaction was deemed appropriate (even though

15. Bogle, *Hooking Up*, 41. The latter terminology can refer to cases where repeat hooking up is taking place and an attempt is made to "hang out" or spend time with the other person in between hooking up. The type of relationship falling under such labels as "seeing each other," "talking," "hanging out," or even perhaps "dating," is characterized as having a low level of commitment (and hooking up with another is still a possibility). Along with this, most of the college women Bogle spoke with indicated it is often the man who decides whether the "couple" will continue "seeing each other" or whether the relationship will end.

16. This desire and hope that some women in Bogle's study have that an exclusive relationship will result from a hookup differs somewhat from Stepp's findings. Some of the women she interviewed had a different operating philosophy. They believed love should wait because they cannot afford to invest time, energy and emotion into a deep relationship. As a result, they see hooking up is a "practical alternative." Stepp writes, "Hooking up enables a young woman to practice a piece of a relationship, the physical, while devoting most of her energy to staying on the honor roll, being accepted into a well-known university and then keeping up her academic scholarship while working ten or fifteen hours a week in the cafeteria, playing lacrosse, working out every day in the gym and applying to graduate programs in engineering" (Stepp, *Unhooked*, 37).

17. Bogle, *Hooking Up*, 43.

18. Ibid., 44.

presumably not all obeyed the limit). Furthermore, it was oftentimes the case that the socially acceptable limit meant no sexual intercourse until marriage or in some rare cases at least until there was some sign of future commitment like an engagement declared or family approval had been given. Nowadays, the practice of hooking up has nearly abolished the importance and usefulness of such "monitoring devices." Hooking up reverses many of the steps within the dating process, especially the timing and meaning of sexual activity.[19] Within the dating script, men and women go on dates first and then, in some circumstances, become more sexually intimate with each other over time. The hookup reverses this sexual norm so that men and women following the hooking up script become sexually intimate prior to *maybe* going on a date.[20] Put differently, it is not that "one night stands" or "casual sex" never took place in the past. Both were alternatives to the more dominant dating script that was present and operating. Stepp affirms this point, arguing that what was called "casual sex" during the 1960s, 70s, and 80s was the exception in college. [21] That is, with some exceptions, most men and women engaged in intercourse within a relationship that, at least on the woman's part, implied some degree of commitment, and it followed several earlier stages of affection. Today, however, hooking up not only is more socially acceptable, but more importantly it functions as the typical site for college-age men and women to begin a romantic relationship. It is not an alternative to the dating/relationship script, but an uncertain potential prelude to it! Hookups might be recreational or they might not; no one seems to know, not even the partners themselves. Hookups reverse previously operating sexual norms (such as go-on-a-date and then hope something might happen at the end of the date) and replaces them with sexual intimacy and interaction prior to *maybe* going on a date.

What significance does this reversal have? The most obvious difference is that, in the more traditional dating process, couples came to know each other better and thus could begin to build a relationship, with

19. Ibid., 47.

20. Ibid. Emphasis Bogle.

21. Stepp, *Unhooked*, 25, affirms this point, though using it to reinforce her previous point that the hookup culture is a time-saving alternative to relationships. According to Stepp, the campus lifestyle of young people today "leaves little time to pursue the finer points of a relationship." Put differently, because hookup partners spend so little time together, jumping into bed together forces decisions they may not be ready to make and destroys any chance of either partner putting their best selves forward (238).

sexual intimacy occurring only after a couple spent a significant amount of time together, and then only gradually. But what is morally significant about this? Why does it matter if couples end up finding relationship partners, one way or another? In order to explore this, I turn to the idea of a practice.

SECTION 2: THE PRACTICE OF HOOKING UP AND THE PRACTICE OF DATING: A COMPARISON

Initially it may appear awkward to refer to hooking up as a practice, but for philosopher Alasdair MacIntyre, practices are central to the moral life. In his view, they provide the arena in which the virtues (i.e., skills) are learned and exhibited (and it is the virtues that are the heart and soul of the moral life). Furthermore, a practice involves standards of excellence and obedience to rules, in addition to the achievement of goods both external and internal.[22] When one enters into a practice, he/she must accept the authority of those standards and the potential inadequacy of his/her own performance as judged by those in authority. Thus participating in a practice requires that a person subject one's attitudes, choices, preferences, and tastes to the standards that currently and partially define the practice. Practices also have a history. Yet the standards of a practice are not immune to criticism, and this is where the concept of virtue becomes important. MacIntyre contends that a virtue is an "acquired human quality the possession and exercise of which tends to enable us to achieve those goods which are internal to practices and the lack of which effectively prevents us from achieving any such goods."[23] It therefore belongs to the concept of a practice that its goods, both external and internal, are achieved only by subordinating one's self within the practice in relationship to other practitioners. In other words, a practice involves learning to recognize what is due to whom because every practice requires a certain kind of relationship between those who participate in it.

For our purposes in this essay, what is helpful about MacIntrye's understanding of a practice is his claim that there are virtues/skills one learns and fosters in a practice, all of which contribute to the development of an individual's moral character, i.e., the type of person one hopes

22. MacIntyre, *After Virtue*, 190.
23. Ibid., 191.

to become. As I indicated earlier, the type of person one is encouraged to become through the practice of hooking up does not cultivate the necessary skills one needs to enter into the practice of marriage. This claim becomes especially relevant when one contrasts the skills a person presumably learns if he/she engages in the practice of dating versus the practice of hooking up.

The moral significance of the practice of dating can be obscured by rhetoric centering primarily on the question of whether or not two people who are dating can engage in pre-marital sexual relations. However, Jason King and Donna Freitas take a different approach in their book, *Save the Date*.[24] They contend the practice of dating can be done in an engaged, intelligent, and loving manner that does not necessarily have to include sexual relations or necessarily lead to marriage.[25] In contrast, they begin by emphasizing how the practice of dating can lead to a shift in one's horizon, i.e., a shift in one's interests and desires. When two people fall in love, they open themselves up to new possibilities for self-understanding, or what King and Freitas call "new ways of being in the world."[26] In the process of dating several things begin to happen to both partners. For starters, what initiates the start of a dating relationship is a simple thing King and Freitas refer to as the "spark."[27] This "spark" is something to be valued because it ultimately draws two people together, piques their mutual interest in each other, and thus begins to inspire a relationship to form beyond the level of friendship. Second, because of this "spark," persons begin to receive vital lessons in intimacy because dating helps focus a person's love and interest in a way that is often deeper than friendship.[28] Along with this, it is through dating that one becomes open to romance. When persons choose to act romantically they begin to learn what it means to consider someone else's likes

24. King and Freitas, *Save the Date.*

25. King and Freitas's claim here runs counter to some contemporary Christian authors who would claim otherwise. In their opinion, not only is it through dating that one is easily exposed to the temptation to commit sexual sins, but the only kind of intimate interaction two people of the opposite-sex should be having with one another is that which will lead toward marriage. That is, two people of the opposite sex should only become "more than friends" if marriage is the intention. For different examples of contemporary Christian authors, see Chediak, *5 Paths.*

26. King and Freitas, *Save the Date*, 81.

27. Ibid., 69.

28. Ibid., 70.

and dislikes and the effort it takes to go about actualizing it. "Far from being egocentric, romance seems to be about our attentiveness outward toward another person, about loving people in their concreteness. It has to do with opening up."[29] King and Freitas contend that dating is important for understanding one's relationship to others, the world, and even to the divine.[30] Persons who begin the process of dating (and falling in love) open each other up to new ways of being in the world (even if that process turns out only to be temporary). As a practice, dating fosters growth of important skills, skills that are not only applicable to many aspects of one's life but are also vital for the practice of marriage.

In contrast, the practice of hooking up fosters neither mutual intimacy nor trust. Rather, the main skill one practices in a hookup is control, control over one's mind, heart, and especially one's body. More specifically, the practice of hooking up fosters the skill of shutting down one's mind and heart and allowing only one's body to function as something to be consumed without any development of emotional or psychological intimacy. Rather than learning to approach the other with openness, the practice of hooking up encourages one to draw near to the other with distrust, doubt, and fear. The latter description might seem like an overstatement, but according to Stepp, hooking up, in its most basic form, is simply all about the ability to become *unhooked* from one's partner.[31] In order to successfully become *unhooked* during a hookup, one must practice being *intentionally uncaring* toward the other and thus view their hookup partner's body as an object of sexual gratification and nothing more. Lost, therefore, in a hookup is the excitement that can come when one physically feels that "spark" for another deep within one's soul and thus acknowledges one's own emotional vulnerability. What happens after a hookup is not intrinsic to the practice itself because one strives to become *un*attached to his/her hookup partner. Openness to the other is eclipsed in favor of a posture of reticence. Thus, the practice of hooking up works directly against the kind of "appropriate vulnerability" Karen Lebacqz deems a necessary part of any exercise of sexuality. "Any sexual encounter that hurts another, so that she or he either guards against vulnerability in the future or is unduly vulnerable in the future, violates the 'appropriate vulnerability' which is part of the

29. Ibid., 77.

30. Ibid., 82.

31. Stepp, *Unhooked*, 5.

true meaning and purpose of our God-given sexuality."[32] Sexual union in its most honest form can only be achieved if both partners are willing to be vulnerable, exposed, and wounded.

Given this brief comparison of the practice of dating versus the practice of hooking up, it is easy to understand why there is reason for concern. The skills cultivated during a hookup are not the skills one needs to enter into and sustain the practice of marriage. While students are aware of this disconnect, there tends to be a failure to understand that one's romantic relationships require the development of certain skills, and do not simply "happen." Thus, the concept of a practice is helpful in analyzing the hookup culture, because it reminds us of the continuity of character that is developed through hooking up. Yet, as explained above, students often seem quite aware of this disconnect. They recognize that hookups do not lead to relationships. The question, therefore, that continues to linger is: why do it? If hooking up is the dominant way to identify personal relationships on a college campus, then how is this practice beneficial toward one-day achieving another goal, i.e., the desire to get married and raise a family? The answer begins to take shape if we consider hooking up as a practice within a larger tradition, the tradition of male power over women.

SECTION 3: HOOKUPS AND GENDER

The hookup culture places unusual burdens on women. This point weighs heavily in Stepp's analysis of hooking up because she argues the aftermath of participating in the practice of hooking up is not only real, but can include serious physical and emotional risks for women. On the one hand, there is what Stepp refers to as "the medical math." Although pregnancy rates for young women age fifteen to nineteen have decreased since 1990, the incidence of sexually-transmitted disease (STD) remains persistently high. "More young women than young men now contract STDs, and the medical community's concerns have shifted from men in their late twenties to teenaged girls."[33] Moreover, infertility rates in the United States continue to climb. Therefore, in addition, to worrying about whether her hookup partner will call the next day, or whether she may be pregnant, Stepp sternly argues a young woman also has to worry

32. Lebacqz, "Appropriate Vulnerability," 259.
33. Stepp, *Unhooked*, 224.

about how many other people her hookup partner may have slept with and whether he has given her a disease with lifelong implications. She may also worry about how many people she sleeps with and whether she may be passing on a disease she does not yet know she has contracted.[34]

In addition to medical risks, there are also emotional risks to consider, especially depression. Stepp writes, a girl "can tuck a Trojan into her purse on a Saturday night, but there is no such device to protect her heart."[35] Put differently, one wonders how attachment-free a hookup actually is if one has to work hard at censoring the natural feelings of connection that develop when two persons engage in sexually intimate behavior (even something as supposedly risk-free as kissing). For Stepp, the connection between hooking up and depression for women demands even more attention because if a woman initiates a hookup or hookup relationship and it goes nowhere, then she cannot hold the man completely responsible and may receive little sympathy from anyone, even her closest female friends. Furthermore, if she turns around and hooks up again, then she takes little time to analyze what happened in the previous encounter or to recover from a disappointment she doesn't want to acknowledge, all the while continuing to fuel in herself more personal doubt and confusion. Thus in the end, the control some women seek in the practice of hooking up turns out to be an illusion; instead feelings of self-doubt and severe loneliness are fueled.

Beyond the numerous physical and emotional hazards one must navigate, there also is a strong sexual double standard operative in the hookup script. Despite the attempts of the women's movement of the late 1960s and 1970s to encourage all women to embrace their sexuality, Bogle notes the lingering presence of the "good-girl" image even in today's hookup culture.[36] That is, when most men and women arrive on college campuses their first year, many students are on the same page. Freshman year is perceived to be a time when limits are tested. Thus, many of Bogle's interviewees, both male and female, indicated that they did not want to be "tied down" during their first year of college because an exclusive relationship may interfere with them experiencing all that college life has to offer. After their first year, however, students reported that things start to change. Men's and women's goals in the hookup cul-

34. Ibid., 225.
35. Ibid.
36. Bogle, *Hooking Up,* 96.

ture begin to diverge in that men are more able to enjoy the status quo while some women begin to want something more. In other words, the hookup script continued to work for some men and thus they did not want another alternative. Women, on the other hand, became more outspoken about wanting hookups to turn into relationships. As a result, Bogle argues that the intimate side of college life can easily become a "battle of the sexes."[37]

One possible reason why some women begin to seek relationships during college is because they are more interested in marrying a few years after graduation than men. (Bogle notes that the women she spoke with often mentioned wanting to be married by age twenty-five.) However, a stronger possibility as to why some women seek relationships during college is because women have considerably less sexual freedom in the hookup script than men. This is the case because oftentimes peers evaluate each other based on the context in which sexual relations with another take place. "In the hookup culture, men and women are permitted to (and do) engage in sexual encounters that are, by definition, outside of the context of a committed relationship. However, there are prejudices against women who are seen as being too active in the hookup scene."[38] In contrast, there are few rules for college men who want to participate in the hookup script; but again, such is not the case for women. Therefore, due to the ambiguous nature of the term "hooking up," women quickly learn they must tread very carefully. They must avoid the potential pitfall of hooking up with two different men who know each other well (especially if both men are members of the same fraternity); they must also consider the time span between hookups. Daring to hookup too soon and not allowing for a "reasonable amount of time" to pass between hookups is grounds for possibly being labeled a "slut." In addition, other behaviors such as dressing too seductively (and thus being called "easy" or "stupid") or hanging around a certain fraternity house (these women in Bogle's study were seen as the lowest of the low) could potentially lead to being negatively labeled. If, however, a college woman is able to find a relationship, then Bogle notes she is freer to engage in sexual activity and thus faces less of a chance of being labeled or shunned.

If it is relatively apparent that college men are in a position of power more so than women and there is an operating sexual double standard,

37. Ibid., 97.
38. Ibid., 104.

then why do women not opt out of participating in the hookup culture? Bogle suggests that there appears to be no clear alternative to the practice of hooking up: "Students who buck the system have few other options for engaging in sexual encounters and forming relationships."[39] Stepp would not disagree, but she also points toward at least three other cultural developments she believes sustain women's participation in the hookup culture.

First, one needs to consider the varying messages promoted by feminism/feminist movements of both the recent past and still operating today. In earlier decades, a woman's worth was determined most often by her ability to find a husband to love. This changed by the 1970s, and instead the most visible leaders of the women's movement were preaching that loving one's self was the preferred goal. For example, Stepp notes that in the United States Betty Freidan and Gloria Steinem helped young, white, middle-class women become more aware of the sexual double standard and thus gave women permission to re-think what they wanted out of both relationships and sex. Second, women interviewed by Stepp repeatedly spoke of messages preached to them by their parents that emphasized such values as self-sufficiency and independence, as well as the influence of their own parents either successful or failed marriage was having on their view of relationships in general and the practice of marriage. Third, the college environment was another factor. Most students go from prescribed course schedules and events calendars to no schedules, from being restricted to doing certain activities to no restrictions, and lastly from negotiating with parents to setting their own rules. Taken either separately or together, each of the above-mentioned cultural developments deserves more attention when trying to discern why some women choose not to opt out of the hookup culture.

CONCLUSION

Hooking up is not simply a meaningless phase some college-age men and women are going through today. Rather, college-age men and women are both giving and receiving distorted lessons in mutual intimacy and trust. Much of the temptation to hookup resides in the illusion that when practiced, one remains in control of his/her mind, heart, and body but that is really only the case in theory. In reality, men and women who

---

39. Ibid., 126.

hookup are learning skills that deter them from knowing what it means to be truly present and mindful of another person's desires because they themselves remain shutdown emotionally and psychologically during a hookup. Oftentimes there is little opportunity to get to know one's hookup partner either before or after a hookup because that kind of information is not valued in the hookup culture. What appears to matter most in the practice of hooking up is the ability to *unhook* from a partner with ease and with as few strings attached as possible. Yet many practitioners of hooking up, especially women, desire just the opposite from a hookup. Many seek to form real intimate relationships with their hookup partner. Until the practice of hooking up is seen for what it really is, young adults risk not only wounding their own minds, hearts, and bodies, but also damaging their chances at learning basic relationship-building skills like mutual trust and intimacy that are the cornerstone of the practice of marriage.

BIBLIOGRAPHY

Bogle, Kathleen. *Hooking Up: Sex, Dating, and Relationships on Campus.* New York: New York University Press, 2008.

Chediak, Alex, editor. *5 Paths to the Love of Your Life.* Colorado Springs: Th1nk, 2005.

Freitas, Donna. *Sex and the Soul.* New York: Oxford University Press, 2008.

Glenn, Norval, and Elizabeth Marquardt. *Hooking Up, Hanging Out, and Hoping for Mr. Right: College Women on Dating and Mating Today.* New York: Institute for American Values, 2001.

King, Jason, and Donna Freitas. *Save the Date.* New York: Crossroad, 2003.

Lebacqz, Karen. "Appropriate Vulnerability." In *Sexuality and the Sacred: Sources for Theological Reflection*, edited by James B. Nelson and Sandra P. Longfellow, 256–61. Louisville: Westminster John Knox, 1994.

MacIntyre, Alasdair. *After Virtue.* 2nd ed. Notre Dame, IN: University of Notre Dame Press, 1984.

Stepp, Laura Sessions. *Unhooked: How Young Women Pursue Sex, Delay Love and Lose at Both.* New York: Riverhead, 2007.

3

Pornography and Penance[1]

MARIA C. MORROW

CORNHOLE HAS BECOME A popular college game in the Midwest. This primarily outdoor game featuring opposing large wooden slabs that have circular cut-outs in them is much like tossing a beanbag in a bucket: cornhole challenges its participants to throw bags of corn into the opposing holes. From my casual observation of this game, it seems that cornhole is best enjoyed as a co-ed game played on sunny afternoons, with alcoholic beverages and as little clothing as the weather permits.

One day I encountered an unusual version of this game while my husband, daughter, and I drove through the student neighborhood at a Catholic university. Most cornhole games that I have seen in a university setting feature the school colors, and often a school logo. This one, however, stood out as different because it was painted in lavender and hues of pink, with curly brushstrokes surrounding the hole. The very brief time in which we drove past it was, unfortunately, enough time for me to comprehend that these cornhole slabs were painted as vaginas. Any doubt I may have had was removed when I caught the slogans painted on them: "Put it in the pussy." A professor at this school, who also happened to see the cornhole game, informed me that each slab had feminine cursive letters painted upon it, which spelled out a girl's name—apparently the girls who had painted them.

1. My thanks to M. Therese Lysaught, Emily Reimer-Barry, David Cloutier, and Jeffrey L. Morrow for their comments on drafts of this paper and other related works.

A friend of mine, to whom I will refer as Leah, entered a Catholic teaching-service program following her graduation from college. This teaching program was attractive to Leah because it advertised itself as taking seriously teaching, faith, and community life, which were all things that Leah valued. When she moved into the apartment with her community, however, Leah quickly discovered—as often happens in these types of community-living situations—that not everybody's commitment to these foundations were the same as her own. More specifically, Leah was offended that one of her male roommates was constantly looking at pornography on the community's computer, which was provided to them so they could do their required online classes.

More than once Leah turned on the computer to find the browser full of porn addresses. Sometimes a porn page was left up on the screen. Knowing that community was a pillar of the program, Leah addressed the conflict and asked her roommate to stop his viewing of pornography. He would not, and most of her community seemed confused at why Leah was making such a big deal out of the situation. Finally, Leah contacted the home office, expecting to receive the support she needed. Instead the program administrators told her she needed to be more tolerant of the preferences and habits of others in her community.

These stories are illustrative for my topic here for several reasons, two of which I will briefly describe. First, the vaginas painted on a cornhole game and Leah's situation are indicative of what secular journalist Pamela Paul has called the "pornification" of American society. While some may continue to assert falsely that pornography can simply be "ignored" by those who choose to do so, my family's chance encounter with vagina cornholes shows that the effects of pornification are everywhere. Leah's repeated encounter with pornography thanks to her roommate also demonstrates that pornography is not simply an issue of personal choice. Instead, both stories illustrate how pornography, and indeed, pornification, is a social rather than an individual issue.

Secondly, both of these stories occurred within settings where "Catholic" is an important part of the identity of the institution or program. The fact that the vagina cornholes were at a Catholic university rather than a state school and that Leah's teaching program was explicitly Catholic rather than government-sponsored, shows that the Church's members and even institutionalized ministries have not been able to escape pornification. That Leah's community members and the administrators of her program did not see the issue of porn consumption within a Catholic-sponsored community as a problem is but a microcosm of the general failure of the Church to address pornography.[2]

Considering pornography in 1981, one Catholic described the issue as "much ado about nothing." Donald DeMarco, writing a few paragraphs in *Communio*, said: "We can counteract pornography only with examples of wholeness in our lives. Nothing else is adequate. . . . We must show the world that pornography is a lame and paltry experience by shaming it with lives that result from sexual love that is whole."[3] Clearly DeMarco wrote before the pornography industry had overtaken the Hollywood box office in revenue.[4] Nonetheless, the real problem with his approach is that it is not instructive enough to be helpful. How should Catholics achieve "wholeness" in their lives? How can Catholics live "lives that result from sexual love that is whole"? Here it is not enough to exhort one to the traditional Church teachings on sexuality; even the few who aspire to adhere to these sometimes fail.

From my own observation and research, DeMarco's position can be seen as representative of the Church's *overall* response to pornography over the past three decades.[5] As a result, even well-meaning Catholics

2. And, of course, most Catholic universities will have a systematized way to deal with pornification issues such as the vagina cornhole. I will note that when the game was left on the front porch with the vagina side facing out during spring break, someone took the initiative to flip it around. Perhaps it was one of the priests or brothers who lived in the house directly across the street.

3. DeMarco, "Pornography," 91.

4. BBC News, "Huge Crowds."

5. Of course, it is difficult to prove an absence of response given the breadth and depth of the Church in the United States. Happily, recent times have brought more attention to the issue, although more at the lay/popular level than institutional. However, there are a few examples that seem to indicate effort on the institutional Church's part to respond to the problem. Cardinal Bernardin, in addition to other Catholics, was involved in the Religious Alliance Against Pornography (RAAP), which focused on political action, for example. The diocese of Washington DC had a "Pornography Awareness" week in 2007. Robert Finn, the bishop of the Kansas City diocese, released a pastoral letter regarding pornography. And finally, the Sabellians, a Catholic apostolate for recovering porn addicts, represent a profound way of addressing pornography struggles. The above responses prove that some Catholics are indeed aware of pornography as a problem and are working to address it as such. However, I was able to find these responses because I was looking for them. To the average Catholic in the pew, pornography likely appears as a non-issue or an issue regarding which the Church has little to offer. Of twenty-six diocesan websites I examined, only three indicate any attention to pornography as an issue beyond the consideration of protecting children from molestation. And, given the

have been unprepared to resist the pornification of U.S. culture and their own lives as a result. In this paper, therefore, I wish to present a different perspective, firstly, as regards pornography and, secondly, regarding how Catholics, as Catholics, can work to counter the pornification of their lives. I will argue that pornography should be understood as an ecclesiological problem—not just an individual one—and therefore should be addressed using ecclesiological resources.

Of these, the sacrament of reconciliation is an important formative tool that is in many ways a counter-practice to pornography and pornification. Whereas pornography objectifies and commodifies the human body, causing a rupture in relationships, the sacrament of confession[6] reconciles sinners with God and with each other, restoring the communal body and re-presenting the human body as a person. Furthermore, as a sacrament it provides God's grace, helping the Church to grow in holiness. In what follows, I will describe key actions and habits in pornography's narrative, then contrast this picture with the key actions and habits of the sacrament of reconciliation, which is a practice of the Church's narrative.

CAVEATS: OBJECTIONS TO SEEING PORNOGRAPHY AS AN ECCLESIOLOGICAL PROBLEM

Before discussing key elements of pornography's narrative, it is necessary to make a few caveats. First, I am aware that the definition of what constitutes "pornography" is contested, as Judge Potter Stewart's well-known line, "I know it when I see it" confirms.[7] Here I will follow Pamela Paul's understanding of pornography as a commercialized means to sexual arousal, i.e., a product on the market for sale and consumption.[8]

---

recent sex-abuse scandal, it may seem to lay Catholics that members of the hierarchy in particular are not credible to address pornography as an issue. This issue has been raised in the past following presentations of my work.

6. The sacrament under consideration can be referred to by several different names: the sacrament of reconciliation, the sacrament of confession, the sacrament of penance, and the sacrament of conversion. Each of these names emphasizes different aspects of the sacrament. Because I do not wish to emphasize any one particular aspect over the others, I rotate use of the most common names, which are the first three listed above. The "sacrament of conversion," however, perhaps best captures the sacrament as a whole and hence could be of great value if used as the primary name for the sacrament.

7. Jacobellis v. Ohio, 378 U.S. 184, 197 (1964) (Stewart, J., concurring).

8. BBC News, "Huge Crowds." While the distinction between erotica and pornography still holds for many, the point here is that an anti-pornography stance, by this

The value of such a definition is that it puts the debate in an economic rather than an "artistic" context; given that the worldwide industry is worth 97 billion dollars, the economic context seems appropriate.[9] Ads from companies like Victoria's Secret and Abercrombie and Fitch may not count as pornography in the strict sense, since they are not selling such images for arousal; however, they certainly fit in with understanding pornification in economic and cultural terms, since these companies use sex to sell their products. The growing market for Victoria's Secret products can be seen as correlative with the increase of pornography as a commercial product. Vagina cornholes, while a self-made creation of undergraduates, may not be bought and sold, but again, can be understood as the products of a general pornification, the ripple effects of the popularity of pornography indicated by the thriving pornography industry. The argument is not over whether such a display is "artistic" or "pornographic," but how such a display is normalized by a larger economic phenomenon of the routine commodification of bodies.

Secondly, it is commonly noted that "pornography" has been around for a long time, and hence it is no more a "new" social problem than it has been in years past.[10] What makes it a more pressing ecclesiological issue now than in the past is the increased privacy of digital media. The VCR was one of the first advancements in privatizing pornography and the DVD has followed suit. The privacy of pay-per-view in hotels, meanwhile, allows Paul to report that half of all hotel guests purchase

---

definition, would not threaten museum paintings or sculptures. Given the greatly increased sexual content of mainstream Hollywood productions, one might wonder if the erotica-pornography debate is worthwhile and if it extends beyond the respective preferences of women and men. In other words, as Pamela Paul notes, "mainstream media, from R-rated movies to HBO television shows, regularly depict erotica that used to be considered pornography." Paul, *Pornified*, 124.

9. Family Safe Media, "Pornography Statistics." Paul notes that pornography "may be the ultimate capitalist enterprise: low costs; large profit margins; a cheap labor force, readily available abroad if the home supply fails to satisfy; a broad-based market with easily identifiable target niches; multiple channels of distribution." Paul, *Pornified*, 247. The pornography industry, moreover, is gaining respectability on Wall Street, as Holmon Jenkins notes: ". . . reputable brokerages have been glad to help porn-related companies win public listings on U.S. stock exchanges." See Holmon Jenkins, "Pornography, Main Street to Wall Street," 7–8.

10. At one conference presentation regarding pornography, I was addressed by an incredulous older man who said he saw pornography when he was much younger and that "it's just not that interesting. I can't believe that people really are interested in something so boring."

pornographic pay-per-view movies, accounting for 70 percent of in-room revenue.[11]

The Internet has also revolutionized pornography in terms of privacy, allowing for accessibility, anonymity, and affordability like never before. The consumer of pornography now has no reason to leave the house to rent, purchase, or retrieve pornography. Pornography statistics are difficult to obtain given that much of the industry remains underground or unacknowledged, and yet the Internet component of "the quietest big business in the world,"[12] was estimated in 2004 as having 260 million pages of pornography online—an 1800 percent increase since 1998.[13] Additionally, each year 25 percent of children who regularly use the Internet encounter pornography accidentally.[14] In sum, digital media—particularly the Internet—has transformed the nature and scope of pornography.

Third, because I wish to reconstrue pornography as a social and ecclesiological problem, I am not going to use the language of "addiction" or discuss the acute struggles that some individual Catholics face, though their battles are important and worthy of attention. An analogy with alcohol on a college campus is useful here. This essay is not concerned with individual alcoholic undergraduates so much as with the general climate of attitudes regarding alcohol; I am addressing pornification and not porn "addicts."

VICES: KEY HABITS OF PORNOGRAPHY'S NARRATIVE

The growth of the porn industry and the pornification of American culture cannot be attributed solely to changes in technology. Pornography is flourishing in part due to the ways in which the key habits of what one might call the narrative of pornography fit with the broader narrative of American culture. Pornography both embodies this narrative and reproduces it. For the purpose of this paper, I will focus on four actions and habits of this narrative: abstraction, commodification, objectification, and self-objectification of the human body. These actions are habituated skills that follow from the more basic practices associated

11. Paul, *Pornified*, 55.

12. Heider and Harp, "New Hope," 286.

13. Paul, *Pornified*, 59. In 2006, this number was estimated at 420 million pages. See Family Safe Media, "Pornography Statistics."

14. Mitchell el al., "Exposure of Youth," 349.

with pornography, for example, the actual viewing of pornography and the masturbation that generally accompanies it,[15] and the absorption of pornographic acts into one's sexual relationships with others.[16]

Abstraction and Commodification

In his book *Consuming Religion*, Vincent Miller describes the abstraction that is a crucial aspect of today's consumer culture when he writes:

> Commodities appear on the scene, as if descended from heaven, cloaked in an aura of self-evident value, saying nothing about how, where, and by whom they were produced. As the market has become ubiquitous—the means by which we satisfy most of our needs—everyday existence has become a constant exercise in taking this abstraction for granted. Our eating, clothing, shelter, labor—all confirm us in this abstraction. We nourish ourselves on food from nowhere and dress in clothes made by no one.[17]

As a commercial product, pornography's source is similarly obscured. Pornographic images appear on the computer screen from Internet nowhere land, and the clips say nothing of how or where they were produced. Most importantly, pornography indicates very little about the actual human beings involved in the clip.

For Miller the paradigmatic example of consumer abstraction is the chicken breast: "Glistening boneless, skinless chicken breasts say nothing of the dangerous production lines on which they are processed."[18] Women's breasts in pornography are abstractions in a similar but even more significant way than the breast of chicken. Whereas the latter is a tangible reminder that a specific chicken once existed and the consumption of chicken serves a caloric purpose, the breasts of pornography are not tangible, nor do they meet a survival need such as nourishment. Pornographic breasts are ephemeral, appearing in a fleeting moment and leaving behind no trace. While one chicken breast enters one home and is consumed by one person, the same pornographic breast can be seen

15. According to the Kinsey Institute poll, 72 percent of respondents said they use pornography to masturbate or achieve physical release. See Paul, *Pornified*, 25.

16. Paul's example is that of an increasing number of men requesting facial ejaculations and anal sex with their girlfriends, both of which are popular in pornography. See *Pornified*, 161.

17. Miller, *Consuming Religion*, 3.

18. Paul, *Pornified*, 38.

simultaneously in diverse geographic locations, can be re-experienced at any time and place without ever bearing a connection to the actual female human being to whom it belongs.

For many, it is precisely this abstraction that makes pornography so attractive vis-à-vis relationships with women. Real women are complicated and difficult in a way that the pornographic images of women are not. Paul describes this situation when she writes: "Compared with the ease of masturbating to women in pornography, sex with real women involves a lot of effort and often time and money to boot. Real women may get angry when men gape, gawk and get hard at inappropriate times. In pornography, the women demand it; sexual arousal and gratification are the whole point."[19] Though there are real women behind the pornographic images viewed by men, there is no need to buy those women flowers on Valentine's Day or help out with housework. With the use of pornographic women, there is no need to abstain from sex when a significant other is tired. The abstracted sex of pornography is seemingly without risk for the man because there is no emotional vulnerability and thus no potential of being hurt or rejected.

This abstraction of the human body from the human person makes commodification of the body possible. Pornography abstracts images of bodies from the people themselves, commodifying human body parts and human bodies, commodifying sexuality and the sex act itself. Hence some anti-pornography feminists define pornography as merely a subset of prostitution.[20] Yet while prostitution is largely illegal in the United States, pornography is not; the bodies of pornography represent a commercial product to be bought and sold. They are images removed from the context of the human person; they are disembodied bodies.

Objectification and Self-Objectification

Objectification can be seen to be the inverse of abstraction as it is played out by the viewers of pornography. On the one hand, the consumer of pornography sexually encounters abstracted, disembodied bodies, but they are appealing precisely because the images represent real human beings; cartoon images are not arousing in the same way.[21] On the other

19. Ibid., 39.

20. See Whisnant and Stark, *Not for Sale.*

21. There are men who enjoy cartoon pornography, but the majority of pornography viewed involves the filming of real people.

hand, the pornographic training in abstraction shapes the encounter with real human beings in a particular way, makes them "less real" and more like the disembodied bodies. Porn viewers are likely to transfer their pornographic gaze to the women they pass on the street, regarding them as body-objects rather than as human beings. This is the habit of objectification. In other words, viewers of pornography consume abstracted images because the images represent real human beings, but they re-conceptualize real human beings because of how they encounter and interact with pornography: formation in abstraction is also formation in objectification.

As men transfer their expectations of porn women onto real women, those real women are regarded not as human beings but as objects. A scene from Disney's *The Little Mermaid* provides one example for understanding how this training in objectification can come by way of media. Ariel the mermaid encounters a fork in one of her explorations. The American children watching this movie know how a fork should be used, and so they laugh when Ariel's seagull friend instructs her to use the fork to comb her hair, and the kids feel her embarrassment when she makes the same mistake at dinner with the prince. Obviously the use of an object such as a fork is not self-evident, but requires training.

The prince, meanwhile, knows how to use a fork because of his upbringing in a world that used forks to eat. We can surmise that Ariel, in her happily-ever-after existence on land with the prince, learned the proper use of a fork by her immersion in the prince's culture. And yet, we can also imagine that Ariel might have learned that forks were used for eating by perusing picture books of people employing forks to eat. Had Ariel watched DVDs or YouTube videos of people eating with forks, her knowledge and understanding would have increased further. Such media training might have saved Ariel embarrassment on dry land at the dinner table.

Women, of course, are human beings and thus quite different from forks. Yet to say that women are objectified in pornography means to assert that men who view pornography begin to see women as though they were something like forks, i.e., mere objects for use. Those who view pornography and use the depicted women for masturbatory purposes begin to see women as objects for purposes of sexual release. Just as Ariel's media training would prepare her to associate forks primarily with eating, men's exposure to pornography trains them to associate women primarily with sex. Simon Hardy supports this when he proposes in his work that the image of a woman's body in a certain position indicates a specific sexual response.[22]

Paul's interviews support this process of the objectification of real women, wherein "a woman is literally reduced to her body parts and sexual behavior."[23] One pornography viewer admitted, "A very common progression addicts describe is that it gets to a point where you can't even look at a woman without first rating her for her physical attributes."[24] Another man interviewed acknowledged, "I've noticed that I find myself thinking more sexually about women I see on the street after I've had prolonged exposure to porn."[25] Those who view pornography frequently begin to transfer pornographic expectations to real life, finding it difficult to compartmentalize their relationships to porn women and real women.[26] Even men who do not view pornography are more likely to see women as sexual objects. They appear as such in the media; the fantasy rape scene depicted in a recent Dolce and Gabbana ad is but an extreme example.[27]

Moreover, as women are regarded as mere objects by the viewer of pornography, so also the pornography consumer can begin to feel like an object, attached to a computer screen, having "sex" with images of women he has never met and will never know. Mark Schwartz, the clinical director of a sex addict program, explains this self-objectification as such: "A man starts to feel like a computer himself when he realizes that he's dependent on computer images to turn him on. . . . You may be mak-

22. Hardy, "Reading Pornography," 15. The example given by Hardy is that the pornographic image of a naked woman bent over a chair with anus exposed indicates anal sex. Men who look at this image and then come upon a clothed woman in the same position in the real world will have the same response evoked; they will think about having anal sex with that woman.

23. Paul, *Pornified*, 80.

24. Ibid., 227.

25. Ibid., 47.

26. Ibid., 230.

27. The controversial Dolce and Gabbana ad featured a scene where a revealingly clothed woman was pinned to the ground by a man, who was surrounded by a crowd of other men. The ad, released in Spain, drew protests and was ultimately pulled. This is another indication of pornification—pornography having an impact beyond the individual viewers who choose to consume it.

ing love to your wife, but you're picturing someone else. That's not fair to the woman, and it's miserable for the man."[28]

The habit of self-objectification is also formed in women living in an increasingly pornified society, which demonstrates that objectification has a powerful influence beyond the people that consume pornography. With America's pornification, including media portrayals of women, the fashion and cosmetic industries, the diet industry, and so on, women are more likely to regard themselves as sexual objects, living out the role in which pornography would have them cast. Hence women's magazines counsel readers on imitating porn moves to keep partners interested, young women take their men to strip clubs as a birthday gift, teenagers look into Jenna Jameson's *How to Make Love Like a Porn Star*, and young girls demonstrate music video dance moves that stylize porn acts.[29] It is perfectly in keeping with the habit of self-objectification that undergraduate females can paint cornhole slabs featuring their disembodied vaginas, carefully write their names on the game, and then laugh while they and their male friends "put it in the pussy."

In summary, pornography, and pornification more broadly construed, serves as training that forms persons in a particular way. The concrete habits of pornography—like using PayPal to purchase online films and masturbating while watching pornography—are instances of individual acts that proceed from and result in the habituated dispositions of abstraction, commodification, objectification, and self-objectification.

STRUGGLE FOR HOLINESS: KEY ELEMENTS
OF THE SACRAMENT OF PENANCE

The terms habit, disposition, acts, and practices hearken to the concepts of virtue and vice. As Thomas Aquinas explains, habits can be good or bad indicating a disposition toward the good or evil acts; those habits that are good are named virtues, whereas those that are bad are called vices.[30] Pornography consumption forms users, and collaterally forms those around them, in habits that are central attributes of the vice of lust. With the vice of lust, the person narrowly seeks sexual pleasure and only

28. Paul, *Pornified*, 105.

29. Ibid., 4–5.

30. ST II–II, Q. 55 intro. See also chapter 3 of Mattison, *Introducing Moral Theology*, 57–74.

considers the body sexually, without the broader appreciation for the person as a human being in all its complexity. The person is consumed and used as an object, even if only in the imagination. Another person becomes a means to the end of self-gratification.[31] As a capital sin, the vice of lust ruptures relationships; for example, pornography usage has become a leading cause for divorce and has led to tensions in relationships and family life across the nation.[32]

When bodies are primarily objects for consumption, purchased contractually by an exchange of credited money, no intrinsic relationship is implied among human persons. Within the context of dating or a marriage, the pornographic habits lead to resentment in response to the normal demands of relationship. Ultimately, pornification represents real life's mimicking of the pornographic narrative. Those who view pornography transfer their expectations onto the world beyond the screen: women are seen only as disposable sexual objects that are easy to please and exist to please men. Sexual desire is largely unchecked, and, by pornography's very nature as a commercial product, sexual desire will never be satisfied.

This is merely one illustration of that which happens with all sin, namely, separation among human beings. The implied anthropology of pornography is one in which human beings, including one's self, are natural objects and disconnected individuals rather than icons of God, united to each other and to God. The vice of lust, like all other vices, fractures relationships. In the Catholic tradition, the overcoming of a vice, such as that of lust, requires two things: the practice of virtues and the grace of God. Hence it should be expected that these two would be involved in addressing the issue of pornography. Additionally, given that pornography is not simply an individual problem but one of broadly distributed cultural practices, an adequate response must offer an embodied, social, institutionally located alternative to abstraction and ob-

31. By far, the most thorough consideration of this can be found in John Paul II, *Theology of the Body*, 278–99. Similar descriptions are also present in Wojtyla, *Love and Responsibility* and the *Catechism of the Catholic Church*, no. 2351.

32. At the 2003 American Academy of Matrimonial Lawyers, two-thirds said they witnessed the sudden rise of Internet-related divorces, and 58 percent of these cases were from a spouse looking at excessive amounts of Internet pornography. As one divorce attorney in Virginia says, "Pornography wrecks marriages." Paul, *Pornified*, 167. For an excellent qualitative analysis of women's experience living with a significant other's pornography habits, see Schneider, "Effects," 32–33.

jectification, by which individuals can be formed and shaped toward a different set of ends within a different narrative.

One practice within the Church that fits all of the above criteria is the sacrament of reconciliation. And while the pornography industry has been rapidly increasing, the reception of this sacrament has been rapidly decreasing. According to sociologist James Davidson, 53 percent of Catholics say they never receive the sacrament of reconciliation and 76 percent say the sacrament is not essential.[33] So what might the sacrament of reconciliation have to offer those Catholics who live in a pornified world? In what follows I will suggest how this sacrament counters the narrative of pornography. I will first discuss the sinners' actions of penance that help form individual Catholics and the Church body in virtue. Here I will particularly consider the virtue of chastity. After this I will discuss God's grace in the absolution of the sacrament.

The key habits of the sacrament of penance are necessarily a part of the larger Christian narrative of which the sacrament is merely one embodiment. Contrary to the abstraction, commodification, objectification, and self-objectification of the human body posed by pornography, the sacrament of reconciliation emphasizes that human beings are persons who always stand in relation to God and to others. The human body is hence not an object to be commodified, but, together with the soul, is a person in the image and likeness of God.

Thomas describes the matter of the sacrament, i.e., the sinner's acts, as having three parts: contrition, confession, and satisfaction.[34] Contrition names what we might think of as the Christian's acknowledgment of sin and struggle with sin, represented in part by the examination of conscience that precedes the sacrament. The verbal confession of sin is made to the priest who represents the entire Church community as well as God. Lastly, satisfaction describes the penance, which is a reparation for sin not in a juridical sense but as something that is transformative. It is not possible to make adequate satisfaction for sin, but the action of penance serves as a testament to the sinner's commitment. These acts of the sacrament of penance become habituated skills; hence Thomas refers to them as acts of the virtue of penance.[35] The form of the sacrament,

33. Davidson, *Catholicism in Motion*, 154.

34. ST III, Q. 84, A. 8–9.

35. For a much fuller consideration of Thomas's treatment of penance as both sacrament and virtue, see Morrow, "Reconnecting Sacrament and Virtue."

represented by the priest's words of absolution, demonstrates the grace of God's merciful forgiveness and reminds the penitent that the sacrament is not about Pelagian self-sufficiency, but rather divine mercy.

Whereas the habits of pornography constitute a vice, the form and matter of the sacrament tend toward virtue; God's grace strengthens human action. Given the topic of this essay, I will examine in particular the virtue of chastity, which provides for the successful integration of sexuality within the person, enabling the inner unity of the bodily and the spiritual. Chastity is understood to be within the cardinal virtue of temperance.[36] As mentioned above, sin tends to reproduce itself: Americans reproduce the narrative of pornography and the habituated vice of lust ruptures relationships. Likewise, the virtues reproduce themselves: the virtue of chastity, for example, "blossoms in friendship," and friendship "leads to spiritual communion."[37]

In sum, the sacrament of reconciliation reinforces the Christian view of the human being as *imago Dei*. It aims toward virtue and the repairing of ruptured relationships among persons and with God. In the sections that follow, I will discuss the examination of conscience, verbal confession, act of contrition, absolution, and penance in regard to how these parts of the sacrament of reconciliation re-present the human body as a human person while forming habits that allow the Christian to grow in the self-mastery required for the virtue of chastity. I will explore the sacrament as an ecclesiological aid that, through God's grace, strengthens relationships among people and repairs the rupture of communion with God and with neighbor.

Countering Objectification: Examination of Conscience and Contrition

Preceding reception of the sacrament of reconciliation, the penitent normally examines his or her conscience. The Ten Commandments traditionally have served as the basis for an examination of conscience, although the Sermon on the Mount and apostolic teachings found within the moral catechesis of the Gospels and Apostolic Letters are also important. Reflecting on one's sins in light of the Word of God enables the person in awareness of how his sin has hurt God, others, and himself. This counters the habit of objectification in that the penitent is forced

---

36. ST II–II, Q. 151, A. 2.

37. *Catechism of the Catholic Church*, no. 2347.

to consider relationships with others and sins against them as persons. Moreover, the person is reminded that sins against other persons are also sins against God.

Consider, for example, the Sermon on the Mount in Matthew, where Jesus says that he has come not to abolish the law but to fulfill it. The "transforming initiatives"[38] that follow the traditional understanding of law emphasize that others must be regarded as persons. Since it seems most apropos to the topic at hand, Matt 5:27–28 reads as follows: "You have heard that it was said, 'You shall not commit adultery.' But I say to you that everyone who looks at a woman lustfully has already committed adultery with her in his heart."[39] To do an examination of conscience in light of this passage means to challenge objectification, discussed above as a facet of the vice of lust. In identifying that sin, the person identifies the woman as a human person and not a sexual object.

In the Catholic tradition, an examination of conscience is done on a daily basis, as a part of Compline, i.e., night prayer. When it is done routinely like this, it becomes habituated; it is a skill of contrition that involves looking for weakness in one's own actions as regards the treatment of other people and God. Whether it is done daily or weekly, a routine examination of conscience enables the person to identify patterns of sin and struggle and hence to identify the vices at the root of these common sins. Naming thoughts, words, and actions as sins that are against the will of God and harm other persons is hence an important step in re-presenting the human body as a human person and not an object.

It is also a valuable tool in developing the virtues, and hence may assist in forming the moral virtue of chastity. As Thomas notes, chastity allows the person "to make moderate use of bodily members in accordance with the judgment of his reason and the choice of his will."[40] The examination of conscience provides an opportunity for identifying the failure to act in accordance with one's reason and will in this area and others. Recognizing the sin and habits of sin is an important step for training in the virtue of self-mastery described by Thomas; the *examen* allows Catholics to grow in necessary self-knowledge that contributes to

38. This is Glen H. Stassen's phrase, from "Fourteen Triads."

39 All Bible quotations are from the RSV, Catholic edition.

40. ST II–II, Q. 151, Resp 1.

attainment of the virtue of chastity, among other virtues. In identifying proclivities toward sin in various forms, one sees how to "avoid the near occasion of sin." For one who struggles with pornography, for example, avoiding the near occasion of sin might involve not having an Internet connection available in one's home.

Most importantly, however, a habituated examination of conscience is a constant reminder of relationships with other people and the way one fails in these relationships, taking persons for granted, treating them unfairly, and so on. Hence the sin of pornography viewing is not solely about breaking a commandment, but about failing to love God, neighbor, and self and hence causing a break in communion. John Paul II notes that "each individual's sin in some way affects others ... a soul that lowers itself through sin drags down with itself the church and, in some way, the whole world."[41] As a practice that precedes the sacrament of reconciliation, the examination of conscience is an ecclesiological aid precisely because it re-presents human beings as persons, against whom greed, anger, envy, lust, etc., are sins. For the one performing the examination of conscience, the practice also re-presents that individual as an acting person connected to other persons—who also are brothers and sisters in Christ, members of one's own community—rather than as an isolated, manipulable object.

The sacrament of reconciliation takes the acknowledgment of sin revealed in the examination of conscience beyond interior reflection, countering objectification at several points. During the spoken confession, the penitent admits aloud that she has sinned against God in treating others as less than persons. In the Act of Contrition, the penitent expresses sorrow for having offended God in these sins against God and against others. The absolution, meanwhile, counters self-objectification in that it presents the penitent with God's forgiveness to him as a human person, made in the image and likeness of God.

Countering Abstraction: Confession, Absolution, Satisfaction

Sacraments are efficacious signs; they present what they represent.[42] Because of this, it is not surprising that the sacrament of reconciliation can be seen as a practice that counters abstraction such as that found

41. John Paul II, "Reconciliation and Penance," no. 16.
42. My thanks to John Cavadini for drilling this particular formulation into me.

in pornography. The sacrament of reconciliation challenges abstraction precisely because it presents what might otherwise be understood primarily in abstracted terms—from sins, to contrition, to forgiveness, to restitution. Many people find the confession of sin to another person to be difficult, bothersome, and seemingly unnecessary—likewise for the absolution from the priest. Ironically, it is precisely this verbalization that concretely renders grace and reconciliation real and resists abstraction.

When the penitent verbally confesses her sins, for example, she takes the results of private, interior reflection and communicates them to another person. In this act of speaking her sins, she admits to the priest that her actions have hurt others. The identification of sin ceases to be unspoken thought and becomes a real confession of sin, witnessed by another person. As the Catechism notes, "The confession of sins, even from a simply human point of view, frees us and facilitates our reconciliation."[43] The priest here is also a presentation of something that might otherwise be abstracted: he signifies the Church community that has been wounded by sin. Likewise, in the spoken Act of Contrition, the penitent expresses his sorrow aloud for his sins. Again, this is not an abstraction, but a real sorrow exposed because admitted in words to the priest who witnesses to the reality of the penitent's contrition.

The absolution is perhaps the most striking counter to abstraction: it presents God's merciful forgiveness to the penitent. Forgiveness is not some abstracted idea floating out there, but is really and truly given by God to the sinner in the sacrament. Yet while absolution takes away sin, it does not magically fix the disorders that sin has caused. Hence in order to regain spiritual health, the penitent makes restitution in what is known as "penance." Penance goes beyond the justice required of repairing harm done to others (e.g., returning stolen goods) and works to configure the sinner to Christ. This means that penance also counters abstraction; making amends requires actually doing something, although this aspect of the sacrament was probably clearer in the manualist era than it is today. A vivid representation of penance can be found in the scene from the film *The Mission* in which Captain Mendoza, in a grueling trek up a mountain, carries the armor so crucial to his slave-trading role and formerly violent way of life. He ascends to the very people he had been abusing, people who might have killed him when he reached their camp, but who instead set him free in an act of mercy.

43. *Catechism of the Catholic Church*, no. 1455.

Countering Individualism: Healing Ruptured Communion

Therese Lysaught notes that liturgical practices "do indeed work on, in, and through 'bodies'—but the primary 'body' upon which they work is the body of Christ. For sacraments, or liturgical practices more generally, are actions that constitute and sustain the church itself."[44] This communal work is evident in the sacrament of reconciliation. Whereas the sinful practices of pornography are rooted in individualism and cause separation from God and among persons, the sacrament of reconciliation is a "sacrament of healing," which is unitive in nature and helps to sustain the Church. The existence of the sacrament indicates that sin is real and causes separation. As is stated in *Lumen Gentium:* "Those who approach the sacrament of penance, through the mercy of God obtain pardon for any offence committed against him, and at the same time are reconciled with the church which they wounded by their sin and which strives for their conversion through charity, example and prayers."[45] The reconciliation provided in the sacrament constitutes and sustains the Church, rejuvenating the Body of Christ, which has sustained injury in the person's sins.

This strengthening of the entire Church is why the sacrament is an apt response to the ecclesiological problem of pornography, even for those who do not personally struggle with the sin of pornography consumption or the vice of lust. Regardless of the sins one confesses, the practice strengthens the whole Church, while also forming the individual in various virtues. In this time period of rapid pornification, the revitalization of the life of the Church would be welcome indeed.

CAVEATS: OBJECTIONS TO SEEING THE SACRAMENT OF PENANCE AS AN ECCLESIAL AID

One cannot propose the sacrament of reconciliation as a response to pornography without being aware of the historical baggage associated with the sacrament. Although it has existed throughout Christian history in various forms, the most recent expression of the sacrament is often associated with the manualist tradition, which delineated specific penance-punishments on the basis of particular sins. In the words of

44. Lysaught, "Liturgy, Health." Thanks to Therese Lysaught for providing me with the unpublished presentation form of this essay.

45. *Lumen Gentium*, no. 11.

Servais Pinckaers, the confessional has in the past—during the manualist era, for example—been "too juridical," leaving little space for mercy.[46] If the sacrament retained this excessively juridical feel, divorcing it, as Pinckaers suggests, from a more comprehensive understanding of Christian struggle toward the final end of beatitude, the sacrament might not be as helpful as a response to pornography.

In the current context, however, those identifying a problem with the sacrament might offer the opposite complaint: confession could never be effective against pornography because in its current form it has become a psychological back-pat more than anything else. James O'Toole identifies this psychologizing of confession as one of the key reasons for the sacrament's decline in the U.S. in the 1960s. As psychology became more popular in the U.S., priests found themselves competing with "professionals," and the sacrament appeared quaint at best, seriously objectionable at worst. In attempts to save the role of confessor, many priests relaxed standards, trying to take on a positive, rather than a negative role.[47] This continues today; knowing that the sacrament is already unpopular, priests fear to make it uncomfortable and can compensate by too much affirmation, sometimes even telling the penitent that his sins are not really sins. Related to this, priests occasionally give unwise advice in the confessional, based on their personal opinions. Once, during confession, a priest asked me about my theological work, and when I mentioned pornography, he imparted his acclamation for pornography as a solution to marital difficulties with sex and wondered how I could possibly find it problematic.

There is no denying that bad counsel from a priest during confession can be harmful, and making the sacrament too psychological or too juridical is also problematic. And yet, so long as the sacrament is valid, grace is bestowed on the penitent; the Catholic understanding of *ex op-*

46. Pinckaers, *Sources*, 273: ". . . the attitudes inculcated by the theology manuals were too juridical to give free scope to mercy, which is so preeminent in the Gospel. It was treated rather as an afterthought, after judgment had been pronounced, and its intervention was often suspect, in moral theology, as possibly opening the door to laxity."

47. O'Toole, "Court of Conscience," 174–77. O'Toole provides an in-depth history, as well as describing several factors in the rapid decline of the practice of the sacrament. When describing psychologization as one explanation for the sacrament's decline, he notes the way the phrase "forgive yourself" undercut the entire theology of the sacrament. If really the important thing is to "forgive yourself" then why bother telling a priest or anyone else about your sins? (176).

ere operato, means that the sacrament of reconciliation is worthwhile in spite of the weaknesses of the priest's part in the sacrament. In this way it is similar to the fact that the congregation still partakes in the Eucharist at a Mass where there is a bad homily or off-key singing. Of course the Mass could be done better, but despite any priest's idiosyncrasies or faults, a valid Eucharist bestows grace on those participating in the celebration. While looking for ways to reform the practice of the sacrament of reconciliation and train seminarians well for their time in the confessional, it is important to recognize the efficacy of God's gracious work despite our faults.

One last objection is that the sacrament of reconciliation seems to be a private and individual sacrament. In proposing it as a response that is counter to the individualism of pornography, then, I should suggest why this sacrament is *not* individualistic, though it might appear to be so at first glance. The days of public confession have moved from the Church onto the afternoon talk show circuit, as Robert Barron notes.[48] And yet, a social aspect remains that contrasts with the individualism of pornography. Whereas that latter individualism does not involve any interaction with another human being, the sacrament of reconciliation requires at minimum speaking to a priest. It often includes going to a Church, which is a public building. Occasionally it even involves standing in line. Perhaps the time that the sacrament feels the most like a social practice is when it is set in the context of a penance service, which is usually held during Advent and Lent.

Yet even without a communal service or 3rd Rite confession[49] service, the sacrament of reconciliation, like the Eucharist, intends a visible practice that is not individualistic, but rather restores the penitent to full communion with the Church.[50] The skilled confessor will press

48. Barron, *Strangest Way*, 99.

49. The 3rd Rite confession service, involving a general absolution, was extremely popular in Australia until recently when it was formally banned. Priests from Australia, whom I met at Tantur Ecumenical Institute in Jerusalem in 2005, contend that 1st Rite reception of the sacrament declined significantly when the 3rd Rite was banned.

50. Similarly, it is important to re-emphasize that I am not proposing the sacrament as a solution to an individual struggling with what some would identify as a "pornography addiction." Just as the sacrament would not cure an alcoholic, it will not cure a serious struggle with pornography, despite the real presence of grace found in the sacrament of penance. It can, however, be an important part of a formative process of acquiring the virtue of chastity and growing in holiness. Moreover, it is helpful even for the few who commit only a very few, venial sins. John Paul II (of happy memory), for example, received the sacrament weekly.

the sinner to think about how her sins weaken or disrupt relationships with others, as well as the Church's relationship with God. Conversely, he will help the penitent to appreciate God's grace as the sacrament restores him to communion. This emphasis on relationships, in highlighting the social aspect of Christian life, also helps fight the individualism inherent in pornography and pornification.

FORMATION BY GRACE

One of the most powerful offerings the sacrament of reconciliation bears as an ecclesiological aid is that it reminds the Church that it is by God's grace that the individual sinner and, indeed, the entire communion of believers is strengthened. As Kelly Johnson notes when considering those who live a life of penance: "the joy of penance is not that the self is abased, but that it succeeds in drawing closer to its truth and its love, going through confrontation with its failure and weakness to find that abounding of grace and mercy."[51] The human effort involved in the examination of conscience and the rite of confession ultimately bears fruit because of the work of the Holy Spirit. Hence it is not surprising that the virtue of chastity is listed as a fruit of the Holy Spirit in Gal 5:22–23.

Whereas the pornographic narrative and the vice of lust would have people believe that images are unconnected to human persons and human persons are only objects, the sacrament of reconciliation re-presents the body as a human person in the image and likeness of God. Because of God's grace, this human person has the potential to grow in virtue and receive fruits of the Holy Spirit, including the self-mastery necessary for the virtue of chastity. Moreover, the person is intrinsically connected to others members of the one Church, such that one person's sin affects the entire Church. As a sacrament of healing, confession repairs the person's ruptured relationship with God and with the Church.

In a world that is increasingly pornified, reproducing the pornographic narrative of individualism, abstraction, commodification, and objectification, the sacrament of reconciliation represents an ecclesiological aid in countering these habits. Far from abstracting human beings in order to objectify them, the sacrament re-presents the person in the context of inescapable relationship with God and others. It does so in a formative process where Christians recognize sin and failings, work

51. Johnson, *Fear of Beggars*, 40.

to repair relationships, and grow in holiness and virtue with the grace of God received in the sacrament.

When considering the immensity of the problem that is pornography, it may seem that the sacrament of reconciliation can only do a very little. For those who lived through the "too juridical" era of confession, this proposal may even seem frightening. And yet, when compared to DeMarco's exhortation for Catholics just to live a moral life of "sexual wholeness," so that pornography can take care of itself, a renewed appreciation for the sacrament of reconciliation provides a concrete way of trying to live a better life—to grow in virtue and holiness by recognizing sin and vice and God's grace in healing the ruptures in relationships caused by sin and vice.

BIBLIOGRAPHY

Barron, Robert. *The Strangest Way: Walking the Christian Path.* Maryknoll, NY: Orbis, 2002.

BBC News. "Huge Crowds at US Porn Convention." January 13, 2007. No pages. Online: http://news.bbc.co.uk/2/hi/americas/6258291.stm.

Davidson, James D. *Catholicism in Motion: The Church in American Society.* Liguori, MO: Ligouri/Triumph, 2005.

DeMarco, Donald. "Pornography: Much Ado About Nothing," *Communio* 8 (1981) 89–91.

Family Safe Media. "Pornography Statistics" (2006). No Pages. Online: http://www.familysafemedia.com/pornography_statistics.html.

Heider, Don, and Dustin Harp. "New Hope or Old Power: Democracy, Pornography and the Internet." *Howard Journal of Communications* 13:4 (2002) 285–99.

Jenkins, Holmon. "Pornography, Main Street to Wall Street." *Policy Review* 105 (2001) 7–8.

John Paul II, Pope. *Man and Woman He Created Them: A Theology of the Body.* Boston: Pauline, 2006.

———. "Reconciliation and Penance." No Pages. Online: http://www.vatican.va/holy_father/john_paul_ii/apost_exhortations/documents/hf_jp-ii_exh_02121984_reconciliatio-et-paenitentia_en.html.

Johnson, Kelly. *The Fear of Beggars: Stewardship and Poverty in Christian Ethics.* Grand Rapids: Eerdmans, 2007.

Lysaught, M. Therese. "Liturgy, Health, and the Lives of the Saints." In *Living Well and Dying Faithfully: Christian Practices for End-of-Life Care*, edited by John Swinton and Richard Payne, 59–85. Grand Rapids: Eerdmans, 2009.

Mattison III, William C. *Introducing Moral Theology: True Happiness and the Virtues.* Grand Rapids: Brazos, 2008.

Miller, Vincent J. *Consuming Religion: Christian Faith and Practice in a Consumer Culture.* New York: Continuum, 2003.

Mitchell, Kimberly, et al. "The Exposure of Youth to Unwanted Sexual Material on the Internet: A National Survey of Risk, Impact, and Prevention." *Youth and Society* 34:3 (2003) 330–58.

Morrow, Maria C. "Reconnecting Sacrament and Virtue: Penance in Thomas's *Summa Theologiae.*" *New Blackfriars* 91 (2010) 304–20.

O'Toole, James M. "In the Court of Conscience: American Catholics and Confession, 1900–1975." In *Habits of Devotion*, edited by James O'Toole, 131–86. Ithaca, NY: Cornell University Press, 2004.

Paul, Pamela. *Pornified: How Pornography is Damaging Our Lives, Our Relationships, and Our Families*. New York: Owl, 2006.

Pinckaers, Servais. *The Sources of Christian Ethics*. Washington, DC: Catholic University of America Press, 1995.

Schneider, Jennifer P. "Effects of Cybersex Addiction on the Family: Results of a Survey." *Sexual Addiction and Compulsivity* 7:112 (2000) 32–33.

Stassen, Glen H. "Fourteen Triads of the Sermon on the Mount (Matthew 5:21—7:12)." *Journal of Biblical Literature* 122 (2003) 267–308.

Whisnant, Rebecca, and Christine Stark, editors. *Not for Sale: Feminists Resisting Pornography and Prostitution*. North Melbourne: Spinifex, 2004.

Wojtyla, Karol. *Love and Responsibility*. Translated by H. T. Willets. New York: Farrar, Straus, & Giroux, 1981.

4

Singular Christianity

Marriage and Singleness as Discipleship

JANA MARGUERITE BENNETT

I F ONLY PAUL HAD not written chapter seven of his first letter to the Corinthians. Christians can fairly easily avoid questions about whether to be married or single when they stick to the Gospels, for Jesus does nothing clear-cut with respect to states of life. He is present at the wedding at Cana in John; in Matthew, he issues a prohibition against divorce; he speaks about being eunuchs for the Kingdom of God, and reconfigures family in his exhortation that the ones who are his disciples are his mother and brothers. Because Jesus does not appear to have much of a line one way or the other, the Gospels appear to allow us not to get too caught up in questions about whether to marry or whether to stay single.

Paul, though, does not let Christians off quite so easily. In verse eight he writes that for the unmarried and widows, it is "*good* for them if they remain as I do."[1] Later in the selection, Paul contrasts the married and the non-married by suggesting that the unmarried virgins can follow Christ, but people who are married are concerned with the world and with family.[2] Paul tempers these points by saying that it is better for people to marry than to be aflame with passion—in other words, do not

---

1. 1 Cor 7:8 (NAB). Various translations use the word "good" here; the New Revised Standard Version uses "well", which tends to decrease the force Paul has on this state of life.

2. 1 Cor 7:34.

strive for remaining unmarried if it will just cause you to sin. Most of the early church fathers interpreted this passage as suggesting that virginity is better, far better, than marriage. For example, John Chrysostom discusses how Paul has saved a thorough discussion of virginity for after he already has spoken about marriage relationships "with the hope that they have learned from his previous words to practice continence, and can now advance to greater things."[3]

Thus Paul's words seemingly set the stage for a debate like that between Jovinian and Jerome in the fourth century, where Jovinian suggested that state of life did not matter as much as some claimed, while Jerome saw marriage as sinful and consecrated virginity as clearly superior. Jovinian wrote, for example, that "our religion has devised a new dogma against nature . . . ," which is the ascetic life of virginity.[4]

One common way to tell the history has been that the elevation of consecrated virginity led to the later medieval sense that vowed celibates, particularly monastics, were holier and superior to those who were married. Protestant reformers questioned this stance, particularly Luther who famously rejected it in his treatise "The Estate of Marriage." Protestants have since tended not to think much about singleness, focusing on marriage as the norm for their adherents. For Catholics, however, it seems that this attitude continued into the twentieth century in various forms, such that Florence Caffrey Bourg is able to note that vocation manuals in the early twentieth century suggested that nuns could follow Jesus, while those who were getting married could not really be disciples.[5]

The force of these arguments shifted mid-twentieth century to focus on families as means for discipleship, and the document *Lumen Gentium* pinpointed that families could be a "domestic church." The latter part of the twentieth century has seen the rise of much literature on the importance of marriage, nuptial theology, and family, to the point that generic searches of literature show far, far more attention paid to marriage and family than to celibacy, virginity, and singleness. Since Vatican II and the document *Gaudium et Spes*, Catholics have become much more inclined to write about marriage and family while paying less attention to, or even maligning single states of life, especially the celibate priesthood.[6]

---

3. John Chrysostom, *On Marriage and Family Life*, 39.

4. Cited in Jerome, "Adversus Jovinianum," (*Patrologiae Latinae* 23, 282).

5. Bourg, *Where Two or Three are Gathered*, 6-7.

6. See, for example, Dennis Coday, "Panel Links Celibacy and Abuse." He writes: "A lay review panel in the Seattle archdiocese said the church's celibacy requirement

While Catholic theology has not wholly turned aside considerations of celibacy, the thrust of the conversation moves toward marriage. One might even go so far as to say that, in the common understanding, celibacy as a state of life has been found wanting and that the best state of life for happiness consists in marriage,[7] or at least, the semblance of marriage, which is perhaps a bit astounding given the rise in divorces since the 1960s.

So much for Paul's words. Yet, if Christians want to take Scripture seriously, there needs to be some accounting of Paul's words to the Corinthians. In addition, there needs to be some accounting for the fact that a very large minority of Christian adults is not currently married. The Pew Forum on Religion and Politics data suggest higher percentages of Christians are married than not (about 60 percent across all denominations); still, about forty percent of all adult Christians are unmarried in some variety (widowed, divorced, never married, cohabitating).[8] The cultural emphasis has become so much about marriage that Christians have neglected to think much about the nearly half of all Americans who are not, in fact, married.

Elsewhere, I have written about a single/married dichotomy in the church that I think ultimately leads to poor ecclesiology.[9] Somewhat ironically perhaps, in this essay I focus on singleness, not as a way to further dichotomize a church that needs no help with dichotomizing, but as a way toward understanding singleness, marriage, and the church rightly. The church needs *both* marriage and singleness to be the church, and married and single need each other in order to rightly understand their own lives. In this essay, I take that argument further, though, to suggest that in a way, what it means to be a member of the Body of Christ is to say that all Christians are married and all are single.

I suggest that a primary reason for the dichotomizing is that views of marriage, family, and singleness unhelpfully map on to heavily ingrained

---

for priests helped 'set the stage for the deviant behavior' of clergy sexual abuse. The 10-member Case Review Board said mandatory celibacy was a 'contributing factor' to the sexual abuse scandal by blurring distinctions between 'deviant or exploitative behavior and normal but unacceptable behavior.'"

7. For example, A Catholic Theological Society of America document, Kosnik et al., *Human Sexuality*, discusses human sexuality. Celibacy is not completely abandoned in this report, but still is given only three pages in a two-hundred-plus page document.

8. See Pew Forum, "U.S. Religious Landscape Survey."

9. See Bennett, *Water is Thicker than Blood.*

cultural views and reinforce them. Contemporary culture names several versions of what it means to be single, and in various ways the church tends to support those views. Thus, the first section of this paper outlines some prominent cultural views of singleness, while the second section suggests ways in which Catholic theology substantiates cultural views. In the third section of this paper, I offer some ways of thinking about singleness that take Paul's words seriously (that singleness is a good) and that end up being rebellious against cultural constraints about marriage and single states of life. Christians can and should be radical witnesses against cultural views that are untruthful, and so I conclude with some possible ways forward for single and married Christians. My focus here is not with those singles who garner more of the focus—celibate priests and religious—though these are very important states of life that need good theological conversation. What I say here may be applicable to vowed celibacy, but my focus is instead with those—never married, divorced, or widowed—who rarely ever get discussed in terms of Christian vocation and discipleship.

THE BRIDGET JONES/"SEX IN THE CITY" VIEW OF SINGLENESS

Cultural icons suggest a lot about attitudes toward things, and for the purpose of discussing contemporary singleness, one of the more famous literary examples is from a popular novel by Helen Fielding. Fielding's book, *Bridget Jones's Diary*, originally emerged as a serial column in a newspaper and became a book and then a film. A sequel, *The Edge of Reason*, came out in both book and film formats, attesting to the ways in which Bridget has captured what it means to be single. Her "singletons," particularly her character Bridget Jones, provide excellent examples of cultural tensions surrounding marriage and singleness. Bridget Jones is a thirty-something unmarried woman and British, and her funny accounts of single life have attracted at least as much attention in the United States as they have across the pond.

What makes Bridget so attractive for followers of her adventures? Bridget wants to be a fabulous woman and show that she's smart, funny, and very adult—but Bridget is single, in and out of love, no steady boyfriends. This makes her the antithesis of what life should be, both on her married friends' views and her own. Many of her friends are now married and have at least one child. These friends once hung out with her and were single themselves, but they have since become a class known as "smug marrieds." They are now the ones who are smart, funny, and sexy. Bridget can't be, because she's *single*. Thus the book and the film both showcase the tensions between being married and being single. In the film, for example, Bridget is invited to a dinner party with "lots of smug marrieds" (her term for those who are married). One of the couples asks her why there are so many unmarried women in their thirties these days, and Bridget replies, "Well, I suppose it doesn't help that underneath our clothing, our bodies are all covered in scales." The suggestion is that that maybe single people seem alien, with scales on their bodies. They look human, speak human languages, but do they really act human?

This sense of alienation is heightened when considering the beginning of the scene. Bridget walks into a dinner party where she is the one single guest among seven couples: the assumption at this dinner party is that normal equals married. And the divide between married and single at the dinner table implies that the vast majority of adults are, in fact, married couples. To heighten the sense of what is normal and abnormal, all seven couples show that they are part of a unity: they dress alike, talk at the same time, one couple cradles their yet unborn child. All of them have the same smiles plastered on their faces. By highlighting the similarities and ties between the couple, the scene also highlights the one person in the room who does not have those ties. Normal is unity with another person.

Some might look at the current array of media and suggest, on the contrary, that there is a shift in the ways people understand singleness—that being single is not only becoming less strange, it is becoming more desired. One example might be the hit TV show "Sex and the City", which depicted four successful women, successful in their own right and not because they were married. These four women also reveled in finding good sex partners and in enjoying the vastness of New York City, which caters to a single lifestyle. Being single, for "Sex and the City," means being hot, sexy, independent, and most of all, free to go and do things that their married friends cannot do. Other 1990s and 2000s shows might typify that same sense to some degree: "Friends," for example, was never primarily about married people with children, but about six young adults living (again) in New York City and finding that each other provided a kind of urban family of support that biological families did not.

What is interesting about these shows, however, is that even if we grant that singleness becomes normalized to an extent, the broader story lines still assume that people will get married, and eventually have children. That is the point toward which each of the women moves in "Sex and the City." The series may have begun with only Charlotte actively seeking marriage and family but by the end of the sixth season all four women are paired up, and by the final episode, Miranda has even bought a house for her burgeoning family of four in (gasp) Brooklyn. Miranda and her husband Steve treat their move to Brooklyn a bit like growing up. The City (i.e. Manhattan) was fine for when they were single and free, but now they have hard difficult choices that are fitting for mature adults.

These cultural icons thus depict both positive and negative images of singleness. On the one hand, singles are glamorized as able to have the best lives, or at least they can attempt to achieve dreams that people who are married with families cannot achieve. On the other hand, singles are depicted as not wanting to be single. The author of *Unhooked Generation: The Truth About Why We're Still Single*, Jilian Straus, proclaims these differences of perception as well, saying of her single friends: "These people have full lives—busy jobs, close friends, and passionate interests. Yet I couldn't help noticing that the topic of our failing relationships dominated almost every conversation."[10] Straus's own argument attempts to provide some conclusive (perhaps correct) ideas for why people remain single, including the notion that television and movies, as well as celebrity fanfare about marriages that ultimately do not last, form peoples' imaginations and visions of what it means to be single. The point, though, is that Straus, like all the media she decries, is pinpointing singleness as a problem and anomaly against a backdrop in which "everyone" gets married or should, particularly when she looks at her own Generation X in comparison with her parents' generation.

It becomes even clearer that something other than our experience is shaping the way we understand marriage and singleness when we look at demographic data. At the very least it is not the case that the vast majority of adult Americans are married. The 2006 data from the U.S. Census Bureau suggest that 47.3 percent of all adults are single in some variety (never married, divorced, separated, cohabitating, widowed). Moreover, looking at the data over the past century shows an interest-

10. Jilian Straus, "Excerpt from *Unhooked Generation*."

ing trend: the percentage of unmarried adults today is lower than it was between 1890 and 1910, and is about equal to the percentage of unmarried adults in the 1920s, 1930s, and is slightly above the percentages in 1940. In mid-century, there is a marked decrease in the percentage of unmarried adults to about 33 percent. Furthermore, there is a dip at the same time (1950s and 1960s) in the average age that men and women get married. Newspapers have made much recently about the current rising marriage age (now 25 for women and 26 for men), but such numbers are not new, at least for men. A century ago, the average age for getting married was 25 for men and 22 for women. In mid-century, the age dipped to 23 for men and 20 for women. Beginning in the 1970s and up to the present day, both the average age of marriage and the percentage of adults who are unmarried gradually increases again. There are numerous reasons for both the lowering and rising of marriage age and percentage of singles, and it would not be a fair historical argument to suggest that contemporary people are simply returning to patterns that their grandparents and great-grandparents had a century ago. What the data do call into question, however, is the idea that "everyone" gets married, by a certain age—the idea that "single" is just a brief stopping point on the way toward being married, or married again.

The cultural assumption goes beyond simply suggesting that the majority of people are married, however. It also presumes that staying single was a choice, and the wrong choice. In *Bridget Jones's Diary*, other (married) characters admonish Bridget throughout the film, saying "You career girls can't wait forever, you know." Those thirty-somethings should have made better choices. *They* should have gotten married when they had the chance. But now they are thirty, and they are not really going to find anyone at all to whom they can be married.

Part of the notion that marriage is a choice goes hand in hand with the view that being married is simply part of adult life. If one is unmarried, one has not yet quite understood adulthood. Singles are depicted as going out drinking and having a good time; married people with children are depicted as paying bills and mowing the lawn. Thus, in *Single in a Married World*, several psychologists discuss what they see generally in their patients who are single—in particular, these psychologists see that their patients do not want to be single in part because it is perceived as childish and as lacking in responsibility. This perception leads, then, to significant problems with depression, anxiety and the like.[11] *Adult* people make choices, and they make the right kind of choices.

The overall result is to suggest that single people are anomalies who can and should have fun, but who should eventually be married and enter the adult world. It is unsurprising that "Sex and the City" ended with all the women finding long-term partners, and with Miranda headed to the outer boroughs to pursue her now more "adult" family lifestyle. The City was fun while it lasted, but once the "singles" fun came to an end, time to pair up the main characters.

CATHOLIC MARRIAGE THEOLOGY

Catholic theologies perpetuate these cultural assumptions in the ways that theologians have tended to focus almost solely on marriage over singleness in recent years. Part of this is because of the dearth of discussion of marriage as a path toward holiness at all, as I noted above and the development of more positive theologies of marriage.

For example, discussion of marriage as a good has developed rapidly in the past few decades, particularly related to the "domestic church" and nuptial theology. Both of these have been developed in relation to the work of John Paul II. The "Domestic Church," a phrase linked to early church fathers, paved the way for serious reflection about ways in which families were wholeheartedly part of the church. The term did not immediately gain widespread usage; Florence Caffrey Bourg notes that it wasn't until John Paul II's Apostolic Exhortation "On the Family" in 1980 that the term gained more import.[12] The pope's document exhorted families to "become what you are": a means by which people are formed in Christian faith and learn to practice discipleship.[13] "Domestic church" became seen as a way in which families could fulfill their lay vocation in part because they were building up the church at home through education of children and the like.

A second development came in the form of nuptial theology, which sees that the ultimate relationship between humanity and God is a nuptial relationship, partially revealed in the marriage relationship between

---

11. Natalie Schwartzberg et al., *Single in a Married World*.

12. Bourg, *Where Two or Three are Gathered*, 13.

13. *Familiaris Consortio*, no. 17.

husband and wife.[14] Eschatologically, the human marriage relationship would cease to exist in the face of the more profound marital relationship between Christ and the Church. In the present era, however, the nuptial relationship between husband and wife can witness to that final relationship. Nuptial theology was further developed by John Paul II in his weekly papal audiences between 1979 and 1983. These weekly talks later became known collectively as *Theology of the Body*. Theology of the Body has been popularized by Christopher West and is the significant underpinning for many diocesan programs about natural family planning and classes for engaged couples seeking to be married in the church. Nuptial theology is not limited to discussion of marriage and family; celibates are typically seen as the culminating example, in this life, of how relationships will be ordered in the next, precisely because they are not dependent on sexual love or present physical needs to live out their relationship with God.

The good that has come from both "domestic church" and "nuptial theology" has been widespread. Married couples and families have received a boost in terms of their identity as Christians within the church, and both theologies have deep roots in much patristic literature. These theologies have enabled those considering marriage to consider themselves as having a vocation, just as members of religious orders or those considering the priesthood have vocations. One of the main thrusts of the theology was to decrease the clericalization of the church, and pinpoint the ways in which lay people, too, were members of the Body of Christ and as such, responsible for tending God's Kingdom. Moreover, on the views of many who write about "domestic church," particularly Lisa Sowle Cahill, Florence Caffrey Bourg, and Julie Hanlon Rubio, the vocation of the family goes beyond divorce, cohabitation, abortion, and the use of birth control that often seem the exclusive focus of theologians discussing family relationships. In this new era of theology about families, familial vocation extends to social justice concerns.

Nonetheless, I contend that "domestic church" and "nuptial theology" both often perpetuate a dichotomy between married people and non-married, between celibate people but also between those singles who are part of households but are unmarried. For example, domestic church is most often linked to families, particularly parents and their children, as in John Paul II's *Familiaris Consortio*. Vowed celibates have

14. See, for example, von Balthasar, *Explorations in Theology*.

little part in this, but non-vowed singles have none. Nuptial theology, too, tends to be discussed in terms of sex, contraception, and bodies, and therefore, married couples. Though nuptial theology ultimately is tied to celibacy as the ultimate nuptial relationship with Christ, singles lack context for understanding their bodies outside of sexual relationships and "total self-giving," and marital relationships are seen as lesser relationships than the celibate ones, further widening a split between the two.

This dichotomy is further heightened by a sense that in the church, too, it is adults who make choices about states of life. States of life are either marriage or vowed religious life. Some people do choose to be single, some in religious life as priests, monks, and nuns. Some make that choice but remain as non-vowed lay people, like Shane Claiborne and others involved in the New Monasticism project.[15] *The Catechism of the Catholic Church* maintains that it is the duty and responsibility of every Christian that "when they become adults, children have the right and duty to *choose their profession and state of life*."[16] While I do think people have the responsibility to question whether they are perhaps avoiding a vocation to religious life or marriage, the tie of adulthood to choosing state of life leaves a quandary for serious Christians. Vocation, if it to be seen truly as a call from God, is not something that can be chosen in the same way that one chooses from among different brands in a grocery store, but that is the way that the current "market" for marriage and even religious life is set up. We advertise ourselves and even our religious communities in online dating ads and religious vocation magazine ads, in the hopes that someone might actually choose my "brand" over that other one.

For many, singleness is not a choice in that way, and the surrounding hype about marriage makes it a serious problem for them. One woman writes:

> I feel that maybe 99% of single people don't feel "called" to be single. They just are. Whether it's the environment we live in . . . or just our bodies . . . or it's how God is . . . most people feel called to be married. But, the problem is . . . you can feel called to be married and still never find the right guy. This is what I deem to be the problem with calling singleness a "vocation." Many times,

15. See www.newmonasticism.org. See also Shane Claiborne, *Irresistible Revolution*.
16. *Catechism of the Catholic Church*, no. 2230. Emphasis in text.

> I think you just feel like you're stuck there. A sort of purgatory.
> Until you either meet the right guy . . . or feel like you are being
> called to remain single.[17]

This person felt as though she was in a personal purgatory of sorts because she was single and not by choice. What does a person do when no vocation has presented itself? What if someone thinks they are called to be married but haven't found someone to marry?

The prevailing assumption by both theologies appears to be that a person either has a vocation for a vowed celibate life, or a vocation for a familial life (variously configured). The church appears to be built on these two pillars. The term "domestic church" cements a view that marriage and family are linked to the church in a close bond, in ways that non-vowed singleness cannot be. Yet living a good Christian life, being part of the Body, no matter what state of life we are in, is something that all Christians are called to do. "Domestic church" as it is discussed, however, causes us to think, not in terms of the Christian life as a whole or the Body of Christ as a whole, but of the subset of parts. This is detrimental both to helping married people understand marriage as a vocation (because it doesn't as readily become linked to Christian vocation) and also to those people who are not married, whether by choice or by chance.

The lack of attention given to the status of the non-vowed laity makes sense in historical context. The rise in divorce rates in the 1960s and 1970s (followed by a leveling off, rather than a decrease in divorce), combined with the rise in average age for marriage, and combined with the fact that many of those who are in their early and mid-twenties who have waited to marry are also no longer living at home, or even in the same state, means that there has been a rather stark demographic shift in the numbers of single people unconnected to families in a traditional sense.[18] Compared to the pre-Vatican II frame of reference, in which the normal state of life for most Americans, married or not, was to be connected to one's family, this demographic shift directs some new theological questions. Much theological energy has been on putting

17. Personal correspondence, September 5, 2008.

18. If anything, the numbers become much starker for Protestant theologians, since it has been far more normalized for Protestant Christians to be married. Most of the early Protestant reformers, for example, advocated that all Christians seek after the married state of life. See John Witte Jr. "Marriage Contracts."

back together some version of the family as it apparently existed prior to the "divorce revolution" and the "sexual revolution."[19] So much attention has been focused to this question, in fact, that very little thought has gone toward other states of life. The result is, as in secular culture, to see marriage and family as normal, more normal than being single, for non-vowed singles.[20]

An important question to ask, then, is how "singleness" fits with ecclesiology. Both "domestic church" and nuptial theology relate to particular ecclesiologies, which do not always adequately account or allow for what some have called the "non-vowed form of the lay state" but the increasing numbers of people who find themselves not led toward any particular vocation at the moment, plus the numbers of people who are divorced, widowed, or find themselves otherwise in the "single" category deserve greater attention in the twenty-first century.[21]

Is all this theological pressure really what Christians are called to do? I fear that for many, being single and Christian means that one has a vocation to find the right person to marry. (With the small caveat that in the relatively unlikely event you are called to a religious vocation, go out and find that.) No wonder people want to get married! Yet still, Paul's letter to the Corinthians, and indeed, the centuries of Christian tradition and witness toward other non-married states of life, should press theologians to ask how to think about singleness alongside marriage. "Domestic church" and "nuptial theology" may still be good views from which to understand singleness, but not as they are commonly discussed.

THAT SINGULAR VOCATION

Paul wrote before monasticism was ever an official state of life, so Patricia Sullivan notes that Paul's own singleness was a form of secular, non-vowed singleness.[22] Single and married appear separate to the extent that

---

19. For example, the Marriage, Family and Culture project, an ecumenical group of theologians, politicians, political scientists and others, has been on the more liberal end of the spectrum, trying to address the problem of lack of marriage in American society and elsewhere.

20. I should note that this is probably even more so the case for vowed celibates, whose state has been quite a bit damaged by the clergy sexual abuse scandal in 2002, even though the church is officially highly supportive of vowed celibate states of life.

21. See Sullivan, "Non-vowed Form."

22. Sullivan, "Non-vowed Form."

there seems to be an us/them divide today, but though Paul advocates for his own state of life, he is decidedly not trying to close off the option to marry. In fact, in the context of the whole, the passage seems to be less about choosing a state of life than it is about not letting any one particular state of life get in the way of the primary vocation of the Christian:

> However that may be, let each of you lead the life that the Lord has assigned, to which God called you. This is my rule in all the churches. Was anyone at the time of his call already circumcised? Let him not seek to remove the marks of circumcision. Was anyone at the time of his call uncircumcised? Let him not seek circumcision. Circumcision is nothing, and uncircumcision nothing; but obeying the commandments of God is everything.[23]

Paul continues by speaking similarly about other states, including marriage and virginity, but also mourning and rejoicing.

Scholars might suggest that Paul's admonitions are quite short-sighted here, because he believes that the Second Coming will happen *very soon*. (As he writes in verse 29: "the appointed time has grown short." And later in verse 30: "For the present form of this world is passing away.") Yet regardless of when Paul thinks the Second Coming will happen (and remember that he does not know precisely when that will be) he still believes that states of life need to be regarded with respect to eschatology. People must live as though they were not married, not mourning, not rejoicing—not because those things are bad, but because those things are not permanent. The Christian's life is always contingent and not ultimate. States of life are gifts (1 Cor 7:7) that we have that might enable us to follow Christ better, or indeed, come to know Christ at all. Thus Paul can say: "Wife, for all you know, you might save your husband. Husband, for all you know, you might save your wife" (1 Cor 7:16).

When Paul speaks of "the call," moreover, he seems to be referring to the point at which people were called to follow Christ. For Paul, that call comes linked to baptism. In his letter to the Ephesians, he writes:

> I therefore, the prisoner in the Lord, beg you to lead a life worthy of the calling to which you have been called, with all humility and gentleness, with patience, bearing with one another in love, making every effort to maintain the unity of the Spirit in the bond of peace. There is one body and one Spirit, just as you were called

---

23. 1 Cor 7:17–20. All quotations in this section are from the NRSV.

> to the one hope of your calling, one Lord, one faith, one baptism, one God and Father of all, who is above all and through all and in all. (Eph 4:1–6)

As in the letter to the Corinthians, Paul here links call not with specific states but with gifts given. "The gifts he gave were that some would be apostles, some prophets, some evangelists, some pastors and teachers, to equip the saints for the work of ministry, for building up the body of Christ, until all of us come to the unity of the faith and of the knowledge of the Son of God, to maturity, to the measure of the full stature of Christ" (Eph 4:11–13).

Each of us at our baptisms was recognized as an individual who dedicated his or her life to God. Each of us received our vocation. As *Gaudium et spes* says, "[The lay faithful] are by baptism made one body with Christ and are constituted among the People of God; they are in their own way made sharers in the priestly, prophetical, and kingly functions of Christ; and they carry out for their own part the mission of the whole Christian people in the Church and in the world."[24] We each *in our own way* were made sharers in Christ's own life and mission.

Which is to say, at heart, *all* Christians are single. We begin our Christian lives, in part, from singleness, from the fact that we are individuals with unique gifts. This is moreover part of the way that we Christians should be giving witness to an alternative message than the world gives. Christians are not, by *default*, married as a state of life. Single is the default of what it means to be Christian. Paul intimates this when he suggests that those who are married should live as though they are not. This Christian life of singleness, though, is marked by very different characteristics than the narrative contemporary culture offers about singleness. This is not a life that involves constant seeking of a new partner, but a life that involves putting down roots in the community in which one has been baptized.

That point leads to my second claim: we also begin our Christian lives, in part, in community, as those who are married. This is, indeed, part of what nuptial theology offers for Christians, but which gets obscured in the overall discussion. As part of the church, all Christians are married to Christ, and moreover all Christians have become part of

---

24. *Gaudium et Spes*, no. 30.

a new family. In one of Augustine's sermon, written on the occasion of Easter baptisms, he suggests of those baptized:

> A short while ago they were called "Askers"; now they're called "Infants." They were called askers because they were agitating their other's womb, asking to be born. They are called infants because they have just now been born to Christ, having previously been born to the world.[25]

The ones who were previously baptized are their parents and they bear the responsibility to raise them and teach them and love them similar to how parents raise and love and care for biological children.

Saying that all are single and all are married in this way serves to highlight the strangeness of the call that Christians have, and the radical witness Christians make to the world about the nature of marriage, singleness, and all the related activities like dating and hooking up. Christ has come and has brought about a very different vision of what marriage and family means, and even what it means to be single.

At the same time, my suggestion that all are single and all are married in this way does not collapse vocation or states of life into broad general categories that become ultimately meaningless. Paul suggests states of life are gifts, and so when it comes to living a particular state, it becomes not a necessity (in the way that marriage so often seems today) but a contingent blessing. States of life do, in fact, mark the ways in which individual Christians live. Individual states of life point toward the full vocation of Christians in the Body of Christ. So, for example, someone who is single and childless might consider that still, she is a "parent" and might offer to teach catechetical classes, which often get taught by biological parents of children.

On the other hand, those states of life cannot become an excuse not to use other gifts that God has given for use in one's "call" as a Christian. For example, those who are single often observe that people expect them to do so much more because they are single and therefore appear to have more time. It is true that people who are married, particularly with children, will find their time truncated. Taking Paul's words seriously, however, suggests that even those who are married with children should consider that still, God might be asking them to use their gifts in ways that get pushed onto those who are single. One example might be medi-

25. Augustine, "Sermon 228," §1.

cal missionary work, which has been successfully negotiated by families, but which (especially for Catholics) often is presumed to be the purview of single people.

In theological accounts, then, there should be neither an elite class in the form of monks and celibates, nor an elite class in the form of married people with families. Single Christians are therefore adults, though not necessarily choosers of the state of life God has given to them at this particular moment. The choice comes instead in determining whether one will follow Christ and live this state of life as a gift now (even if in the future, marriage might well be a possibility), or whether the option taken will be conforming to cultural assumptions about marriage that run counter to Christian witness. The overabundant focus on marriage that "domestic church" and nuptial theology offer is rightly tempered by recognition that states of life are gifts toward living out the one vocational call that we all have.

BIBLIOGRAPHY

Augustine, "Sermon 228." In *Sermons (184–229z) on the Liturgical Seasons*, edited by John E. Rotelle, OSA, trans. Edmund Hill, OP, 257–79. New Rochelle, NY: New City, 1993.

Bennett, Jana Marguerite. *Water is Thicker than Blood: An Augustinian Theology of Marriage and Singleness*. New York: Oxford University Press, 2008.

Bourg, Florence Caffrey. *Where Two or Three are Gathered: Christian Families as Domestic Churches*. Notre Dame, IN: University of Notre Dame Press, 2004.

Claiborne, Shane. *The Irresistible Revolution: Living as an Ordinary Radical*. Grand Rapids: Zondervan, 2006.

Coday, Dennis. "Panel Links Celibacy and Abuse." *National Catholic Reporter* (October 29, 2004) 3.

John Chrysostom. *On Marriage and Family Life*. Translated by Catherine P. Roth and David Anderson. Crestwood, NY: St. Vladimir's Seminary Press, 2000.

Kosnik, Anthony, et al. *Human Sexuality*. Paramus, NJ: Paulist, 1977.

Pew Forum on Religion and Public Life. "U.S. Religious Landscape Survey." Online: http://religions.pewforum.org/.

Schwartzberg, Natalie, et al. *Single in a Married World: A Life Cycle Framework for Working With the Unmarried Adult*. New York: Norton, 1995.

Straus, Jilian. "Excerpt from *Unhooked Generation: The Truth About Why We're Still Single*." Online: http://www.unhookedgeneration.com/excerpt.php.

Sullivan, Patricia A. "The Non-vowed Form of the Lay State in the Life of the Church." *Theological Studies* 68 (2007) 320–47.

von Balthasar, Hans Urs. *Explorations in Theology: Spouse of the Word*. San Francisco: Ignatius, 1989.

Witte, John, Jr. "Marriage Contracts, Liturgies and Properties in Reformation Geneva." In *To Have and to Hold: Marrying and its Documentation in Western Christendom, 400–1600*, edited by Philip L. Reynolds and John Witte Jr., 453–88. Cambridge: Cambridge University Press, 2007.

5

Understanding Sexual Orientation as a *Habitus*

Reasoning from the Natural Law, Appeals to Human Experience, and the Data of Science[1]

REV. NICANOR PIER GIORGIO AUSTRIACO, O.P.

I N AN ADDRESS TO the participants of the International Congress on the Natural Moral Law several years ago in Rome, Pope Benedict XVI called for an urgent renewal of the natural law tradition in moral theology.[2] According to the Holy Father, extraordinary developments in the human capacity to decipher the rules and structures of matter—here he is clearly talking about progress in the empirical sciences—have led to much advance and progress in human civilization. However, they have also made us blind to the moral message contained in the order of creation, a message that the perennial tradition calls the *lex naturalis* or the natural law. He attributes this blindness to changes in our understanding of nature. Nature has ceased to be a robust metaphysical reality. Instead, it has become a mere object of empirical analysis. As a result, the Pope argues, nature—in fact, being itself—is no longer transparent to moral analysis, creating a sense of disorientation that renders the choices of

1. I thank the parishioners of the Cathedral of St. Matthew the Apostle in Washington, DC, for motivating me to write this paper; my fellow participants at the 2008 New Wine, New Wineskins Conference at the University of Notre Dame for responding to and criticizing an earlier version of this paper; my Dominican brothers for commenting on several drafts of the manuscript; and Lawrence J. Goodwin for challenging me to clarify my argument.

2. Benedict XVI, "Address of His Holiness Benedict XVI to the Participants in the International Congress on Natural Moral Law."

daily life precarious and uncertain. The Pope points out that this disorientation strikes younger individuals in a particularly poignant way because it is they in particular who must make fundamental choices for their life without the clear guidance of the natural law. Thus, the Pope concludes, there is an urgent need to recover such a clear understanding.

As a contribution to the renewal of the natural law tradition called for by the Holy Father, this paper will explore the relationship between natural law reasoning, appeals to human experience, and the data of science, using homosexuality as a test case.[3] More specifically, I want to answer this question: How should moral theologians working on the natural law appropriate insights from the natural sciences to renew their tradition?

I will make three observations, one for each of the three parts of my paper. First, I will sound a caution: Moral theologians cannot use the data of science alone to determine the good in a morally normative sense. They need to contextualize all the findings of science by reflecting upon the teleological pattern of creation from which we can understand the ideas of God and the right way to live. Next, I will propose that moralists can use scientific data to help them respond to questions raised by natural law arguments that appeal to human experience for their justification: Whose experience is normative? Whose experience is privileged? How do we know if we have sampled all the relevant human experiences associated with a particular behavioral pattern? Third, I will propose that moral theologians can use the findings of empirical studies to articulate and, in some limited cases, to justify those virtuous practices that must accompany natural law reasoning if it is to be an effective moral guide, especially for those young people who are struggling to make decisions about their lives. As an example, in light of recent scientific findings, I would like to suggest that it may be helpful to understand sexual orientation as a *habitus*, a stable disposition towards acts, in this case, sexual

3. Why homosexuality? Several years ago, I spent two years serving at the Cathedral of St. Matthew the Apostle in Washington, DC. During that time, I had the opportunity to meet several Catholic men who were struggling with same-sex attraction. Listening to their stories and witnessing their often heroic attempts to live chaste lives that are faithful to the Lord and to the teachings of his Church made me realize that their experience as persons struggling with same-sex attraction had been overlooked in the theological debate over homosexual experience. Sharing their narratives with my colleagues and fellow moral theologians remains a primary motivation for the writing of this paper.

acts, which may be shaped by frequently repeated action in the context of virtuous practices. In the course of my paper, I will respond to several Christian scholars who have used natural law arguments to call for a revision of the Church's teaching on the immorality of homosexual acts.

I

How are moral theologians working in the natural law tradition called to appropriate scientific discoveries that link human behavior to the biological constitution of the human being? Or to put it another way, how do we determine if a behavior that arises from the biological nature of an individual is good or bad?

On June 7, 2008, a scientific paper entitled, "Genetic and Environmental Effects on Same-sex Sexual Behavior: A Population Study of Twins in Sweden," involving the largest twin study of same-sex sexual behavior attempted so far, reported that genetics can explain approximately 35 percent of the variation associated with male homosexuality and about 18 percent of the variance associated with female homosexuality.[4] The rest of the variation could be explained by random environmental factors including hormonal influences.[5] In the end, it is likely that homosexuality will eventually be explained by appealing both to biological and to societal causes.

What is the moral significance of this scientific finding? In a speech to the annual meeting of the United Society for the Propagation of the Gospel on July 4, 2008, the Most Rev. Alan Harper, OBE, the Anglican Archbishop of Armagh and the Anglican Primate of All Ireland, argued that the Christian Church would have to accept that homosexuals commit "natural"—and thus, good—rather than "unnatural"—and thus, bad—sexual acts with each other if science could definitively prove that they were born homosexual.[6] The archbishop's proposal echoes many other authors and writers who conclude that homosexuality is natural

---

4. Langstrom et al., "Genetic and Environmental Effects on Same-sex Sexual Behavior."

5. To put these findings into context, studies of twins also show that up to 60 percent of the variation between children in their ability to learn to read is shaped by genetic factors. In other words, our reading and spelling ability is more genetically determined than our sexual orientation. For discussion and references to the literature, see Raskind, "Current Understanding of the Genetic Basis of Reading and Spelling Disability."

6. Harper, "Holy Scripture and the Law of God."

and good precisely because homosexuality is influenced and shaped by biological—and more specifically, genetic—factors.[7] According to this argument, genetics determines the good.

This argument is flawed. It is erroneous because it is clear that there is a biological basis for other behaviors that we would still consider disordered. For instance, there is convincing evidence for a biological basis for the propensity towards violent behavior, including the identification of genetic variants in three specific genes, *MAOA, DRD2,* and *DAT1,* which predispose individuals to violent acts.[8] In other words, in the same way that genetics informs one individual's predisposition to same-sex acts, genetics also informs another person's predisposition to violent acts.[9] From this, it should be apparent that natural law reasoning cannot always move legitimately from the scientific conclusion that a behavior has a biological basis to the moral judgment that the particular behavior pattern is normatively good. Otherwise, violent acts, including acts of rape, could be considered natural and good.

In sum, scientific analysis alone cannot determine what is perfective for the human person. Rather, natural law reasoning has to locate its reflections in the rational and teleological order of creation that examines the human being within the context of his natural and supernatural ends. As Pope John Paul II taught in *Veritatis splendor:* "The natural law is called the natural law not because it refers to a generic nature common to all animal species but because it refers specifically to man's proper and primordial nature, the 'nature of the human person,' which is the person himself in the unity of soul and body, in the unity of his spiritual and biological inclinations and of all the other specific characteristics

---

7. For one popular example, see Reuters, "The naturalness of homosexuality." In contrast, Edward Stein has argued that the biological argument for lesbian and gay rights—the proposal that the findings of science are relevant to making the case for lesbian and gay rights—is misguided and not pragmatic. For discussion, see Stein, *Mismeasure of Desire,* 277–304.

8. For discussion and references to the literature, see Guo, et al., "Integration of Genetic Propensities."

9. There is even some suggestion that pedophilia may have a biological basis, though the data is still not conclusive. Two research groups, one in Toronto, Canada, and the other in Magdeburg, Germany, have shown that the brains of pedophilic men are structurally different from the brains of non-pedophiles in regions critical for sexual development. For discussion, see Cantor et al., "Cerebral white matter deficiencies," and Schiltz et al., "Brain pathology."

necessary for the pursuit of his end."[10] To put it another way, natural law reasoning is grounded in an anthropological account that implicitly acknowledges that the human person is created by God for particular ends.

How do we determine the teleological ordering of the human person? As St. Thomas Aquinas explained, natural law reasoning discovers four subordinate ends, life, procreation, community, and truth, either from immediate experience or from reflection and inference, which are required to attain our ultimate perfection.[11] Ordained by God, these goods—these perfective ends—are inter-related and mutually support each other. First, we need life to strive for our goals and for our perfection. This is the most basic end necessary to achieve all our other natural ends. Next, we need to procreate to preserve the human community. Third, we need the human community because as social creatures, we can only attain our perfection in communion with others. Finally, we need to know truth because it is truth that gives our lives meaning and purpose. Ultimately, of course, we need to know the truth about God who is the cause of all that exists, in order to attain, with the help of his grace, the happiness that is friendship with him.

Ordained by God, human sexuality too has a teleological ordering. As the Second Vatican Council taught, a reasoned reflection upon the personal and biological meaning of human sexuality reveals that conjugal love is ordered towards two complementary ends, the procreation of children and the union of the spouses:

> The intimate partnership of life and the love which constitutes the married state has been established by the creator and endowed by him with its own proper laws. . . . By its very nature the institution of marriage and married life is ordered to the procreation and education of the offspring and it is in them that it finds its crowning glory. Thus the man and woman, who "are no longer two but one" (Matt 19:6), help and serve each other by

10. *Veritatis splendor*, no. 50.

11. St. Thomas Aquinas, *ST* I–II, Q. 94, A. 2. Other authors have proposed more elaborate lists of human ends. For example, Grisez, *Way of the Lord Jesus*, 115–40, has suggested that human beings have seven categories of human goods that perfect persons and contribute to their fulfillment both as individuals and as communities: self-integration, practical reasonableness and authenticity, justice and friendship, religion, life and health, knowledge of truth and appreciation of beauty, and satisfaction in playful activities and skillful performances. John Finnis, *Natural Law*, 85–92, proposes a similar list of basic human goods.

their marriage partnership; they become conscious of their unity
and experience it more deeply from day to day."[12]

In light of these truths about human sexuality, to choose someone
of the same sex for one's sexual activity is to annul the rich symbolism
and meaning, not to mention the teleological ordering, of the Creator's
sexual design. Same-sex union by its nature is unable to transmit life
and as such is inherently non-procreative. It is also not a complementary
union. In other words, the union in same-sex unions can never be the
complete and total self-gift that is properly associated with the conjugal
act because same-sex partners can never share their powers to procreate.
Of course, as the Church notes, this does not mean that homosexual
persons are not often generous and giving of themselves. However, when
they engage in homosexual activity, they confirm within themselves a
disordered sexual inclination that is essentially self-indulgent because
it is not self-giving. It is behavior that prevents the human person from
attaining his own fulfillment and happiness because it is contrary to the
creative wisdom of God. As such, it is immoral.[13]

II

It is becoming commonplace for Catholic individuals and moral theologians to appeal to human experience to morally justify human behavior,
especially homosexual behavior. Such positive experience is thought to
offer the decisive counterargument to the classic natural law account
above, which, the authors contend, needs to be revised in light of the
positive experience. In an essay published in *Commonweal*, Professor
Luke Timothy Johnson, a renowned Catholic biblical scholar, appeals
to the experience of numerous individuals including his own lesbian
daughter to argue for the naturalness and goodness of homosexuality.
He writes: "We appeal explicitly to the weight of our own experience and
the experience thousands of others have witnessed to, which tells us that
to claim our own sexual orientation is in fact to accept the way in which
God has created us."[14] According to Johnson and other Catholic com-

12. *Gaudium et spes*, no. 48.

13. This paragraph is indebted to the CDF document, *Letter to the Bishops of the Catholic Church on the Pastoral Care of Homosexual Persons*, no. 7. For a comprehensive explanation and defense of the Church's teaching on homosexuality, see Latkovic, "Homosexuality." Also see the insightful book, Harvey, *Truth about Homosexuality*.

14. Johnson, "Scripture & Experience," 16.

mentators including Todd Salzman and Michael Lawler, and Margaret Farley, Catholic moralists should examine human experience to evaluate the morality of biological behaviors including homosexuality.[15] If so, they would discover that the testimony of gay and lesbian couples affirms both the goodness of their sexual relationships and the judgment that their relationships draw them closer to God, neighbor, and self. In other words, human experience can help us better understand human flourishing.

But arguments that appeal to experience raise several questions: Whose experience is normative? Whose experience is privileged? How do we know if we have sampled all the relevant human experiences associated with a particular behavioral pattern?

I propose that at times, Catholic moralists can use empirical data to help them respond to these questions. For instance, in opposition to Johnson, Salzman, and Lawler, and others who appeal to the positive testimony of gay and lesbian couples, there is mounting scientific evidence that demonstrates that homosexuality is associated with a greater risk for mental disorders.[16] It is becoming clearer that homosexual persons are more likely to experience mental illness than their heterosexual counterparts.

Three papers published in the peer-reviewed and well-respected journal, *Archives of General Psychiatry*, are representative. In the first study, Herrell et al., used a powerful technique, the co-twin control method, to look at the psychological health of self-identified and sexually active homosexual men in the United States.[17] The study concluded that on average, male homosexuals were five times more likely to show suicide-related behavior or thoughts than their heterosexual counterparts. Significantly, most of the findings were valid even after the researchers accounted for the influence of substance abuse and depressive symptoms other than suicidality. The second study followed a large New Zealand group from birth to their early twenties.[18] Corroborating the first

15. For discussion, see Salzman and Lawler, "Catholic Sexual Ethics" and "Truly Human Sexual Acts"; and Margaret Farley, *Just Love.*

16. For a recent review of the literature, see Herek and Garnets, "Sexual Orientation and Mental Health." Also see the study by King et al., "Systematic review of mental disorder."

17. Herrell et al., "Sexual orientation and suicidality."

18. Fergusson et al. "Is sexual orientation related."

study, this independent report showed a significant increase of depression, anxiety disorder, conduct disorder, substance abuse and thoughts about suicide among those who were homosexually active. As one scientist commentator has pointed out, these two studies "contain arguably the best published data on the association between homosexuality and psychopathology, and both converge on the same unhappy conclusion: homosexual people are at a substantially higher risk for some forms of emotional problems, including suicidality, major depression, and anxiety disorder."[19] Finally, the third and most recent paper of the three studies showed that there was an increase in mental health problems associated with homosexual persons in the Netherlands.[20] Remarkably, HIV status was not a factor. From this scientific data, there is reason to think that homosexual persons are inherently predisposed not only towards homosexual acts but also towards those self-destructive acts associated with mental illness.

Critics could object by proposing that societal and not biological factors may be the cause for the higher incidence of mental illness found in homosexual persons: Homosexual individuals may suffer from mental distress because of the social marginalization that they experience in non-tolerant societies. In other words, critics could argue that the homosexual heterosexual orientation is not *intrinsically* associated with the observed mental distress.

In response, it is clear that societal factors can and probably do contribute to the higher incidence of mental illness in homosexual persons. One study has shown that youth who were considered gender atypical in childhood experienced verbal, physical, and sexual victimization, which, not unexpectedly, led to mental distress.[21] However, as one commentator has pointed out, this argument—which some have called the minority stress hypothesis—cannot completely explain the elevated incidence of mental distress in gay individuals because the observed differences in mental health status between homosexuals and heterosexuals are just as great in the Netherlands and in New Zealand, two societies which are relatively more tolerant of homosexuality, as they are in the United

19. Bailey, "Homosexuality and Mental Illness," 883.

20. Sandfort et al., "Same-sex sexual behavior and psychiatric disorders."

21. D'Augelli et al., "Childhood gender atypicality." Also see the study by Ploderl and Fartacek, "Childhood gender nonconformity."

States, a society which is relatively not as tolerant.[22] If social ostracism is indeed a significant factor in influencing the mental health status of homosexual persons, then one would expect to see differences in the incidence of mental illness in homosexuals among societies with varying tolerances to homosexuality. These differences do not exist. Indeed, a more recent population-based study in the Netherlands suggest that even in a country with a comparatively tolerant and accepting climate regarding homosexuality—97 percent of the Dutch people think that "homosexuals should be left as free as possible to lead their own lives," while 93 percent think that homosexual couples "should have the same rights as ordinary married couples to inherit from each other"[23]— homosexual men were still at much higher risk for suicidality than heterosexual men.[24] Therefore, it appears that the heightened risk of mental illness among homosexuals cannot be completely explained by appeals to social marginalization, suggesting that biological causes are also involved.[25]

From a cursory glance at the theological literature, it is clear that the experience of homosexual persons struggling with mental illness has not been heard in the debate surrounding the morality of homosexual acts. There is also no mention of the experience of the gay couples who have embraced promiscuity as part of their committed relationships[26] or the experience of lesbian couples who struggle with problems related to alcohol consumption at a significantly greater rate than heterosexual couples[27] or even the experience of Catholic homosexuals who have

22. Whitehead, "Homosexuality and Mental Health Problems."

23. West and Green, *Sociolegal Control of Homosexuality*, 300.

24. R. de Graaf et al., "Suicidality and sexual orientation." Note that the study also concluded that this pattern appears not to hold with women.

25. I think that it is important to emphasize that the heightened risk of mental illness among homosexuals does not mean that all homosexual individuals are mentally ill or that all homosexual individuals will develop mental illness. As comparison, note that not all smokers develop lung cancer though it is clear that smoking is a primary cause for lung cancer in those smokers who do develop that malignancy and that in general, smoking causes lung cancer.

26. One study in the Netherlands has revealed that for homosexual men with steady partners, the rate at which they acquire casual partners averaged eight per year. Homosexual men without a steady partner, on the other hand, were found to acquire an average of twenty-two casual sex partners per year. See Xiridou et al., "Contribution of steady and casual partnerships."

27. For details and discussion, see Drabble et al., "Reports of alcohol consumption and alcohol-related problems."

chosen to live chaste lives because of the disorder they encountered in the gay lifestyle.[28] Their experience—in direct opposition to the experiences that undergird the arguments proffered by Johnson, Salzman, and Lawler—would affirm that the homosexual condition is not inherently good for the human person. Their experience is evidence that it undermines human flourishing. It is intrinsically disordered.

To conclude, the moral structure of the natural law should resonate with human experience, but this experience cannot be limited to the experience of a select, privileged few, in the case of this discussion, to the experience of some primarily white, Western homosexuals living at the turn of the twenty-first century. An examination of the available empirical evidence suggests that Catholic moral theologians who have appealed to human experience to justify homosexual acts have been too selective in their choice of personal testimonies. It is likely that a more inclusive study would reveal the disorder of many same-sex relationships.

III

In this final section of this paper, I would like to propose that the data of science can also help us to articulate and, in some cases, justify those virtuous practices that must accompany natural law reasoning if it is to be an effective moral guide. I am convinced that the natural law cannot be divorced from a virtue ethic because moral theology as a practical science is ordered ultimately not towards conceptual discussions regarding the morality of human acts, but towards particular actions done here and now by a particular human agent. Thus, it is not enough for a Catholic moral theologian to make natural law arguments about homosexuality. He or she also needs to be able to formulate that argument so that a 19-year-old college student struggling with same-sex attraction can act and live out its truth. This is an integral part of the science and the art of moral theology.

What would a virtue ethic for an individual struggling with same-sex attraction look like? In a paper published in the journal *Archives of Sexual Behavior*, Dr. Robert L. Spitzer, Professor of Psychiatry at Columbia University and chairman of the 1973 American Psychological Association (APA) committee which recommended that homosexual-

---

28. For example, see Morrison, *Beyond Gay* and Tushnet, "Experience and Tradition." Also see the personal narrative and insightful analysis by Selmys, *Sexual Authenticity*.

ity be removed from the official diagnostic manual of mental disorders, interviewed men and women who had experienced a significant shift from homosexual to heterosexual attraction and had sustained this shift for at least five years.[29] To his surprise, he discovered that contrary to his own expectations, some highly motivated individuals, using a variety of change efforts, were able to make a substantial change in multiple indicators of sexual orientation and achieve good heterosexual functioning.

In his study of 200 individuals, Spitzer reported that after their change efforts, 17 percent of the men and 55 percent of the women interviewed claimed that they were now exclusively heterosexual in their orientation. Furthermore, 66 percent of the men and 44 percent of the women also reported that they had achieved good heterosexual functioning defined in the study as being in a sustained heterosexual relationship within the past year, rating emotional satisfaction from the relationship a seven or higher on a 10-point scale, and having satisfying heterosexual sex at least monthly. The study concluded that some change in sexual orientation is possible.

Two points should be made here to put the findings of the Spitzer study in a proper context. First, it is important to note that the subjects in the Spitzer study were not chosen at random from among homosexuals who had gone through therapy. Thus, the results should not be considered typical. As Spitzer himself remarked, a significant majority of his subjects were "highly motivated" to change. Second, given the difficulty he had in finding volunteers for his study, Spitzer has acknowledged that a complete change in sexual orientation is probably uncommon. Rather, according to Spitzer, a better way to conceptualize "sexual reorientation" is to see it as the diminishing of unwanted homosexual potential with a concomitant increase in the heterosexual potential of a particular individual.

Since the study was made public at the annual meeting of the American Psychological Association on May 9, 2001, the conclusions of Spitzer's report have been heavily criticized. Typically, there are two main objections.[30] First, critics charge that the study did not include data on the subjects' original sexual orientation. Thus, they assert that the study could not rule out the possibility that all the individuals inter-

---

29. Spitzer, "Can Some Gay Men and Lesbians Change Their Sexual Orientation?"

30. For critical analysis and discussion of the Spitzer study, see Drescher and Zucker, *Ex-Gay Research.*

viewed were not true homosexuals, who by definition are persons who are sexually attracted *exclusively* to members of the same sex. Hence, these critics assert that the study was probably limited to individuals who had had a bisexual orientation and had previously engaged in at least some homosexual activity. After therapy, these critics propose that the subjects remained bisexual though they now feel that they have successfully developed a relationship with a person of the opposite gender. Thus, they conclude that the sexual orientation of the subjects really did not change.

To respond to these critics, I note that the study did report that 42 percent of the men and 46 percent of the women interviewed said that they were exclusively homosexual before they engaged in the reparative therapy. Furthermore, only 9 percent of the men and 26 percent of the women had opposite sex masturbatory fantasies before their treatment. Together, both these results indicate that prior to therapy a significant number of the subjects were probably not bisexually orientated as the critics claim.

Second, critics charge that the study was limited to a very select group of individuals that is not representative of the gay community. The subjects were predominantly Evangelical Christians associated with groups who condemn homosexuality: Of those who participated in the study, 78 percent had spoken publicly in favor of efforts to convert homosexuals to heterosexuality; 93 percent said religion was "extremely" or "very" important in their lives. From this, critics conclude that these subjects were atypical and thus cannot be compared to the majority of persons in the gay community. To support their claim, they contrast Spitzer's study with another study reported by psychologists, Ariel Shidlo and Michael Schroeder, who found that the vast majority of the subjects in their group, individuals recruited through the Internet and direct mailings to groups advocating reparative therapy, reported failure in their efforts to change through reparative therapies.[31] The participants of this second study were largely non-Christian since this study was supported by a pro-gay advocacy group. Intriguingly, however, Shidlo and Schroeder did report that 4 percent of their subjects had reported a successful change of sexual orientation. They were surprised when they discovered that these individuals were all Christians who attributed their success to their faith. Nevertheless, critics take the great

31. Shidlo and Schroeder, "Changing sexual orientation."

disparity in the findings between the Spitzer and the Shidlo/Schroeder studies and conclude that the former is biased and thus, unreliable. Some even charge that the subjects of Spitzer's study, given their anti-gay sentiments, probably lied about their behavior and exaggerated their success stories by constructing elaborate self-deceptive narratives.

To respond to these critics, Spitzer points out several things. First, if there was significant bias, one might expect that many subjects would report complete or near complete change in all sexual orientation criteria after therapy. Only 11 percent of the males and 37 percent of the females did so. One might also expect that many subjects would report a rapid onset of change in sexual feelings after starting therapy. In fact, subjects reported that it took, on average, a full two years before they noticed a change in sexual feelings. Next, if systematic bias were present, one would expect that the magnitude of the bias for females would be similar to that for males. However, marked gender differences were found. These gender differences are consistent with previously published literature suggesting greater female plasticity in sexual orientation. Thus, Spitzer concludes that it is reasonable to believe that the subjects' self-reports in this study were by-and-large credible and that probably few, if any, elaborated self-deceptive narratives or lied.

How can moral theologians appropriate the findings of the Spitzer study and other similar reports?[32] I would like to suggest that it may be helpful to understand an individual's sexual orientation as a *habitus*, a stable disposition towards acts, in this case, sexual acts, which may be formed and shaped by frequently repeated actions within the context of particular practices.[33] This would explain the essential findings of the

---

32. For a comprehensive and recent overview of reparative therapy for male homosexuality, see Joseph Nicolosi, *Reparative Therapy*. Also see the discussion in the literature review by Hughes, "A general review of recent reports on homosexuality and lesbianism." Finally, for case stories of reparative therapy see Nicolosi, *Healing Homosexuality*.

33. A *habitus* is often translated in English as a habit. However, the English word can be misleading because it is often used to refer to any routine performance of an act no matter how trivial, including involuntary habits like the scratching of one's nose. In contrast, a *habitus* is a durable characteristic of the acting person that inclines him to certain actions, either good or evil. Thus, it is better to understand a *habitus* as a skill, a settled disposition, which, with much practice, can become natural and enduring, a "second nature," if you will, that makes the person a virtuoso cellist, a brilliant scientist, or a faithful friend. For more discussion, see Kent, "Habits and Virtues" and the seminal essay by Pinckaers, "La vertu est tout autre chose qu'une habitude."

Spitzer study. First, it would explain why it takes a long time—months and, in most cases, years—to diminish unwanted homosexual desires with a concomitant increase in heterosexual inclinations. By definition, a *habitus* is hard to change, though it can be changed.

Next, it would also explain the importance of the Christian faith in those subjects who were capable of altering their sexual desires. Rather than pointing to bias, the need for religious faith may be evidence for the need of particular virtuous practices that support a homosexual individual's efforts to develop the contrary sexual *habitus*. Within Christian groups, therapeutic interventions involve more than just counseling.[34] Individuals are invited to join a network of supportive friends who encourage them to embrace social and religious practices that reinforce their desire to modify their sexual behavior. In contrast, secular attempts to modify sexual orientation usually involve counseling alone and do not usually include any associated practices to reinforce the behavior modification.

Finally, and most importantly, the finding that Christianity is associated with any attempt to diminish one's homosexual tendencies may also be proof that the grace offered through Jesus Christ is a necessary element for any successful attempt to develop chastity when one is struggling with same-sex attraction. As the Congregation for Doctrine of the Faith correctly noted, "As in every conversion from evil, the abandonment of homosexual activity will require a profound collaboration of the individual with God's liberating grace."[35]

Within the context of the empirical findings discussed above, a virtue ethic for an individual struggling with same-sex attraction would include not only a call to develop chastity gradually but also an invitation to grow in the theological virtues. As a priest, I have had the opportunity to meet several men who were striving to live chaste lives despite their struggles with same-sex attraction. They ground themselves in lives of prayer with daily attendance at holy mass, the regular use of the confessional, and the discipline of moderate ascetical practices. They also surround themselves with supportive friends who invite them to develop

---

34. For a description of self-therapy for homosexuality written from a Christian perspective, see van den Aardweg, *The Battle for Normality*. Also see the insightful analysis in Wolkomir, *Be Not Deceived*.

35. Congregation for the Doctrine of the Faith, *Letter to the Bishops of the Catholic Church on the Pastoral Care of Homosexual Persons*, no. 11.

healthy and intimate relationships that are not erotic. Finally, by shunning television and Internet use unless absolutely necessary, they distance themselves from a popular culture that would not only undermine but also condemn their efforts to modify their unwanted sexual desires as homophobic. Not surprisingly, over time these men develop virtues and virtuous practices that allow them to live wholesome and fulfilled lives. Incidentally, I do not know if they have become heterosexual individuals, but I would argue that this is not crucial.[36] What is evident is that they have modified their sexual appetites within a continuum of sexual preferences—they have ordered their sexual *habitus*—in such a way that they are able to live lives that are not dominated by same-sex attraction. They have been able to develop intimate, chaste, and fulfilling friendships with other men.

To end this third section of my paper, I emphasize once again that any effort to develop a natural law argument should include an account of the virtues and the virtuous practices that would allow someone to live the truth of that argument. This proposal should not be alien to natural law reasoning since virtue ultimately involves the perfection of one's nature.

IV

Finally, to conclude my paper, I would like to make a comment on the relationship between natural law theory and narrative ethics. In a study of the natural law and homosexuality, Stephen Pope once referred to a wall between natural law theory and narrative ethics.[37] In his view, this wall

---

36. A recent report from the American Psychological Association has concluded that "the results of scientifically valid research indicate that it is unlikely that individuals will be able to reduce same-sex attractions or increase other-sex sexual attractions through SOCE [sexual orientation change efforts]" (3). However, the report went on to admit: "The available evidence, from both early and recent studies, suggests that although sexual orientation is unlikely to change, some individuals modified their sexual orientation identity (i.e., individual or group membership and affiliation, self-labeling) and other aspects of sexuality (i.e., values and behavior). . . . For instance, in some research, individuals through participating in SOCE, became skilled in ignoring or tolerating their same-sex attractions. Some individuals report that they went on to lead outwardly heterosexual lives, developing a sexual relationship with another-sex partner, and adopting a heterosexual identity" (3). In other words, according to the APA, sexual orientation change efforts can help an individual develop a virtuous life. For discussion, see *Report of the American Psychological Association Task Force*.

37. Pope, "Scientific and Natural Law Analyses of Homosexuality," 117.

exists because Catholicism's natural law proscriptions appear to be irreconcilable with the narratives of homosexual persons. Again, however, arguments that appeal to personal narrative and thus to personal experience raise the questions: Whose narrative is normative? Whose narrative is privileged? No wall exists between the natural law and the narratives of those homosexually-inclined men whose experience I described above and others like them who have developed a sexual *habitus* that allows them to live chaste lives in accordance with the gospel. They have discovered that the natural law has helped them to narrate meaningful lives that have led to authentic human flourishing. They have discovered that the natural law points them towards happiness not only in this life but also in the life to come.

BIBLIOGRAPHY

American Psychological Association. *Report of the American Psychological Association Task Force on Appropriate Therapeutic Responses to Sexual Orientation* (2009). Online: www.apa.org/pi/lgbc/publications/

Bailey, J. Michael. "Homosexuality and Mental Illness." *Archives of General Psychiatry* 56 (1999) 883–84.

Benedict XVI, Pope. "Address of His Holiness Benedict XVI to the Participants in the International Congress on Natural Moral Law," February 12, 2007. Online: http://www.vatican.va/holy_father/benedict_xvi/speeches/2007/february/documents/hf_ben-xvi_spe_20070212_pul_en.html.

Cantor, J. M., et al. "Cerebral white matter deficiencies in pedophilic men." *Journal of Psychiatric Research* 42 (2008) 167–83.

Congregation for the Doctrine of the Faith, *Letter to the Bishops of the Catholic Church on the Pastoral Care of Homosexual Persons* (1986). Online: http://www.vatican.va/roman_curia/congregations/cfaith/documents/rc_con_cfaith_doc_19861001_homosexual-persons_en.html.

D'Augelli, A.R. et al. "Childhood gender atypicality, victimization, and PTSD among lesbian, gay, and bisexual youth." *Journal of Interpersonal Violence* 21 (2006) 1462–82.

Farley, Margaret. *Just Love: A Framework for Christian Sexual Ethics*. New York: Continuum, 2006.

de Graaf, R., et al. "Suicidality and sexual orientation: Differences between Men and Women in General Population-based Sample from the Netherlands." *Archives of Sexual Behavior* 35 (2006) 253–62.

Drabble, et al. "Reports of alcohol consumption and alcohol-related problems among homosexual, bisexual, and heterosexual respondents: Results from the 2000 National Alcohol Survey." *Journal of Studies on Alcohol* 66 (2005) 111–20.

Drescher, Jack, and Kenneth J. Zucker, editors. *Ex-Gay Research: Analyzing the Spitzer Study and Its Relation to Science, Religion, Politics, and Culture*. New York: Harrington Park, 2006.

Fergusson, D. M., L. J. Horwood, and A. L. Beautrais. "Is sexual orientation related to mental health problems and suicidality in young people?" *Archives of General Psychiatry* 56 (1999) 876–80.

Finnis, John. *Natural Law and Natural Rights.* Corrected ed. Oxford: Clarendon, 1982.

Grisez, Germain. *The Way of the Lord Jesus: Christian Moral Principles.* Quincy, IL: Franciscan, 1983.

Guo, G., et al. "The Integration of Genetic Propensities into Social-Control Models of Delinquency and Violence among Male Youths." *American Sociological Review* 73 (2008) 543–68.

Harper, Alan. "Holy Scripture and the Law of God in Contemporary Anglicanism in the light of Richard Hooker's 'Lawes,'" Address to the United Society for the Propagation of the Gospel, July 4, 2008. Online: http://www.ireland.anglican.org/index.php?do=news&newsid=2242.

Harvey, John F., OSFS. *The Truth about Homosexuality: The Cry of the Faithful.* San Francisco: Ignatius, 1996.

Herek, Gregory M., and Linda D. Garnets. "Sexual Orientation and Mental Health." *Annual Review of Clinical Psychology* 3 (2007) 353–75.

Herrell, R., et al. "Sexual orientation and suicidality: a co-twin control study in adult men." *Archives of General Psychiatry* 56 (1999) 867–74.

Hughes, John R. "A general review of recent reports on homosexuality and lesbianism." *Sexuality and Disability* 24 (2006) 195–205.

John Paul II, Pope. *Veritatis Splendor.* Online: http://www.vatican.va/holy_father/john_paul_ii/encyclicals/documents/hf_jp-ii_enc_06081993_veritatis-splendor_en.html.

Johnson, Luke Timothy. "Scripture & Experience." *Commonweal* 134:12 (June 15, 2007) 14–17.

Kent, Bonnie. "Habits and Virtues (Ia IIae, qq. 49–70)." In *The Ethics of Aquinas,* edited by Stephen J. Pope, 116–30. Washington, DC: Georgetown University Press, 2002.

King, M., et al. "A systematic review of mental disorder, suicide, and deliberate self harm in lesbian, gay and bisexual people." *BMC Psychiatry* 8 (2008) 70.

Langstrom, N., et al. "Genetic and Environmental Effects on Same-sex Sexual Behavior: A Population Study of Twins in Sweden." *Archives of Sexual Behavior,* Epublished ahead of print on June 7, 2008.

Latkovic, Mark S. "Homosexuality, Morality, and the Truth of Church Teaching." *The Catholic Truth* 6 (2000) 29–33.

Morrison, David. *Beyond Gay.* Huntington, IN: Our Sunday Visitor, 1999.

Nicolosi, Joseph. *Healing Homosexuality: Case Stories of Reparative Therapy.* Northvale, NJ: Jason Aronson, 1993.

———. *Reparative Therapy of Male Homosexuality: A New Clinical Approach.* Northvale, NJ: Jason Aronson, 1997.

Pinckaers, Servais, OP. "La vertu est tout autre chose qu'une habitude." *Nouvelle revue theologique* 80 (1960) 387–403.

Ploderl, M., and R. Fartacek. "Childhood gender nonconformity and harassment as predictors of suicidality among gay, lesbian, bisexual, and heterosexual Austrians." *Archives of Sexual Behavior* 38 (2009) 400–10.

Pope, Stephen. "Scientific and Natural Law Analyses of Homosexuality: A Methodological Study." *Journal of Religious Ethics* 25 (1997) 89–126.

Raskind, Wendy H. "Current Understanding of the Genetic Basis of Reading and Spelling Disability." *Learning Disability Quarterly* 24 (2001) 141–57.

Reuters, "The naturalness of homosexuality: Sexual Identity Hard-wired by Genetics, Study Says." Online: www.libchrist.com/other/homosexual/genetics.html.

Salzman, Todd A., and Michael G. Lawler. "Catholic Sexual Ethics: Complementarity and Truly Human." *Theological Studies* 67 (2006) 625–52.

———. "Truly Human Sexual Acts: A Response to Patrick Lee and Robert George." *Theological Studies* 69 (2008) 663–80.

Sandfort, T. G. M., et al. "Same-sex sexual behavior and psychiatric disorders." *Archives of General Psychiatry* 58 (2001) 85–91.

Schiltz, K., et al. "Brain pathology in pedophilic offenders: Evidence of volume reduction in the right amygdala and related diencephalic structures." *Archives of General Psychiatry* 64 (2007) 737–46.

Selmys, Melinda. *Sexual Authenticity: An Intimate Reflection on Homosexuality and Catholicism.* Huntington, IN: Our Sunday Visitor, 2009.

Shidlo, Ariel, and Michael Schroeder. "Changing sexual orientation: A consumer's report." *Professional Psychology: Research & Practice* 33 (2002) 249–59.

Spitzer, Robert L. "Can Some Gay Men and Lesbians Change Their Sexual Orientation? 200 Subjects Reporting a Change from Homosexual to Heterosexual Orientation." *Archives of Sexual Behavior* 32 (2003) 403–17.

Stein, Edward. *The Mismeasure of Desire: The Science, Theory, and Ethics of Sexual Orientation.* Oxford: Oxford University Press, 1999.

Tushnet, Eve. "Experience and Tradition." *Commonweal* 134:12 (June 15, 2007). Online: http://www.commonwealmagazine.org/article.php3?id_article=1957.

van den Aardweg, G. J. M. *The Battle for Normality: A Guide for Self-Therapy for Homosexuality.* San Francisco: Ignatius, 1997.

West, Donald, and Richard Green, editors. *Sociolegal Control of Homosexuality: A Multi-nation Comparison.* New York: Plenum, 1997.

Whitehead, N. E. "Homosexuality and Mental Health Problems." *NARTH Bulletin* 11 (2002) 25–28. Online: www.narth.com/docs/whitehead.html.

Wolkomir, Michelle. *Be Not Deceived: The Sacred and Sexual Struggles of Gay and Ex-Gay Christian Men.* New Brunswick, NJ: Rutgers University Press, 2006.

Xiridou, et al. "The contribution of steady and casual partnerships to the incidence of HIV infection among homosexual men in Amsterdam." *AIDS* 17 (2003) 1029–38.

6

Cohabitation and Marriage

David Matzko McCarthy

In *The Marriage-Go-Round*, Andrew Cherlin identifies a pattern of multiple partnerships (cohabitation, marriage, or a combination) that is distinctive to American culture.[1] Compared with other Western nations, Americans have a higher rate of marriage, a higher rate of divorce, and shorter term, more frequent cohabitation. Cherlin provides evidence that "having several partnerships is more common in the United States not just because people exit intimate partnerships faster but also because they *enter* them faster and after a breakup *reenter* them faster."[2] Cherlin's metaphor of the "merry-go-round" is not particular to marriage (despite the title of his book), but is really a "partnership-go-round." For most people, marriage and cohabitation are both derivative of the intimate relationship. They have differences; however, marriage and living together have the same internal, relational rationale: self-development and self-expression. The "partnership-go-round" is moved by the needs of the self. In this regard, cohabitation is hardly a challenge to marriage; it is a sign of how we have come to think about marriage. It is a sign that our understanding of marriage corresponds to the rise (and logic) of both cohabitation and divorce. In the logic of the present system, breakup and divorce are often required but never desirable at the outset. Marriage is desirable as a goal but not necessary along the way—not necessary to set

---

1. Cherlin, *Marriage-Go-Round*, 11.
2. Ibid., 15.

up a home or have children. It is living together (in marriage or cohabitation) that is the necessary, even if temporary, form of life.

Cohabitation is a sign that we have to think differently about marriage. Our current theology puts the weight of marriage on the interpersonal union and the strength of a "relationship," but this personalist fix is
a fragile antidote to cohabitation and its logic of individualism. On the
basis of this fix, it is not clear how we can come to understand marriage
in a way that offers a strong challenge to the logic of relationships-as-
personal-expression and the essentially private and self-defining nature
of intimate relationships. Modern personalism, the primary strategy in
contemporary theology, narrates interpersonal union as a bond of self-
giving and other regard rather than self-interest. After a discussion of
cohabitation and individualism, the chapter will critique the personalisms of Michael G. Lawler and Christopher West. Each is inadequate in
its attempt to account for distinctiveness of marriage as a sacrament and
life-long union.

The chapter then will turn to a focus on marriage, in its institutional features, as the ground work for the distinctiveness of marriage
and nuptial union. In contrast to personalism, neither the friendship of
spouses nor the sexual union is basis of the marital relationship. The
social and communal structure of marriage is a framework for a different kind of interpersonal union and self-discovery—a different kind of
spirituality than provided by personalism or our cultural practices of
cohabitation. The vocation of marriage (as public and communal) allows
us to think in term of stages of development—not relationship development but marriage development—in ways that give room for a variety of
models, change, and dysfunction. In this narrative of change and growth,
a husband or wife experiences, at certain points, dissatisfaction or a lack
of trust in the process of personal growth and the development of the
relationship. In contrast to focusing on the interpersonal union, this
third possibility is able to distinguish cohabitation from marriage in a
way that emphasizes the procreative, public, and communal purposes
of family and the character of marriage as a vocation. If this strategy is
taken seriously, we would have to hold that our marriages might not be
a primary source of interpersonal contentment. We would need connections to a wider set of relationships, networks of families and single
people who carry the institutional practices of marriage. This assertion
would clearly delineate marriage from cohabitation, but in our culture

of the "partnership-go-round," such a view would not seem inviting and advantageous. These appearances might have to be risked.

I. MARRIAGE AS A PERSONAL CAPSTONE

Cherlin's study of the marriage-go-round represents a broad consensus on marriage and cohabitation in the United States.[3] The rise of cohabitation is not a positive development at a social and economic level. Cherlin's main concern is its negative effects upon children. There is clear evidence that periodic changes in home life (of the partnership-go-round) instigate behavioral and developmental difficulties for children.[4] The United States Conference of Catholic Bishops, specifically the Department of Laity, Marriage, Family Life, and Youth, summarizes the social scientific evidence in an attempt to dissuade cohabitation, not only for the sake of children but also for its negative impact upon marriage as steadfast union.[5] "Forty percent of cohabiting households include children. After five years, one-half of these couples will have broken up, compared to 15% of married parents."[6] Cohabitation makes women more vulnerable to abuse, and women who bear children in the context of cohabitation are more likely to raise these children alone.[7] Cherlin holds that cohabitation delineates a wide, grey area for men in the household.[8]

Most couples believe that living together will have a beneficial effect on marriage—in choosing and learning to live with a partner. But there is evidence that the impermanence of cohabitation cultivates a mindset that "increases the chance of future marital problems and divorce."[9] Since 1970 the marriage rate has dropped by almost 50 percent while the figures for cohabitation have risen from a half million to over five million people.[10] Those who live together with the intent to marry are more likely to stay together; persons who cohabit without marriage in

3. Kline Rhoades et al. "Pre-engagement Cohabitation"; Smock et al, "Everything's There Except Money"; Hohmann-Marriott, "Shared Beliefs and the Union Stability."

4. Cherlin, *Marriage-Go-Round*, 19-23.

5. USCCB, "Making a Case for Marriage."

6. Ibid., citing Whitehead, "Patterns and Predictors."

7. Ibid.; Ambert, "Cohabitation and Marriage."

8. Cherlin, *Marriage-Go-Round*, 101.

9. USCCB, "Making a Case for Marriage"; Ambert, "Cohabitation and Marriage"; Stanley et al., "Inertia Hypothesis."

10. Popenoe and Whitehead, "State of Our Unions 2005."

view tend to follow a pattern of "serial" cohabitation.[11] Less than half of cohabitation unions end in marriage. "Currently, 60 percent of all marriages are preceded by cohabitation;" yet, those who cohabit before marriage are 46 percent more likely to be divorced.[12] Despite these numbers, most people assume that cohabitation is a sensible option. Couples live together in order to pool resources (renting one apartment rather than two) and to negotiate the practical complexities of relationship, schedules, household, work, and raising children.[13] All of these practical matters are joined together by the personal needs and benefits of companionship and intimacy.

In Cherlin's analysis, the basic problem for marriage is not cohabitation *per se* but individualism. In general, most Americans believe that marriage is an essential part of the life plan, that it is faithful and forever, and that divorce is a last resort.[14] However, when given specifics, the same people justify divorce and cohabitation in terms of what Cherlin calls expressive individualism. Expressive individualism is a term used by Robert Bellah, in *Habits of the Heart*, to identify how people give reasons for engagement (or lack of engagement) in social life and common pursuits.[15] In the case of marriage, it means that a partnership is an instrument for self-development. Marriage is permanent, except when we grow out of it or have needs that the marriage does not fulfill.[16] Marriage is still a high ideal, but the tenants of individualism are elevated as well. The ideal of lifelong intimacy and fidelity is sustained alongside the view that "one's primary obligation is to oneself," one develops living arrangements and partnerships in a variety of ways according to what is needed for personal needs and growth, and dissatisfaction is a perfectly acceptable reason to end a marriage or intimate partnership.[17]

It is possible to sustain the ideal of marriage alongside expressive individualism when the ideal is transformed by the primacy of personal concerns. The transformation is described by Cherlin as a shift

11. Popenoe and Whitehead, "Should We Live Together?"

12. USCCB, "Making a Case for Marriage"; Popenoe and Whitehead, "Should We Live Together?"

13. USCCB, "Making a Case for Marriage."

14. Cherlin, *Marriage-Go-Round*, 25.

15. Bellah et al., *Habits of the Heart*.

16. Whitehead, *Divorce Culture*.

17. Cherlin, *Marriage-Go-Round*, 31.

from role to self.[18] In a survey of Catholics in the U.S. by the Center
for Applied Research in the Apostolate (CARA), the shift is noted as a
generational difference. Those born before 1943 are far more likely to
hold that marriage is a vocation, "is shared with extended family members of the couple," and "contributes to the common good of society."[19]
More recently, marriage has become more of a private endeavor for the
purposes of personal satisfaction and growth and less a set of obligations
and social roles. Marriage is still connected to economic prospects and
social standing, but these also have been personalized. They pertain to
individual rather than familial and broader "household" economic interests and to a lifestyle and achievement rather than a life course. With
this shift to self-development and individual interests, cohabitation has
been integrated into a culture of expressive marriage. "By the early 1990s
cohabiting relationships . . . were an entrenched part of the American
family system."[20] Living together makes sense when marriage is elevated
as an interpersonal ideal and is disconnected from the practical matters
of the household and raising children. In way of thinking, marriage is
the highest expression of cohabitation.

Cherlin notes that the usual image of cohabitation—the trendset-
ting, well educated, childless couple—is inaccurate. Less educated men
and women with less income (and less potential income) are more likely
to live together and less likely to marry. In the current economy, wage
earners without college degrees are vulnerable, earning less in real income than twenty years ago.[21] Marriage, for them, remains an ideal.[22] But
they lack the income and income security to fulfill the ideal. If the ideal
of marriage is an interpersonal union for rest of one's life, cohabitation
is the better option for dealing with the practical, variable problems of
money and children. The couple will share a household and raise children together (frequently not "their" children), but marriage offers no
benefit in these practical arrangements. Marriage constrains too much.
The financial difficulties intrude too much. In contrast, college educated
couples are likely to follow a more traditional path, or rather, to cohabit

18. Ibid., 90.

19. Center for Applied Research in the Apostolate, *Marriage in the Catholic Church*,
48–49.

20. Cherlin, *Marriage-Go-Round*, 98.

21. Ibid., 163.

22. Edin et al., "Peek Inside."

briefly on the way to what looks like the more traditional path. Marriage is promising long term, given the prospects of dual incomes or a sizable single income. Neither low-income cohabitation nor higher-income marriage is outright materialism. On the contrary, each separates material concerns from the relationship. Each reflects a common understanding of the priority of the intimate partnership and the companionate goal of marriage.

Cohabitation is the setting where both the wage earning couples and the upwardly mobile professionals work out the practical matters and enjoy a good measure of relational intimacy. If it works, then marriage might be on the horizon. Cohabitation is supposed to be a stepping stone to a better relationship. The wage earning couple is likely to separate if they have no means to move forward. Without means for independence, they will cohabit and enjoy the partnership while it lasts. With good education and prospects for a down payment on minivan and home, the professional couple has the self-reliance and autonomy needed to reach the goal of interpersonal stability. The difference between the lower income and higher income narratives is not the ideal of marriage or the logic of expressive individualism. The difference is that those with a good income and promising future are able to move confidently from a brief cohabitation to the long term prospect of marriage. The reader is sure to balk at this claim. There will always be counter examples of upper and lower income couples who do not cohabit before marriage. But the fact of the matter is that brief cohabitation, whether ending in marriage or simply ending, has become part of the life course for the majority of people in the U.S. Cherlin is faithful to evidence that marriage is a high ideal for both those on the way to marriage and the serial cohabiter, and that it is most often explained in personal rather than public or communal terms.

In short, marriage is a personal capstone, rather than a social foundation. As Cherlin explains: "Although the practical importance of marriage has declined, its symbolic importance has increased."[23] He provides a narrative of this transformation. "In the mid-twentieth century . . . , being married was not a symbol of being special but rather a mark of fitting in."[24] Beginning in the 1970s other options started to emerge, both for living together and raising children. Sexual intimacy was detached

23. Cherlin, *Marriage-Go-Round*, 139.
24. Ibid., 139.

from marriage and raising children. Being married started to become optional but was still the preferred state of life. By the 1990s, it is not the preferred start to the course of life.

> Now ... getting married is a step one does not take until one's life course is further along than in the past. Being "ready" to marry may mean that a couple has lived together to test out their compatibility, saved up for a down payment on a house, and possibly had children to judge how good they are at parenting together. Marriage's place in the life course used to come before those investments were made, but now it often comes afterward. Whereas marriage used to be the foundation of adult family life, now it is often the capstone.[25]

Marriage is a mark of achievement (the upwardly mobile are far more likely to marry). According to Barbara Dafoe Whitehead and David Popenoe (and their research in 2001), marriage is "emotionally deep and socially shallow."[26] While it has a diminished social role, "it is gaining popularity as a SuperRelationship, an intensely private spiritualized union, combining sexual fidelity, romantic love, emotional intimacy and togetherness."[27]

The shift from role to self and from foundation to capstone has obvious implications for an understanding of marriage as a sacrament. As a sacrament, marriage is a covenant of grace, which provides a foundation for a vocation and way of life. It is a way of life where a couple first pledges and then learns fidelity and steadfast love through moments of hardship and the regular course of day-to-day life. Marriage is essentially open to children; becoming father and mother is not a personal or lifestyle choice but is considered a vocation and a natural part of being husband and wife. Marriage is not the capstone of these achievements, but the context for their realization—fidelity, enduring love, generativity, and service to the common good. Marriage is a biblical sign of Christ's relationship to the Church and of our social nature as human beings.[28] As such, it is necessarily a communal and public sign. When marriage in our culture becomes, instead, an expression of private options and personal achievements, then the sacrament can no longer draw on com-

---

25. Ibid., 139.

26. Popenoe and Whitehead, "State of Our Unions 2001," 5.

27. Ibid.

28. *Gaudium et Spes*, no. 12.

mon habits and understandings. It will require an alternative form of enculturation.

The shift from social foundation to personal capstone has implications for Catholic social thought as well. In modern Catholic teaching, marriage and family take on importance as a basic social form—a fundamental human institution and basic cell of society. The modern economy and politics are governed by instrumental logic. Individual interests are fundamental, and social relations as well as economic exchange are governed by utilitarian contracts. Robert Bellah shows, in *Habits of the Heart*, that this utilitarian individualism produces expressive individualism in the personal sphere (as a kind of reaction to utilitarianism). In this context, marriage and family become important as an alternative social form. In *Rerum Novarum* (1891), Leo XIII appeals to family, on natural law grounds, as a principle to limit the modern (contractual) state and as a means to understand the just wage apart from merely contractual and market relations.[29] John Paul II, in his *Letter to Families*, contrasts the civilization of love, of which family is organically related, and the civilization of use (utilitarianism) where people are treated like things— valued only insofar as they are useful.[30] What happens when marriage in society is governed by expressive individualism—the very instrumental logic against which it is supposed to offer an alternative?

This question is, first of all, a pastoral problem—a practical issue of formation and how a couple is situated in common life. The pastoral problem comes to the surface when a cohabiting couple comes to a parish for marriage preparation. Close to half of the couples in marriage preparation are living together.[31] The Bishop's Conference recommends that pastors avoid the extremes of out-and-out condemnation and silent approval. The USCCB document, "Marriage Preparation and Cohabiting Couples," counsels an attitude of hospitality and a program of instruction on the differences between cohabitation and marriage.

> The Church has consistently taught that human love "demands a total and definitive gift of persons to one another" that can only be made in marriage (*Catechism of the Catholic Church*, #2391). ... The general goal of marriage preparation with all couples is the same: To create a clear awareness of the essential characteristics

29. Leo XIII, *Rerum Novarum*, nos. 5, 20, 37, 39.
30. John Paul II, *Letter to Families*, no. 13.
31. USCCB, "Marriage Preparation and Cohabiting Couples."

of Christian marriage: unity, fidelity, indissolubility, fruitfulness; the priority of the sacramental grace that unites the couple to the love of Christ; and the willingness to carry out the mission proper to families in the educational, social and ecclesial areas. (Pontifical Council for the Family, *Preparation for the Sacrament of Marriage, #45*)[32]

In the main, the USCCB (like John Paul II and most theologians) puts the marital relationship first, before attending to procreation and the mission of families. Social scientific and statistical evidence is marshaled to show that cohabitation weakens the interpersonal relationship, in terms of sex, conflict resolution, a sense of trust, and working out practical difficulties of household and money.[33] Little attention, however, is given to the proper mission of families in "social and ecclesial areas." This sense that the social of nature of marriage is secondary (or at least builds on the base of the interpersonal relationship) parallels our cultural situation where cohabitation and marriage are (in Whitehead and Popenoe's phrase) "emotionally deep and socially shallow."

II. THEOLOGICAL PERSONALISM

Thus, the personalist approach is the standard. At the beginning of the chapter, I noted that one prominent strategy to distinguish the goods of marriage is to focus on an intimate partnership and self-development (like expressive individualism), but to emphasize that the union requires self-giving love. I will review two different versions of this approach. The first, by Michael G. Lawler, emphasizes the priority of interpersonal union and proposes that "prenuptial cohabitation" can serve, in certain situations, the good of unity in marriage. In this proposal, Lawler narrows our focus to the well-educated, economically secure couple that lives together briefly with the clear intent to marry. In doing so, he does very little to challenge the expressive individualism that is at the heart of cohabitation. The second approach, by Christopher West, also emphasizes interpersonal union. But he offers an alternative to expressive individualism through what could be called a role and duty centered personalism. Insofar as West's approach provides an alternative to cohabitation, it seems that his personalism is a rhetorical flourish and that

32. Ibid.

33. "Experiences From Cohabitation Itself" in USCCB, "Marriage Preparation and Cohabiting Couples." Also see Diocese of Saint Cloud, "Seven Reasons."

marriage is grounded, instead, by its institutional (and what West calls its "objective") character.

Lawler and West share a starting point: the shift in the second half of the twentieth century (especially Vatican II) from a legal framework for understanding marriage to a focus on the interpersonal relationship.

> The Second Vatican Council marked a shift from a merely "juridical" presentation of marriage, typical of many previous Church pronouncements, to a more "personalist" approach. In other words, rather than focusing merely on the objective "duties," "rights," and "ends" of marriage, the Council Fathers emphasized how these same duties, rights, and ends are informed by the intimate, interpersonal love of the spouses.[34]

The quotation is provided by West. Lawler also highlights the basic contrast between juridical and personalist approaches, although he and West will disagree on how objective ends and duties are "informed" by interpersonal love. In any case, West would agree with Lawler that the most important development in a theology of marriage is that "the union of spouses and its importance in both marriage and family moved into focus."[35] The procreative end of marriage is sustained, but its context is unitive, interpersonal love, a love that is self-giving and oriented to the other. The procreative end is located in the unitive, and the core of unitive love is the will and commitment, rather than mere emotion. The "I do" of marriage means "I love you as Christ loves his church, steadfastly and faithfully."[36]

Lawler is a consistent personalist. Personalism holds that the individual is always the person-in-relation, that the person-in-relation is the fundamental human reality, and that the experience of the person is a fundamental way of knowing. Personal experience is an epistemological category. In dealing with a theology of marriage, personalism begins with a structure of human relationships and shows how the sacrament of marriage confirms and sustains the meaning of this structure. For example, in Lawler's *Marriage and Sacrament*, he gives a phenomenology of friendship, without which we "will fail to become integrated human beings."[37] Friendship is the ground work for love—the love of

34. West, "A Basic Theology of Marriage."
35. Lawler, *Marriage and the Catholic Church*, ix.
36. Ibid., 14.
37. Ibid., 1.

friendship—when we love not for something we gain but for "someone who is good in *himself* or *herself*."[38] Love, as a matter of self-giving will and choice for another, seeks to endure, and may lead to a public commitment and partnership for the whole of life. This is marriage (added to the base of friendship and love). Christian marriage is yet another level. Marriage is theologically elevated by the sacrament of marriage, which is a prophetic symbol. The couple "images and represents the union between Christ and the Church."[39] This personalist approach puts the structure of reality far before the institutional reality and provides a standpoint from which to judge the duties, public roles, and legal framework for marriage. A married couple sustains a vital marriage, not by attending to marriage as an institution, but by cultivating their more fundamental relationship.[40]

Personalism has its origin in a critique of rule-governed institutions and rationalist structures of thought. It emerges in the early twentieth century in response to the reduction of the human being and human knowing by disembodied forms of modern rationality and scientific positivism. This tenor of critique does not necessitate a criticism of Christian marriage. However, it does imply an attitude of criticism within the framework, noted above, of the shift from a "merely juridical" view of marriage to a personalist approach. The personal relationship becomes the measure. When personal experience comes into conflict with a traditional (presumably outdated?) legal framework, personalism gives the benefit of the doubt to the way of knowing grounded in interpersonal relations. Likewise, Lawler develops a theology of Christian marriage that gives a rich display of interpersonal love and friendship, and he looks for ways to create latitude and autonomy for interpersonal relationships within the institutional structure.

Before we consider Lawler's view of cohabitation, it will be helpful to take a brief look at his treatment of divorce and remarriage, a topic of pain and struggle for Catholics in the traditional, juridical frame. Lawler's first and main point follows from his personalist approach. The

38. Ibid., 4.

39. Ibid., 16.

40. Ibid., 66–87. My purpose is not to discuss Lawler's understanding of the sacrament, but it seems to me that his personalism holds with sacraments in general. The reality of the sacrament is internal to the person and not primarily "objective" in a substantive sense. See *Marriage and the Catholic Church*, 43–61.

reality of marriage is internal to the couple, not the institutional aspect and certainly not its structure in Canon Law; therefore, when the marriage dies, "it makes no sense to claim that they [Christian marriages] are binding ontologically."[41] This argument is not constructive, in the sense that it says nothing about what kinds of reasons count for the death of a marriage. It simply places the judgment in the realm of the interpersonal experience. Once this point is made, Lawler clears space within the tradition. Scripture and Canon Law show variations which can be attributed to historical and cultural situations. Further, there is historical record of remarriage in some situations. Therefore, current Canon Law ought to accommodate a situation where 40 percent of marriages end in divorce and the experience of second marriages, for many, is good and faithful. In the end, Lawler draws on the Orthodox practice of *oikonomia* (compassionate exception-making), which soberly permits "the remarriage of an innocent or repentant spouse."[42]

With *oikonomia*, Lawler offers an intriguing and promising idea. However, to make it more than "no fault" divorce (especially in a culture of no fault divorce), it would require some kind of institutional process (like annulment) and some paradigm cases, such as the traditional cases in the Orthodox tradition of adultery and abandonment. How do we judge "innocent" and "repentant"? Seven years of "penance with tears"?[43] I don't think so, not within the personalist frame. Lawler transplants *oikonomia* from a culture where marriage (like penance) is primarily public to one where it is primarily private. He makes clear the need for compassion for the divorced and remarried. But that is all. He does not broach or point us toward justifiable reasons for the death of a marriage or communal practices of evaluation—and certainly not to communal practices of repentance and penance. His initial personalist point (that the "reality" of marriage is internal to the interpersonal relationship) seems to suggest that an institution or a community cannot make a claim when a marriage lives or dies. It can only respond to what the couple determines. At the end of Lawler's proposal, we are left with this uncertainty. We know that the good reason for marriage is that a couple

41. Lawler, *Marriage and the Catholic Church*, 94.

42. Ibid., 112.

43. Lawler notes that Basil (d. 379) records a case when a man who leaves his wife and remarries is accepted back in the church after seven years of penance. *Marriage and the Catholic Church*, 98.

loves one another and promises to do so for the whole of life. Is the good reason for divorce just the inverse, that they no longer love one another and no longer promise to do so? He may not want to confirm our culture's expressive individualism, but in the case of divorce, Lawler offers us little alternative to it.

Lawler's qualified acceptance of cohabitation follows a similar line of argument. It locates the reality of marriage in the interpersonal bond, independent of the institutional and juridical aspects of marriage. He notes variations in the broad history of the Catholic tradition. Like his treatment of *oikonomia*, however, the historical examples of betrothal and cohabitation are taken out of historical context. His examples of practices in Africa and the medieval West fail to note that these forms of cohabitation and betrothal makes sense, not in terms of a personalist view of marriage, but amid social forms of marriage which make procreation and the household economy primary, not to mention the rule of the husband and father.[44] He identifies a kind of cohabitation that fits with the goods of marriage—a couple who initiates cohabitation with the intent to marry. However, he leaves open the actual reasons for living together before marriage. Convenience? Economic necessity? Whatever the reasons, they are private. He leaves open the reason why the couple would not get married sooner (before cohabitation) rather than later. He does suggest, however, that marriage is, indeed, a capstone. His personalist perspective easily fits with the idea that marriage is a personal achievement rather than a social foundation. Can his proposal on cohabitation provide an alternative to expressive individualism?

In Lawler's arguments on cohabitation, he narrows his proposal to "pre-nuptial cohabitation and cohabitants, that is, those who are already committed to marry each other."[45] He is clear that many live together without the intention to marry and that this cultural practice undermines the practices of marriage. Like the USCCB, he would cite social scientific evidence that non-nuptial cohabitation weakens the interpersonal bond and perpetuates dysfunctions. Lawler looks at the data carefully. He recognizes (like Andrew Cherlin) that the distinction between non-nuptial and pre-nuptial cohabitation corresponds to socio-economic class. His paradigmatic example of the non-nupital, serial cohabitor is a twenty-three year old man, with divorced parents, only a high school degree,

---

44. Lawler, *Marriage and the Catholic Church*, 164, 166, 174.

45. Ibid., 166. See also Lawler, "Cohabitation."

and employment, "but moves from job to job." After living with two girlfriends, he marries an unemployed twenty year old after they have a child. Lawler's constructive example is quite different: the paradigmatic pre-nuptial cohabitants include a twenty-eight year old man with a master's degree and job security and a twenty-four year old graduate student with a part time job. They live together for six months while they are engaged. They are active in their church.[46]

Lawler holds that these pre-nuptial cohabiters will do fine, that living together is part of their process of getting married, and that they are likely to have a faithful and steadfast union. He is right. The trouble is that his positive example corresponds to Cherlin's example of the upwardly mobile couple who thinks of marriage in terms of expressive individualism. We do not know what Lawler's couple thinks. But the parallel with Cherlin's account of expressive individualism and marriage is striking: Marriage is not a social foundation, but a personal goal and mark of prestige that the upwardly mobile couple is able to attain and that the twenty-three year old wage earner is not likely to reach. The high school graduate and serial cohabiter is likely to hold the same ideal of a process toward marriage: secure an income and develop a relationship, live together, then get married. Cherlin notes that for wage earners the inability to secure an income prolongs the stage of cohabitation, to cohabitations, and puts raising children in the sequence. The point for Cherlin is that both cases (working class and upper middle class) do not think of marriage as a foundation of common life. It is an expressivist goal. Lawler proposes a ceremony of betrothal for the pre-nuptial couple, in order to solidify the process and give it a clear direction toward marriage. But he also seems to be confirming the view that marriage is primarily a personal achievement rather than a basic social form.

Lawler recommends betrothal for a specific group of cohabiters who are going to get married anyway and are likely to have marriages that last. They may live together before marriage. But by making their cohabitation public, betrothal will make living together the paradigmatic process for marriage. Will "betrothal" simply baptize the expressive individualism? Does it confirm what we know, that American individualism is far less destructive for the upwardly mobile? Will marriage in the church as well as our culture simply become a personal capstone for those with means? Lawler thinks that his betrothal proposal offers a

46. Lawler, *Marriage and the Catholic Church*, 167.

parallel to "pre-modern, pre-Tridentine, pre-Victorian" practices.[47] It is parallel if the modern view of the individual self and personal development makes no difference to history. Will marriage, post-betrothal, look anything like medieval marriage? Will laborers wait for permission to marry from their feudal lord? It is at least true that marriage will be a better prospect for the nobility—for well-educated professionals. They have the resources (both economic and interpersonal) for the capstone of marriage.

In response to Lawler's paradigmatic case, we have to ask why the couple that cohabits for six months does not get married six months earlier, or why they do not wait six months (until they are married) to live together. Convenience? Waiting to finish graduate studies so that marriage can be a way to cap things off? Sharing rent and saving for an expensive wedding (which, on average, costs $21,000–$24,000)?[48] Lawler does not offer any indication. Living together is simply an option available for couples to decide according to what suits their interpersonal relationship. We should not single out Lawler; he simply puts a common view on paper. Most members of Generation X and the Millennial generation consider cohabitation and marriage a private concern, the excessive wedding a standard, and marriage a prudent idea once we resolve all the practical questions of education and income.[49] I was married at age thirty, less than a month after I finished my PhD and my wife her master's degree. And we are doing fine. In fact, theologians ought to admit that our theologies of marriage from Vatican II onward are directed primarily to the well-educated and upwardly mobile: to a class of highly articulate, expressive and interpersonally savvy individuals who have enough economic security for private marriage. Most of our personalist accounts of marriage, like Lawler's proposal for betrothal, give us little means to offer an alternative to expressive individualism. The fact that cohabitation works for some of us is a bad sign for all.

A stance against all forms of cohabitation outside of marriage is provided by Christopher West, who also claims a personalist perspective. He rejects expressive individualism and develops what might be called an expressivist account of duty, objective roles, and obligations. West, like John Paul II's theology of the body, uses personalist language

47. Ibid., 175.

48. "They'll Never Know."

49. Whitehead, "Changing Pathway."

as a tool, but he does not hold to the epistemological commitments of personalism. The individual is always the person-in-relation, and the person-in-relation is a fundamental human reality; however, personal experience (as affective and contingent) is not the fundamental way of knowing. West calls John Paul II's personalism a "reformed phenomenological approach"—something like Immanuel Kant's objective structure with Max Scheler's account of affectivity and experience of value.[50] This reformed phenomenology is not bound to a particular culture, but is the structure of human sexual relations as such. It begins with a theological anthropology (in terms of Genesis 1) and authoritative Church teaching. In West's *Good News about Sex and Marriage*, chapter one treats Genesis, and chapter two, the Church's Magisterium.[51] West (like John Paul II) uses personalism to fill out a subjective experience within a principled, institutional frame.

The conceptual, philosophical frame pertains to an act-centered account of sexual intercourse. A comparison with Lawler will be helpful. Lawler's personalism highlights a relational process rather than act, so that sex gains it meaning not in the context of a single act, but in a sexual relationship as it develops.[52] This process is one reason why it is not necessary to draw the line of sexual activity at the inception of a marriage. Marriage will elevate the commitment of an already existing sexual relationship. West, in contrast, is concerned with a phenomenology of the sexual act in itself. The act is the total self-giving of the partners, and there is a clear difference between marital and non-marital sexual intercourse. The covenant of marriage is consistent with the meaning of the sexual act, while non-marital intercourse is self-deceptive and dishonest.

> Two consenting adults who *truly* love one another and want to express that love through sexual intercourse are two adults who want to consent to marriage. Out of their love for each other, and out of their desire never to speak dishonestly to each other, they won't speak the "language" of their bodies through intercourse until that language is an expression of the commitment they have *already made* in their wedding vows.[53]

50. West, *Theology of the Body Explained*, 36.
51. West, *Good News*.
52. Lawler, *Marriage and the Catholic Church*, 179.
53. West, *Good News*, 67.

In short, the sexual act expresses the commitment of marriage through bodily language, and sex outside of marriage will contradict itself. Non-marital sex will lead to more frustration than fulfillment. It will express a longing, yet aggravate rather than satisfy. It will create the kind of culture we have, a confusing set of options for frustrating sex—pornography, hook ups, cohabitation, and so on. West's personalist theme is that we are fulfilled sexually and personally when we conform ourselves to the sacrament of marriage.

West's personalism is rhetorical rather than epistemological. This point is not necessarily a criticism; rhetoric is important as "public speaking." In this regard, West's work is impressive for its attention to sexual practices. He faces up to questions that most of us keep private. His *Good News about Sex and Marriage* deals with a host of difficult questions: the line between sensual contact and sexual intercourse, masturbation, pornography, oral sex and stimulation, and anal intercourse as foreplay. The appeal of his personalism, it seems to me, is that it offers a public language for talking about sex. There are limits, however. For example, West has to drop personalist language altogether when dealing with divorce. Regardless of personal experiences of bad marriages, "the permanence of marriage is an objective reality to which the Church must bear witness."[54] Or, when speaking of a divorced and remarried person: "Objectively speaking, such a person is living in direct contradiction to what the Eucharist means."[55] Personalism goes only as far as the description of the sexual act in itself. It does not provide an expressive display of the goods of marriage—of permanence and life-long exclusivity: these are given by an "objective" structure of obligation and law.

In terms of expressive individualism and personalism, West's work and popularity shows us two things. First, personalist language is appealing, and second, personalism is not sufficient to account for marriage. West's personalism does not extend to difficulties in marriage and what might count for as a reason for separation (leaving aside the question of divorce). It does not help with the ongoing struggles of marriage, like raising children, maintaining a home, and figuring out how to pay for cars and school clothes. The ready answer to relationship and practical questions seems to be, for West, a constant return to the sexual act and to the "I do" moment of the marriage vows. (The sexual act is a reliving

54. Ibid., 59.
55. Ibid., 60.

of the "I do" moment.) For people looking to be married for decades, this kind of personalism will not be of help for very long, probably not past the honeymoon period when sex is the center of the relationship. The real trajectory of West's personalism is objective conformity to the teachings of the Church.[56] Yet, he does not use these teachings and the Church's claims about marriage to give a practical picture of how marriage, from day-to-day and year-to-year, looks different than cohabitation, other than the dishonesty of the sexual act. Certainly, the difference extends to the interpersonal and social character of the relationship as a whole. West gives us a definition of sex that shows the failing of sex within cohabitation as an instance non-marital sex, but he does not attend to the ways that the practices of marriage (apart from the sexual act in itself) are different than cohabitation.

III. MARRIAGE AS AN INSTITUTIONAL PATH

Given this failure, the priorities of personalism need to be reordered to reflect the actual nature of marriage. Lawler begins with a basis in the relationship of friendship and love, and then adds on, first, marriage as a lifelong commitment and, second, the prophetic symbolism of Christian marriage. This ordering—a private and personal relationship with an institutional superstructure—confirms, or at least does not do much to reject, the popular idea that marriage is simply an elevated form of living together—value-added cohabitation. However, long-lasting marriages do not follow this personalist ordering. A marriage is likely to begin with a romantic process that goes from friendship to love to marriage, but I am not sure that even this process holds for all cases. Some people (by their late twenties) are tired of having "relationships" and are looking to be married. The process might be: identify those with characteristics of a future husband or wife and subsequently hope to develop a relationship. Whether a couple begins with the "relationship" or the virtues of a good spouse, the institutional features of marriage make the relationship distinctive. It is not a value-added friendship. It is a marriage, not reducible to a general idea of an "intimate relationship" that endures. The public structure of fidelity, permanence, and openness to children gives shape to the relationship, day-to-day and over time.

56. West focuses on faithful self-giving (surrender) to the structure of subjectivity provided by the duties and obligations of marriage as self-giving, faithful, permanent, and open to children, *Good News*, 28–29, 36.

This point can be made philosophically and experientially. Philosophically, personalism exaggerates the role of the personal sphere in friendship and love. It draws a picture where a couple creates their own common life. But classic accounts of friendship (Aristotle, Cicero, and Augustine) assume that friends are bound, not simply by a view of the good and a sense of the good in each other, but largely by the political order—by public and shared activities that are sustained outside (or regardless of) the friendship. In the classic account, the context for the possibility of friendship is the city, and here Augustine develops the complex relationships of friends in the earthly city and the city of God.[57] In effect, when the institutional features of marriage are made secondary, marriage loses its coherence as a friendship. Friendship is not itself a practical context for common life, but a common bond and context for personal engagement in common life. Friendship needs goods and practices external to the friendship. A friendship without external social practices is not a friendship at all. Likewise, companionate marriage is its own undoing.[58] The "community of two" cannot be sustained as a stable way of life apart from the *priority* of institutions.

Experientially, this need for a social context is true of friendship in general. Friends come and go; they become old friends when institutional and practical structures in our lives change. We have friends from our hometown, school friends, colleagues, coworkers who become friends, neighbors, fellow members of the parish, friends who have children in school or on the soccer team with our children, and so on. Old friends are not friends in an Aristotelian sense; we have affection for them, but we do not share day-to-day pursuits and work on common projects. Our contact is sporadic and occasional. We have to add the friendship on to what we do in our ordinary day; we have to work to give it room with cell phone calls while driving to the store, texting at a baseball game, or emailing while at work. The memory of common endeavors sustains a bond; the relationship is sustained, but it does not grow. The relationship is not a friendship; it is a relationship with a past friend who is now a sounding board or advisor. When a married couple becomes this kind of "old friends," they see no reason to be married. Often, divorced couples

57. See Collinge, "St. Augustine of Hippo"; Crosson, "Structure and Meaning"; McNamara, *Friends and Friendship*; Cicero, "Laelius De Amicitia,"; Aristotle, *Nicomachean Ethics*.

58. Coontz, *Marriage, A History*.

remain friends in relationship to common practices that continue to be sustained, like raising children or running a business.

Marriage is distinctive because it is an institutional practice. It is not a coherent set of practices in American culture on the whole, where legally it is merely a contract and socially an endeavor of expressive individualism. In the Church, however, it is a covenant and a sacrament. It is by definition, faithful, steadfast, procreative, and a school of charity and forgiveness. It is not a friendship but there are analogies to friendship, not a relationship of colleagues but there are analogies to co-workers and allies, not companionship but there are analogies to those with whom we share good company.[59] It is distinctive because the vows are public and are not defined by the married couple. Marriage is an institutional context where married couples have a role. One key element of that role is to stay together faithfully and learn to love one another as God loves us. Here I am reversing Lawler's view that the relationship is the foundation and marriage an additional "meaning" or superstructure. Certainly, in our culture, a couple is most likely to develop a romantic relationship and then enter marriage. However, the marriage is the beginning of something entirely new. The couple vows (for richer and for poorer) that their life together is no longer based on the satisfaction and harmony of the relationship.

Experientially, the social role of husband and wife—the fact that the basis of their life together is no longer a simple interpersonal bond—impels many of us to have good, workable, satisfying, and life giving relationships. But because the relationship is not the *basis*, we have freedom to develop relationships that work through a life time and the freedom to have relationships that are not satisfying. We are freed from the straight-jacket of total satisfaction and romantic ideas about sharing the "total self." We are freed from the myth of the soul mate. Some marriages will look like school friendships (sharing ideas and ambitions), others like allies in common work (arguing passionate about how to get the work done), still others like affectionate companions (staying close but saying little). A wide array of interpersonal forms can be sustained within the institution. In fact, these different sorts of relationships might be found over time in the same marriage: romantic lovers, "old friends" barely managing to keep in contact, co-workers in raising children, allies

---

59. The distinctions between allies, companions, and friends are taken from Lewis, *Four Loves.*

in community endeavors, companions on the long journey, frustrated or alienated partners, romantic lovers again, care-giver and patient, and so on. It is the vocation to lifelong fidelity and generativity that sustains the changing relationship, not the relationship itself that sustains the vocation. When a couple has vowed faithfulness for life, they have committed themselves to learning, over time, what the calling requires.

Through the joy, dysfunction, and dissatisfaction, we carry on in hope that with honest repentance, forgiveness, grace, and reconciliation, we will find the depth of God's love in our marriages. West proposes that the whole of self-giving and the "I do" of marriage are expressed in the sexual act. He may be right in theory, but it is hard to see how it reflects both the wonder of a sexual relationship and its pedestrian times in marriage. West puts the relationship between marriage and sex backward. He holds that the sexual act *per se* expresses the meaning of marriage at the level of personal experience. The reality is that because a couple is committed to sexual fidelity for life the sexual relationship gives a variety of experiential and interpersonal meanings to sexual acts. Ironically, he approaches sexual acts in a way that parallels, even when it contrasts, our secular culture's definition of the sexual act, as a context in itself—as love making, mere pleasure, and so on. The wonder of sex in marriage is that a single encounter can be wonderful, and it can be, on its own, experientially almost meaningless or routine or self-absorbed. Because husband and wife made vows and have entered into a relationship that they do not define, they keep having sex with each other and endure times when they don't. Because they are committed to being bound through their sexual relationship, they learn the full meaning (for richer and for poorer) of sexual union and bodily belonging.

The institutional and communal foundation of marriage—the vows, expectations, and social relationships structured on the basis of family, the social tasks of sustaining productive households, and the common callings of raising children—give marriage purposes that an interpersonal relationship cannot sustain. Marriage and family naturally give rise to social networks and habits of reciprocity that help support the vocation. Like the ideal of the autonomous relationship, the self-sufficient, nuclear family in the age of individualism is an almost impossible burden to bear. It is the privilege of the upper middle class, who strategically keep the size of their families small and manage to sustain an isolated family unit. Likewise, the interpersonal relationship of married couples will need help, not because the marriage is not all that it should be, but because marriage is the kind of interpersonal relationship that is sustained, acutely at times, by external and institutional supports.

A good example of external support is offered by the USCCB's program, "For Your Marriage."[60] One key element of the perspective given to couples is that marriage undergoes stages, some very difficult, but that we can hope in a good end. There are more than a few ways to understand the stages of marriage: romance, disillusionment, mature love; romance, commitment, settling down, rebellion, power struggles, reconciliation, beginning again; the struggles of being newly married, the struggles of the raising children and the middle years of marriage; the struggles of the empty nest and growing old together.[61] We could develop these stages further: stories about just scraping by, living with parents, renting cheap apartments, stories about depending upon neighbors, losing a job and learning to be a househusband, stories about shoestring weddings, hand-me-down clothes, big gardens, stories about "down-sizing" and living an alternative way, stories about living as a witness, as family.

Although making reference to stages and struggles appears to be trivial, it is an important shift. Personalism assumes that marriage can be defined by its beginning, by the friendship that forms the marriage. In Lawler's personalism, a marriage confirms a relationship; in West's duty-centered personalism, the meaning of marriage is expressed in a single, sexual act. The stages in "For Your Marriage," in contrast, indicate that the fullness of a marital relationship is known and experienced only when we make it through good times and bad, harmony and discord, romance and disillusionment to a deep sense of reconciliation and trust. "Contemporary culture wants answers and certainty; faith requires trust and surrender. The invitation to the marital journey, and the resources to undertake it, come from God. God gives us enough clarity to take the next few steps, even if we cannot see the entire road and where it will end."[62] In this account of the journey, marriage is no capstone. It is the foundation and pathway.

Marriage and family life require a kind of asceticism and spirituality of poverty. Couples suffer through because they are married. People who are living together might suffer through relationship troubles, but

60. USCCB, "For Your Marriage."
61. USCCB, "Stages of Marriage."
62. Giblin, "Stages of Growth in Marriage."

it appears, statistically speaking, that couples live together so that they do not have to. They can take the good times as long as they last. One of the limitations of personalism is that it implies that the relationship is always good; it must be in order to carry the marriage. For West, sex is always a good experience, and if it is not, he simply shifts his rhetoric to objective norms. It seems to me that one of the challenges of marriage is to develop a language of spiritual poverty and to become, practically and communally, a foundation available to the poor (rather than a capstone for the upwardly mobile). In a culture where marital vows are feared as a limitation to our happiness, we are quick to respond and cite statistics to say otherwise. Marriage is not for the weak; that is clear. It is a pilgrimage, a real pilgrimage (rather than a holiday trip) which begins at a point where we are not sure we will get to the end. The challenge is to develop practices and a spirituality of marriage, where we, the weak, can be strong in networks of families and married couples. Let those who live together take their happiness while they can, but let us invite them to a common struggle and adventure to see what kind of love we find when we live out marriage to the end.

BIBLIOGRAPHY

Ambert, Anne-Marie. "Cohabitation and Marriage: How are they related." Online: http://www.vifamily.ca/library/cft/cohabitation.html

Aristotle. *Nicomachean Ethics*. Translated by Terence Irwin. Indianapolis: Hackett, 1999.

Bellah, Robert, et al. *Habits of the Heart*. 2nd ed. Berkeley: University of California Press, 1996.

Center for Applied Research in the Apostolate (Georgetown University, Washington, DC). *Marriage in the Catholic Church: A Survey of U.S. Catholics* (October 2007) 48–49. Online: http://cara.georgetown.edu/MarriageReport.pdf.

Cherlin, Andrew J. *The Marriage-Go-Round*. New York: Knopf, 2009.

Cicero. "Laelius De Amicitia." In *De Senectute, De Amicitia, De Dviniatione, with English Translation*. Translated by William Armistead Falconer. The Loeb Classical Library. Cambridge: Harvard University Press, 1964.

Collinge, William. "St. Augustine of Hippo—Love, Community, and Politics." In *The Heart of Catholic Social Teaching*, edited by David M. McCarthy, 73–84. Grand Rapids: Brazos, 2009.

Coontz, Stephanie. *Marriage, A History: From Obedience to Intimacy or How Love Conquered Marriage*. New York: Viking, 2005.

Crosson, Frederick J. "Structure and Meaning in St. Augustine's *Confessions*." In *The Augustinian Tradition*, edited by Gareth B. Matthews, 27–38. Berkeley: University of California Press, 1999.

Diocese of Saint Cloud. "Seven Reasons Why Living Together Before Marriage is not a Good Idea." Online: http://www.stcdio.org/omf/marriage-ministry/7ReasonWhy .htm.

Edin, Kathryn, et al. "A Peek Inside the Black Box: What Marriage Means for Poor Unmarried Parents." *Journal of Marriage and Family* 66 (2004) 1007–14.

Giblin, Paul R. "Stages of Growth in Marriage: An Overview." Online: http://www .foryourmarriage.org/interior_template.asp?id=20398992.

Hohmann-Marriott, Bryndl E. "Shared Beliefs and the Union Stability of Married and Cohabiting Couples." *Journal of Marriage and Family* 68 (2006) 1015–28.

John Paul II, Pope. *Letter to Families* (1994).

Lawler, Michael G. "Cohabitation: Past and Present Reality." *Theological Studies* 65 (2004) 623–29.

Lawler, Michael G. *Marriage and Sacrament: A Theology of Christian Marriage.* Collegeville, MN: Liturgical, 1993.

———. *Marriage and the Catholic Church: Disputed Questions.* Collegeville, MN: Liturgical, 2002.

Leo XIII, Pope. *Rerum Novarum* (1891). Online: http://www.vatican.va/holy_father/leo_ xiii/encyclicals/documents/hf_l-xiii_enc_15051891_rerum-novarum_en.html.

Lewis, C. S. *The Four Loves.* New York: Harcourt Brace, 1960.

McNamara, Marie Aquinas. *Friends and Friendship for Augustine.* Staten Island: Society of St. Paul, 1964.

Popenoe, David, and Barbara Dafoe Whitehead. "Should We Live Together?" Online: http://marriage.rutgers.edu/Publications/SWLT2%20TEXT.htm.

———. "The State of Our Unions: The Social Health of Marriage in America 2005." Online: http://marriage.rutgers.edu.

———. "The State of Our Unions 2001." Online: http://marriage.rutgers.edu/ Publications/SOOU/TEXTSOOU2001.htm.

Rhoades, Kline, et al. "Pre-engagement Cohabitation and Gender Asymmetry in Marital Commitment." *Journal of Family Psychology* 20 (2006) 553–60.

Smock, Pamela J., et al. "'Everything's There Except Money': How Money Shapes Decisions to Marry Among Cohabitors." *Journal of Marriage and Family* 67 (2005) 680–96.

Stanley, Scott M., et al. "The Inertia Hypothesis: Sliding vs. Deciding in the Development of Risk for Couples in Marriage." Online: www.bgsu.edu/organizations/cfdr/ cohabitation/lead_papers/inertia_hypothesis.pdf.

"They'll Never Know: Eight Hidden Ways to Cut Wedding Costs." *Wall Street Journal Digital Network* (June 11, 2008). Online: http://www.smartmoney.com/personal- finance/marriage-divorce/theyll-never-know-eight-hidden-ways-to-cut-wedding- costs-13918/.

United States Conference of Catholic Bishops (USCCB). "For Your Marriage." Online: http://www.foryourmarriage.org/home.asp.

USCCB Department of Laity, Marriage, Family Life, and Youth. "Making a Case for Marriage." Online: http://www.usccb.org/laity/marriage/cohabitation.shtml.

———. "Marriage Preparation and Cohabiting Couples: An Information Report on New Realities and Pastoral Practices." Online: http://www.usccb.org/laity/marriage/ cohabiting.shtml.

———. "Stages of Marriage." Online: http://www.foryourmarriage.org/interior_ template.asp?id=20398766.

West, Christopher. "A Basic Theology of Marriage." Online: http://www.christopherwest.com/page.asp?ContentID=72.

———. *Good News about Sex and Marriage*. Ann Arbor: Servant, 2000.

———. *Theology of the Body Explained: A Commentary of John Paul II's 'Gospel of the Body'*. Boston: Pauline, 2003.

Whitehead, Barbara Dafoe. "The Changing Pathway to Marriage: Trends in Dating, First Unions, and Marriage among Young Adults." In *Family Transformed: Religion, Values, and Society in American Life*, edited by Steven M. Tipton and John Witte Jr., 168–84. Washington, DC: Georgetown University Press, 2005.

———. *The Divorce Culture*. New York: Knopf, 1997.

———. "Patterns and Predictors of Success and Failure in Marriage." Online: http://www.usccb.org/laity/marriage/Whitehead.pdf.

Coming Home

7

Multi-Dimensional Marriage Vocations and Responsible Parenthood

FLORENCE CAFFREY BOURG

S INCE VATICAN II, THE Catholic Church has committed itself to read-ing and scrutinizing signs of the times, and interpreting them in light of the gospel. In the U.S. and elsewhere, we see spouses striving for an egalitarian relationship wherein both contribute their talents in professional, community, parental, and household roles. This pattern ex-ists among lay Catholic theologians and pastoral ministers, a majority of whom are married. For the first time in a very long time, the Catholic community has a cadre of scholars and professional ministers who can bring their theological tradition into creative interaction with lived experience of marriage. As thoughtful believers articulate multifaceted dimensions of Christian marriages, a foundation may be laid for consen-sus-building around a neuralgic issue of Catholicism—family planning, or responsible parenthood.

READING SIGNS OF THE TIMES

Five Cultural Signs

First, the National Marriage Project has found that the primary purpose of marriage cited by young American adults (94 percent) is "finding a soul mate."[1] A 2007 survey of U.S. Catholics across several generations also found 77 percent somewhat or strongly agreeing that a spouse

---

1. Whitehead and Popenoe, "Who Wants to Marry a Soul Mate?"

should be a soul mate, first and foremost.[2] "Soul mate" means different things to different people, since contemporary descriptions of marriage can be privatized and devoid of religious awareness. Eighty percent of young adults surveyed by the National Marriage Project agreed that "marriage is nobody's business but the two people involved"; the directors remark that mainstream understanding of "soul mate" marriage is typically "emotionally deep but socially shallow."[3] Catholic social teaching echoes their concern. Still, the soul-mate understanding of marriage has Christian precedent. St. Thomas Aquinas described marriage as the greatest friendship.[4] Protestants describe Christian marriage as a covenant, reflecting God's covenant with humans. Orthodox Christianity says the primary goal of Christian marriage is for the couple's union to provide a sacramental manifestation of Christ's love for the Church. For centuries, Roman Catholicism has likewise taught that Christian marriage is a sacramental sign of Christ's love, and moreover that a couple's free consent creates a marriage bond. Vatican II adopted language such as covenant, partnership, and union of life and love to describe marriage.

Secondly, between 1900 and 2007, the percentage of married American women employed outside the home rose from 5.6 percent to 60 percent.[5] Married women's employment is no longer perceived primarily as an indicator of a husband who cannot support his family (though that may be true). Employment can be a path to women's personal enrichment, and a way to contribute their talents to society in ways unavailable to prior generations. Christians can connect these values to the concept of vocation.[6]

Third, hormonal pills and other birth control methods developed since the 1960's have been hailed as crucial to self-determination within marriage, especially for women. Refined "natural" methods based on fertility awareness (including high-tech options) can also be used to prevent or plan pregnancy.[7] Development of effective means of fertility

2. Center for Applied Research in the Apostolate, *Marriage in the Catholic Church*.

3. Whitehead and Popenoe, "Who Wants to Marry a Soulmate?"

4. *Summa Contra Gentiles* 3.123.6.

5. Romanowski, "Take Your Girlie," 200; U.S. Bureau of Labor Statistics, http://www .bls.gov/cps/wlf-table6-2008.pdf.

6. See McLemore, *Also a Mother*, and Rubio, *Marriage and Family*, esp. chapters 5 and 6.

7. The rhythm or calendar method, endorsed by the Catholic Church implicitly in 1930, and explicitly in 1951, earned its reputation as unreliable. Improved under-

management has coincided with emergence of responsible parenthood as a core value of Catholic teaching on marriage. This idea bespeaks a shift in interpretation of God's providence and of human freedom. Humans are considered more active than passive in cooperating with God as co-creators of human life and as stewards of fertility.

Fourth, fertility control doesn't exist in a vacuum, but in a culture dominated by capitalist pursuit of maximum efficiency. This ethos pervades the non-profit sector too, including church-related institutions. Workplaces are structured around the model of an unencumbered "ideal worker" without other obligations. Vowed celibacy in Catholicism functions as a parallel model. The maximum efficiency work ethic poses hardships even for celibates; research shows workload is one of the top stressors on today's priests.[8] It's not hard to appreciate the strain on those who feel called to combine parenthood, volunteerism, and professional service in a multi-faced vocation, especially if their employers don't provide paid family leave or a living wage.[9] In prior generations, stay-at-home wives, who managed households and children while husbands worked elsewhere, sustained the "ideal worker" model. The cost of doing business was shifted off companies' books and onto unpaid women. Women's entry into professions previously dominated by men has come at a price, for women are often expected to behave as unencumbered "ideal workers."[10] Employed parents, especially mothers, commonly work a "second shift" managing family responsibilities.[11] In this context, effective fertility control contributes to an environment wherein spouses (especially women) may be pressured to have fewer children than they might wish for, or to schedule pregnancies and childcare such that par-

standing of fertility means "natural family planning" techniques are now more reliable. See the U.S. Catholic Bishops' website http://www.usccb.org/prolife/issues/nfp/index. shtml and Weschler, *Taking Charge*; also http://www.ovusoft.com/. Besides low tech NFP methods which monitor temperature, vaginal mucus, and cervical position, some high-tech options monitor fertility based on a daily temperature reading analyzed by a hand-held computer. Others analyze saliva or urine samples.

8. Dean Hoge, "Current State of the Priesthood."

9. See Bourg "Dual Vocation." In Catholic social teaching, a living wage means payment high enough that a typical size two-parent family with dependent children, with one full-time worker, can maintain frugal-yet-dignified existence and keep themselves out of poverty.

10. See Williams, *Unbending Gender.*

11. See Hochschild, *Second Shift*; Hochschild, *Time Bind*; Schor, *Overworked American.*

enthood doesn't inconvenience an employer or impede their own professional advancement. This pattern may be considered a form of social sin. John Paul II used the expression "contraceptive mentality" to describe the habit of viewing children as an inconvenience rather than a gift from God.[12] These realities will be foremost in consciences of contemporary Christians discerning how to exercise responsible parenthood.

Fifth, increased life expectancy means that in a marriage of 50 or 60 years, 20 or 30 may be spent as post-menopausal empty-nesters.[13] Surely this "sign of the times" ought to profoundly impact Catholic reflection on marriage, for until the 1960s, Catholic teaching called procreation and nurture of children the primary purpose of marriage; other purposes were called secondary.[14] Medical advances give us added reason to assume marriage vocations can be multidimensional.

To sum up cultural signs: In the U.S. and similar cultures, typical adults of marrying age think marriage should complement and promote, rather than stifle, each spouse's unique talents. They will likely find theological references to partnership, mutuality, and communion between spouses attractive. They will likely be wary of references to pre-ordained marital duties and natural/God-given gender roles, especially if interpreted to imply male dominance and female submission. The connection of marriage, sex, and parenthood is certainly appreciated, but their linkage is often conceived as more malleable than previous generations imagined.

Ecclesial Signs

A key development in recent decades has been John Paul II's "theology of the body." Its devotees, including a vibrant youth contingent, exude evangelical zeal disproportionate to their numbers among Catholics as a whole.[15] Echoing the "soul mate" ideal of marriage in their theme of

12. For example, John Paul II's *Evangelium Vitae* (1995), no. 13, also *Familiaris Consortio* (1981), no. 30, which uses the expressions "consumer mentality" and "anti-life mentality."

13. See the National Marriage Project, "Life Without Children."

14. Whitehead and Popenoe report that among the general U.S. population, almost 70 percent disagree with the statement that "the main purpose of marriage is having children;" among 20–29 year olds, only 16 percent agree ("Who Wants to Marry a Soul Mate?").

15. See John Paul II, *Theology of the Body*. On "evangelical Catholics," see William Portier, "Evangelical Catholics." See also youth festivals sponsored by the Franciscan University of Steubenville, OH. Online: http://www.franciscanyouth.com.

"total self-giving," they aim to redress excesses unleashed by the previous generation's sexual revolution. Even scholars who are uncomfortable with some aspects of theology of the body acknowledge that it addresses a true human need. The search for an alternative to trivialized sex is a "sign of the times" appreciated by many people of good will. Some theology of the body advocates employ esoteric scriptural and theological language, along with sound bites intended for shock value. Janet Smith likens contraceptive marital intercourse to junk food, racial segregation, marital rape, and adultery; Christopher West likens it to blasphemy, adultery, and killing one's own grandmother, and to spouses spaying/neutering themselves as they would a pet dog.[16] Whatever the rhetoric used, objective norms presented are the same, familiar to Catholics everywhere—monogamous, life-long, heterosexual marriage; sexual intercourse reserved for marriage and non-contraceptive. These norms are understood as essential to God's design for human fulfillment; there are no circumstances that justify a different path to fulfillment.

Catholics who embrace these norms—interpreted in this exceptionless manner—are a minority. A 2005 survey of U.S. Catholics found 75 percent agreed someone could be a "good Catholic" while disobeying the hierarchy's teaching on contraception, and only 13 percent agreed the hierarchy has final authority to determine whether using contraceptives is right or wrong.[17] A separate survey of American Catholics married from 1995–1999 determined only 12 percent had *ever* tried natural family planning methods;[18] other studies estimate the percentage using NFP consistently is perhaps 3–4 percent.[19] While a conservative cohort

---

16. See Smith, *Humanae Vitae*, 82, 92–93; West, *Theology of the Body for Beginners*, 108, 110. West believes that in contracepted sex, spouses say to each other, "We prefer the momentary pleasure of a sterilized orgasm over the opportunity of participating in the inner-life of the Trinity . . . Bad choice!" (115). Expanding the junk food analogy, West says couples who embrace John Paul II's theology of the body are enjoying luscious food at a banquet, while those who accept the vision of sexuality promoted by the media (including approval of contraception) are settling for "maggot ridden scraps at the bottom of a dumpster" (126). Elsewhere West says, "When we override the divine language written in our bodies with contraception, we speak against the 'great mystery' of God's life and love that our bodies proclaim. We blaspheme. And it is never okay to blaspheme. Not even once." ("A Response to Luke Timothy Johnson's Critique of John Paul II's Theology of the Body").

17. D'Antonio et al., *American Catholics Today*, 177, 175.

18. Creighton University Center for Marriage and Family, *Time, Sex, and Money*, 26.

19. Rubio, "Beyond the Liberal/Conservative Divide," 274.

of priests, especially younger ones, exhibits strong allegiance to official teachings, other priests are resigned to an uneasy truce over controversial sexual issues.[20] Meanwhile, one in ten Americans raised Catholic leaves the Church; for every person who joins as an adult, four depart. Disagreement with teachings on sexuality is often cited as a reason, especially by those now unaffiliated with any religion.[21] Commenting on American Catholic laity, sociologist William D'Antonio says even those "committed to the church as regular Mass goers, who would never leave the church, and who say the church is one of the most important influences in their lives, nevertheless distance themselves from the church's formal teachings on marriage and sexual issues. . . ."[22] Catholics who love their Church, but do not fully support official interpretation and application of marital/sexual norms (distinguishable from *rejection* of them) can be dismayed when their respectful critiques seem to be treated dismissively.[23] The devil is in the details, even when the same basic goods are sought by all.

A LOOK AT HISTORY

A person's willingness to remain part of the Church—despite being unconvinced by certain teachings—can depend on whether such teachings seem immutable. Today, Catholicism has detailed teachings and policies concerning sex and marriage. Many people don't know that for much of its history, the Church carried on without all the same formalities—for instance, that weddings haven't always happened in churches with priests officiating,[24] or that natural family planning hasn't always been

20. For comparison of the youngest cohort to older colleagues, see Hoge, "Current State of the Priesthood."

21. Pew Forum on Religion in Public Life, *Faith in Flux*.

22. Quoted in McCormick, "Catholicism and Sexuality," 193.

23. Julie Hanlon Rubio notes, "Even the Common Ground Initiative, founded by Cardinal Bernardin in 1996 to encourage dialogue between liberals and conservatives in the church, only took up the issue of sexual ethics in 2004." Having participated in this 2004 event, she reports, "Because of the delicate nature of the discussion, for the first time proceedings were not made public and participants were asked not to take the content of the conversations outside the confines of the conference. Dialogue itself was a scandal!" ("Beyond the Liberal/Conservative Divide on Contraception," 271). Of note, the U.S. Bishops have begun a pastoral initiative on marriage involving significant consultation. See preliminary reports at http://www.usccb.org/laity/marriage/npim. shtml. It remains to be seen what the responses to respectful critique will be.

24. The sixteenth-century Council of Trent implemented a requirement that marriage vows be witnessed by a priest and two additional persons. This is known as "canoni-

promoted. Knowing these practices haven't always existed, we shouldn't assume it was wrong for them to have developed. But we can recognize that some practices appropriate for a given context aren't essential in every context. Timeless Christian convictions can be expressed in multiple ways. Or, sometimes practices which seemed essential in a certain context are later set aside, because believers recognize they aren't essential after all. To illustrate: for centuries, Catholic spouses were instructed to abstain from sexual intercourse at least half the liturgical year, more if the wife was pregnant![25] By learning about continuity and development in Catholic tradition, we realize we're in good company whenever we ponder how to incarnate Christian discipleship more fully in marriage.

Contemporary Roman Catholics often describe "marriage vocations" in contrast to a "religious vocations," as if a person cannot be *both* married and religious. If asked how these vocations differ, many will reply that one involves sex and parenthood, and the other doesn't. Or, married people do "ordinary" things, while "religious" people do "holy" things. "Christian" marriages may be distinguished from others based on whether a cleric officiated at the wedding. The earliest Christians didn't think in these categories. For them, the vocation of Christian marriage, if we wish to call it that, was foremost the calling to be a disciple of Jesus, accepted by a married couple. There was no required Christian wedding

---

cal form." Previously in Roman/Western Catholicism, marriages were considered valid and sacramental by virtue of the spouses' consent, even without witnesses, although wedding ceremonies at churches had been customary in various areas of Europe by the twelfth century. See Martos, *Doors to the Sacred*, 368–82.

25. This information comes from penitential books used, beginning in the 6th century, to guide confessors in assigning penances. See Payer, *Sex and the Penitentials*. Payer says each period of abstinence "is associated with times of penance (the three Lents, Wednesdays, Fridays) or has unmistakable Biblical justification (menstrual period, after childbirth) or is allegorically associated with a Biblical episode (before communion)." (27; also 23–28 and 127–28) Most penitentials regard pregnancy as a time for abstinence, perhaps because procreation isn't possible, but only one penitential alludes to this connection; concern about inappropriate sexual positions may have played a role. The 'three Lents' refer to forty days before Christmas and Easter, and after Pentecost. Several penitentials assign penances for intercourse on Saturdays and Sundays. Spouses would have had precious few times available for intercourse without guilt! Assuming a couple uses present-day NFP methods to avoid pregnancy for most menstrual cycles during their fertile years, abstinence is typically needed for 7–10 per cycle, perhaps more if the couple abstains during menstruation. Thus, by comparison, the Catholic Church asks less asceticism of contemporary spouses than was expected in centuries past. Perhaps this is an unspoken reason John Paul II insists the difficulties of NFP shouldn't be experienced as overwhelming!

ritual, but Christian spouses could be identified as they shared Eucharist together—perhaps in their own homes! St. Paul writes, "Give my greetings to Prisca and Aquila; they were my fellow workers in the service of Christ Jesus and even risked their lives for the sake of mine. Not only I but all the churches of the Gentiles are grateful to them. Remember me also to the congregation that meets in their house" (Rom 16:3–5).[26] Married clergy were common. There were families with multiple generations of clergy, including saints, bishops, and popes.[27] Besides worshipping together, what did Christian spouses do? Those who opened their homes to community gatherings, including unsupervised women or slaves who joined the new sect apart from heads of their own households, put their reputations at risk. Some endured persecution and execution. Promiscuity, adultery, and easy divorce were inappropriate. A second-century observer remarked, "Like others, [Christians] marry and have children, but they do not expose [=abandon] them. They share their meals, but not their wives."[28] Converting to Christianity might mean changing jobs, since certain occupations (e.g., government/military) were difficult to reconcile with the faith. Financial and social habits were also at stake. Justin Martyr testifies in the second century, "We who valued above all else the acquisition of wealth and property now direct all that we have to a common fund, which is shared with every needy person. We who hated and killed one another, and who, because of differing customs, would not share a fireside with those of another race, now, after the appearance of Christ, live together with them."[29]

Ambivalence toward marriage, especially sex, grew in the third to fourth centuries, partly as a byproduct of honor attached to monasticism, which attracted Christians who sought a rigorous countercultural lifestyle.[30] Several regional church councils, beginning with Elvira in 306, instructed married clergy to abstain from intercourse.

26. Other ancient authors praised Christian households as "little churches." See Bourg, *Where Two or Three Are Gathered*, 10–11.

27. See Mark 1:30–31, 1 Cor 9:5, 1 Tim 3:1–7, Titus 1:5–9; and Kowalski, *Married Catholic Priests*, 3–13.

28. "Letter to Diognetus."

29. Justin Martyr, *First Apology*, chapter 14, in Michael Pennock, *This is Our Church*, 53.

30. Sexual asceticism existed in Judaism and other Mediterranean sects, which were often dualistic. Virginity "for the sake of the kingdom" or to be "free from distraction" gained credibility from Matt 19:10–12 and 1 Corinthians 7.

Celibacy (=being unmarried) wasn't required, but rather continence (=sexual abstinence).[31] The ideal of sexually abstinent clergy became prominent in the Western Church, but decisions by regional councils weren't binding everywhere, and some councils issued opposite opinions.[32] As Christianity expanded into far-flung lands, awareness and enforcement of continence instructions dwindled. Early medieval Catholics were often served by married priests.[33]

St. Augustine had lasting influence on Catholicism's sense of marriage and sex. He thought marriage was good, but sex was almost inevitably sinful. Responding to debate between St. Jerome, who promoted virginity, and Jovinian, who believed marriage was equally honorable, Augustine said virginity was more excellent, but also articulated three goods of marriage: *fides, proles,* and *sacramentum.* Augustine believed spouses' desire to have intercourse for the purpose of *proles* (children) was rational, but otherwise sexual desire was disordered lust.[34]

31. Kowalski, *Married Catholic Priests,* 9. There is a link to monasticism. Originally, monks weren't priests, but lay people who adopted ascetic lifestyles, including celibacy and continence. Eventually their holy lives became the ideal for priests. Some monks were ordained, and priests were expected to be continent. Jewish priests abstained from intercourse with their wives before offering sacrifices, and this purity ritual also influenced Christian priesthood. St. Ambrose wrote in the fourth century, "You have received the grace of the sacred ministry with an untouched body, an undefiled modesty and an unfamiliarity with carnal relations. You are aware that you must continue a ministry which is unhampered and spotless, one which should not be profaned by conjugal intercourse.... If even the [Israelite] people were forbidden to take part in the offering without having washed their clothes, would you dare to make an offering for others with a defiled mind and body? Would you dare to act as their minister?" (*On the Duties of Ministers* I, 50, cited in Martos, *Doors to the Sacred,* 423) In Western Christianity, the Eucharist came to be celebrated daily, unlike Eastern Christianity, where weekly Eucharist was typical. This may have influenced divergent histories regarding married priesthood. In John Paul II's theology of the body, priestly continence is portrayed as a self-giving way of loving, a complementary counterexample to marital self-giving. This is an improvement over explanations which portray marital intercourse as a source of contamination!

32. See Kowalski, *Married Catholic Priests,* 10, 12–13; he cites the Synod of Ancyra (314), the Council of Gangra (345), and the Council of Trullo (692) which is regarded as ecumenical by the Orthodox. It set the practice of allowing deacons and priests to marry before ordination. Bishops must be unmarried, widowed, or separated by mutual consent. These customs also apply to Eastern-rite Catholicism.

33. Martos, *Doors to the Sacred,* 428.

34. "Marriage has also this good, that carnal or youthful incontinence, even if it is bad, is turned to the honorable task of begetting children, so that marital intercourse makes something good out of the evil of lust." *The Good of Marriage,* chapter 3, in Clark, *St. Augustine,* 46.

Fides (fidelity) entailed providing sex when lust couldn't be controlled. Such intercourse was venially sinful, but pardonable since it prevented fornication or adultery.[35] Augustine seems unable to conceive of sexual passion as a positive expression of marital companionship, good in its own right, independent of a procreative intention.[36] He says as couples age and "the ardor of youth has cooled," their marriage will be "better in proportion as they begin the earlier to refrain by mutual consent from sexual intercourse."[37] Augustine called marriage a *sacramentum* (sacrament) because according to Ephesians 5, it was a sign of union between Christ and the Church.

Penitential books give insight into sexual expectations of medieval Christianity.[38] They evolved into textbooks which confessors relied upon until the mid-twentieth century. These books focused overwhelmingly on vices and sins. Meanwhile, monastic asceticism was regarded as the epitome of virtue. Penance and asceticism became lenses through which Catholics saw their moral lives. For too long, the Catholic community neglected to sufficiently balance penitential and ascetic impulses with positive affirmation of human sexuality.

35. *Good of Marriage,* chapter 6 in Clark, *St. Augustine,* 47–48.

36. Smith, *Humanae Vitae,* says this common interpretation of Augustine (particularly by those who disagree with Catholicism's ban on contraception, and trace its roots to Augustine) "has not gone uncontested." (54) She cites two sources from the 1960s but doesn't provide details. John Paul II's theology of the body, and interpretation by West, acknowledge a positive, unitive purpose to sexual "body language" occurring during infertile periods with a deliberate intent to avoid procreation. In this respect, they differ from Augustine. Yet, echoing Augustine, they insist that desire for intercourse using contraception is an expression of lust or concupiscence, and that contraceptive intercourse *cannot* have any positive, unitive purpose.

37. *Good of Marriage* chapter 3 in Clark, *St. Augustine,* 45–46. A married couple beatified by John Paul II, Luigi and Maria Quattrocchi, abstained from sex for the last 26 years of their 46 year marriage. Some commentators consider a continent married couple an odd choice of role models for contemporary times. See McBrien, "Benedict XVI and Saint-Making."

38. Penances took account of age, clerical/lay status of the penitent, and whether sins were accidental, intentional, or habitual. For example, from the *Penitential of Cummean* (c. 950): "He who for a long time is lured by imagination to commit fornication, and repels the thought too gently, shall do penance for one or two more days, according to the duration of the imagination. . . . But he who kisses and embraces, [shall do penance for] one year, especially [if the sin occurred] in the three 40-day periods [see note 25, above]. . . . If, however, he has spoken but has not been accepted by her, forty [days] . . ." See Wogaman and Strong, *Readings in Christian Ethics,* 84–85.

In the eleventh and twelfth centuries, a campaign to enforce continence and celibacy among Roman Catholic clergy escalated. Families were forcibly separated; children and wives were enslaved![39] Married priests were prohibited from celebrating the Eucharist; Catholics were ordered not to attend masses they offered. Thus, married clergy were deprived of their honor and livelihood. The crackdown was part of a campaign to prevent churchmen from passing titles and land benefices to relatives. But it was influenced by an assumption that sexual asceticism modeled on the monastery was holier than chaste sex within marriage.[40] As the clerical celibacy requirement became firmly established, a sense that ministry and marriage could be combined in a multi-dimensional vocation eroded.

In the twelfth and thirteenth centuries, the heretical Albigensians promoted the dualistic opinion that marriage was sinful. In reply, Aquinas said marriage is part of God's natural design for procreation and nurture of children; from a supernatural perspective, sacramental marriage directs children to God.[41] Unlike Augustine, he distinguished lust from "proportionate" sexual desire and pleasure accompanying the intent to procreate within marriage.[42] Still, because sexual pleasure involves a loss of reason, Aquinas assumed the "marriage act" needed another justification. He thought spouses sinned at least venially if they had sex motivated by pleasure, *without* intent to procreate or pay the marriage debt (=to prevent one's spouse from committing adultery).[43] Aquinas's critique of extramarital sex centers not simply on lust, but on restricting intercourse to a setting conducive for children's welfare. The worst sexual sins, he thought, were acts without procreative potential, like masturba-

39. Kowalski, *Married Catholic Priests*, 14–15, 34–35; also O'Malley, "Some Basics About Celibacy"; and "Celibacy."

40. Pope Gregory VII, a.k.a. Hildebrand, reigned from 1073 to 1085. A monk from the prominent and rigorous Cluny community, he was the foremost advocate of the celibacy campaign. Catholicism still teaches that virginity or celibacy for the sake of the kingdom is superior to sacramental marriage. John Paul II insists this "superiority" doesn't diminish the dignity of marriage, but presupposes it; he cites St. John Chrysostom: "What appears good only in comparison with evil would not be particularly good. It is something better than what is admitted to be good that is the most excellent good." See *Familiaris Consortio* (1981), no. 16.

41. *ST*, Supplement 49.5 ad. 1.

42. *ST*, II–II 153.2 & ad. 2.

43. *ST*, Supplement QQ. 49.1, 5 & 6.

tion and homoerotic behavior. Rape, adultery, and incest were serious sins, but maintained a semblance of conformity with reason. If Aquinas understood menstrual cycles and knew women are infertile more often than not, he might have thought sex was designed by God for purposes besides procreation, and adjusted his sense of sin accordingly. Aquinas analyzes sex "primarily in relation to the total project of married life. This is probably as it should be, but the importance of sexual intimacy as an expression and enhancement of the 'friendship' of which Thomas speaks surely deserves more attention than he gives it."[44]

SOMETHING OLD AND SOMETHING NEW

Vatican II's *Gaudium et Spes* (GS) maintained elements of traditional marriage theology, yet interpersonal and vocational dimensions were emphasized as never before. Previously, procreation was called the primary purpose of marriage; other purposes, including mutual help and remedying of concupiscence/lust, were called secondary.[45] This ranking disappeared in GS. Most commentators[46] say Vatican II affirmed unitive and procreative purposes of marriage as equally important.[47] Before Vatican II, marriage was commonly called a contract. The 1917 *Code of Canon Law* stated, "[E]ach party gives and accepts a perpetual and exclusive right over the body for acts which are of themselves suitable

44. Cahill, *Between the Sexes*, 113.

45. For example, in his 1951 "Address to Midwives," Pius XII states: "The truth is that marriage, as a natural institution, is not ordered by the will of the Creator towards the personal perfection of the husband and wife as its primary end, but to the procreation and education of new life. The other ends of marriage, although part of nature's plan, are not of the same importance as the first. Still less are they superior." (In Liebard, *Official Catholic Teachings,* 116.) Concupiscence means desire for sensory gratification (from food, drink, sex, etc.) without regard for what is reasonable and good for our overall well-being.

46. For exceptions, see Smith, *Humanae Vitae*, 42–54.

47. "*While not making other ends of less account*, the true practice of conjugal love, and the whole meaning of family life which results from it, have this aim: that the couple be ready with stout hearts to cooperate with the love of the Creator and the Savior, who through them will enlarge and enrich His own family day by day.... *Marriage is not instituted solely for procreation*; rather, its very nature as an unbreakable compact between persons and the welfare of children both demand that the mutual love of spouses be embodied in a rightly ordered manner, that it grow and ripen. Therefore, marriage ... maintains its value and indissolubility even when despite the often intense desire of the couple, children are lacking." (*Gaudium et Spes,* no. 50, emphases added)

for the generation of children."[48] GS avoids portraying marriage as a contractual exchange of bodily rights. Marriage is a committed union of entire persons, a "covenant of irrevocable personal consent." Expressions like "communion of life and love," "mutual gift of two persons," partnership, and friendship are used. Language referring to interpersonal cooperation isn't totally absent in prior tradition, as in Aquinas or in Pius XI's *Casti Connubii*,[49] but it is shrouded by language of contract and primary/secondary ends. The majority of delegates at Vatican II seemed intent, in their choice to de-emphasize certain terms, to turn Catholic discourse on marriage in a new direction.

How is marriage a sacrament? The sacramental reality had been associated especially with *permanence* of the bond, considered a sign of Christ's union with the Church. GS indicates that *love* is at the core of the sacrament. "[Christ] abides with them . . . so that just as he loved the Church and handed Himself over on her behalf, the spouses may love each other with perpetual fidelity through mutual self-bestowal. Authentic married love is caught up into divine love. . . ." Christian families should "manifest to all men the Savior's living presence in the world, and the genuine nature of the Church . . . by the mutual love of spouses, by their generous fruitfulness, their solidarity and faithfulness, and by the loving way in which all members of the family work together."[50] The Council clarified that there's more to being a sign of Christ's love than mere endurance! Repeatedly, GS calls marriage a vocation, correcting the misconception that marriage is for Catholics who *don't* have a vocation. Vatican II revived the permanent diaconate. Married deacons and

---

48. Canon 1013.1. See also Pius XI, *Casti Connubii* (1930), especially introduction and part I.

49. Although *Casti Connubi* repeats the formula that procreation is the primary purpose of marriage, a curious text from part I reads, "This mutual inward moulding of husband and wife; this determined effort to perfect each other, can in a very real sense, as the Roman Catechism teaches, be said to be the chief reason and purpose of matrimony, provided matrimony be looked at not in the restricted sense as instituted for the proper conception and education of the child, but more widely as the blending of life as a whole and the mutual interchange and sharing thereof." (in Liebard, *Official Catholic Teachings*, 31) This passage was cited by the majority report of papal birth control commission (see below) as one of the precedents for its recommendations (in Liebard, *Official Catholic Teachings*, 305).

50. *Gaudium et Spes*, no. 48.

their families help debunk the myth that marriage must be separate from "religious" vocations to pursue service and holiness.[51]

GS's description of *sex* is strikingly positive. Sex expresses and perfects marital love, which is a "merging [of] the human with the divine." It isn't inherently lustful, nor is it designed only to produce children, but also to "promote that mutual self-giving by which spouses enrich each other."[52] A papal commission had been convened to study birth control, and since results were still pending, the Council spoke about family planning only in general terms: "When harmonizing conjugal love with responsible transmission of life, the moral aspect of any procedure does not depend solely on intentions, but must be determined by objective standards. These, based on the nature of the human person and [human] acts, preserve the full sense of mutual self-giving and human procreation in the context of true love."[53] In other words, both unitive and procreative purposes of marriage and sex are natural for humans.

What do these standards imply in practice? As for numbers and spacing of children, there can be legitimate variety. GS assumes, yet goes beyond, guidelines in Pius XI's *Casti Connubii* and Pius XII's "Address to Midwives" (1951). *Casti Connubii* admitted it isn't "against nature" for spouses to "use their [sexual] right in the proper manner, although on account of natural reasons either of time or of certain defects, new life cannot be brought forth," and said sex during infertile times could be legitimated in consideration of secondary ends of marriage.[54] The "Address to Midwives" took this premise further, permitting spouses to deliberately avoid pregnancy by monitoring women's cycles and confining intercourse to infertile periods. Previously, extending back at least to Augustine, Catholics were taught it was always sinful to seek intercourse while excluding the intent of procreation, or indeed, without positively intending to procreate. Though the "Address to Midwives" said it was legitimate to avoid pregnancy only for "grave reasons," many were cited: financial, medical, social, and eugenic. These could justify confining intercourse to infertile times "even for the duration of the marriage."[55]

51. See Ditewig, "Married and Ordained.".

52. *Gaudium et Spes*, no. 49.

53. Ibid., no. 51. An alternate translation from Austin Flannery reads "respect the total meaning of mutual self-giving and human procreation in the context of true love."

54. See Liebard, *Official Catholic Teachings*, 42.

55. Liebard, *Official Catholic Teachings*, 112–13.

While Pius XII portrays family planning as an exceptional practice, GS suggests it's a normal aspect of marriage. Subsequent magisterial texts call it 'responsible parenthood.'[56] GS didn't evaluate specific planning methods, with notable exceptions of condemning abortion and infanticide. It simply said birth control must employ "methods not found blameworthy by the teaching authority of the Church."[57] This left the door open to revised teaching on specific techniques.

The papal birth control commission included demographers, physicians, theologians, bishops, and married couples. It was an advisory group without authority in its own right; this became apparent when Paul VI rejected recommendations supported by a very large majority, including a majority of bishops.[58] Vatican II's fresh approach to marriage led many Catholics to expect relaxation of the contraception ban. It was proposed that self-giving and procreation "in the context of true love" could be compatible with contraception, if the overall context of a loving marriage welcomed children. Commission members Pat and Patricia Crowley, leaders of the Christian Family Movement, surveyed 3,000+ couples from eighteen countries on experiences with periodic abstinence. "Though most couples said the method worked well enough, and 64 percent said it helped them grow in self-sacrificial love, 78 percent believed that it was harmful to their marriage, in that it increased tension and reduced spontaneity." Some respondents found the result of periodic abstinence wasn't mutual self-giving. "Rhythm leads to self-seeking, promotes excess in infertile times and strain in fertile times," or, it "seriously endangered [their] chastity" or "[made them] obsessed with sex throughout the month."[59] The commission's majority report concluded that contraception by married couples wasn't intrinsically evil, though contraception could be used in evil, selfish ways. It noted that prior teaching on procreation developed largely in response to dualistic,

---

56. *Gaudium et Spes* says, "[Spouses] will thoughtfully take into account both their own welfare and that of their children, those already born and those which may be foreseen. … they will reckon with both the material and the spiritual conditions of the times as well as with their state in life. Finally, they will consult the interests of the family group, of temporal society, and of the Church herself. The parents themselves should ultimately make this judgment in the sight of God" (no. 50). See also Paul VI, *Humanae Vitae*, no. 10; John Paul II, *Familiaris Consortio*, nos. 6, 11, 28, 31, 33.

57. *Gaudium et Spes*, no. 51.

58. For details on votes, see Salzman and Lawler, *Sexual Person*, 44.

59. Rubio, "Beyond the Liberal/Conservative Divide," 273–74.

heretical sects who opposed *all* transmission of life. "The tradition has always rejected seeking this separation with a contraceptive intention for motives spoiled by egoism and hedonism, and such seeking can never be admitted. . . . The opposition is really to be sought between one way of acting which is contraceptive and opposed to a prudent and generous fruitfulness, and another way which is in an ordered relationship to responsible fruitfulness . . . In such a conception the substance of the tradition stands in continuity and is respected."[60] The majority condemned abortion at any point after conception, and specifically attached this condemnation to "interventions which give serious grounds for suspecting that they are abortive."[61] Commission reports were leaked

60. Liebard, *Official Catholic Teachings*, 305. The final sentence is reminiscent of a famous quote from John XXIII's opening address to the Council: "[T]he substance of the ancient doctrine of the deposit of the faith is one thing, and the way in which it is presented is another."

61. In subsequent years several methods have been implicated as abortifacient in their primary mode (IUDs) or secondary modes of operation (hormonal methods), for they have the potential to prevent implantation of an early embryo by altering the endometrium. While the majority of medical literature acknowledges these methods may prevent implantation, it labels them as contraceptive rather than abortifacient. Why? In recent decades an influential portion of the medical profession has "redefined" pregnancy as beginning with implantation, rather than conception. Pro-life medical professionals have expressed concern that the definition of pregnancy was changed so that IUDs and hormonal methods would not be labeled as abortifacients. To be more precise, there is medical consensus hormonal birth control methods don't always prevent ovulation (especially if a woman forgets to take a pill every day). [Progestin-only pills fail to prevent ovulation more often than estrogen-progesterone combination pills.] There is also medical consensus that hormonal methods thin the endometrium (=uterine lining) to a level unsuitable for implantation. However, there isn't research available to conclusively answer a key question among pro-life medical professionals re: *how often* the hormonal surge at the time of conception will *override* previous thinning of the endometrium. It seems there is a minority of pro-life physicians who think that in the event of break-through ovulation and conception, the woman's normal hormonal surge will ALWAYS override the prior thinning of the endometrium, and thus, hormonal birth control methods do not have abortifacient potential. The majority medical opinion (among pro-life and pro-choice medical professionals, and in FDA labeling guidelines for hormonal birth control methods) is that a 'hostile endometrium' *does* contribute to the 'effectiveness' of hormonal methods; in other words, the hormonal surge that occurs with conception DOES NOT ALWAYS override prior thinning of the endometrium. For details, see Genovesi, *In Pursuit of Love*, 210–22; Kilner et al., "Bioethical Decisions," 177–201; Larimore and Stanford, "Postfertilization Effects"; and the American Association of Pro-life Obstetricians and Gynecologists website, http://www.aaplog.org/, particularly the link http://www.aaplog.org/PositionsAndPapers/OralContraceptiveControversy.aspx?fileID=1.

to the press in 1967. When *Humanae Vitae* appeared in 1968, dissent was widespread.

What did *Humanae Vitae* teach? Paul VI said sexual self-giving and procreation have an "inseparable connection, willed by God and unable to be broken by man on his own initiative" (no. 12). He concludes, "[E]ach and every marriage act must remain open to the transmission of life" (no. 11). Any action "which, either in anticipation of the conjugal act, or in its accomplishment, or in the development of its natural consequences, proposes, whether as an end or a means, to render procreation impossible" (no. 14) is considered unacceptable. While couples using both artificial and natural birth control methods have the "positive will of avoiding children for plausible reasons, seeking the certainty that offspring will not arrive" (no. 16), the two methods are considered qualitatively different. Why?

1. Periodic abstinence is understood to "make legitimate use of a natural disposition," the infertile part of the menstrual cycle God designed. Other methods are said to "impede the development of natural processes" and to assume "dominion over generative faculties" which God hasn't delegated to us (nos. 16, 13).

2. The "positive will of avoiding children" may be acted upon in different ways. One option is a 'positive act' of separating unitive and procreative meanings of conjugal intercourse. Paul VI thinks having sex while using contraceptives is this sort of act. Another option is abstaining from sex. This is considered a morally different act that doesn't "make into the object of a positive act of the will something which is intrinsically disordered" (no. 14).

3. Spouses who avoid procreation by periodic abstinence "give proof of a truly and integrally honest love," while those who have sex "which is deliberately made infecund" do something "intrinsically dishonest" (nos. 16, 14).

Humanae Vitae doesn't explain why one method might be more honest than another. But John Paul II's theology of the body focuses intently on this theme. He says for humans, sex is a symbolic body language meant to incarnate the interface of human and divine love—precisely because it communicates self-giving and union, and generates new life.[62] Like the Eucharist, which symbolically re-creates Jesus' self-gift to humanity, and allows communicants to accept it, sex allows spouses to symbolically re-exchange marriage vows. Christian marriage, symbolically captured in these vows, reflects Christ's love for the Church and love among divine persons of the trinity. The problem with contraception, says John Paul II, is that it drastically alters what couples are saying in their sexual body language by "altering its value of 'total' self-giving. Thus the innate language that expresses the total reciprocal self-giving of the husband and wife is overlaid, through contraception, by an objectively contradictory language, namely that of not giving oneself totally to the other. This leads not only to a positive refusal to be open to life but also to a falsification of the inner truth of conjugal love, which is called upon to give itself in personal totality."[63] In other words, contraception *always* negates *both* procreative and unitive dimensions of marriage. Theology of the body interpreters say contraception destroys marital union as much as adultery and marital rape do.[64] John Paul II reiterates that there's no contradiction between unitive and procreative dimensions of conjugal love. Any so-called contradictions people claim to experience arise from concupiscence and lust, for which the proper remedy is self-control.[65] God strengthens us to refrain from acting upon lust, if we're open to receiving that grace.

Paul VI predicted acceptance of contraception would lead to increased marital infidelity, and to disrespect of women by men who would treat them as sex objects. He feared young people might more easily be tempted to immoral behavior, and governments might impose contraception.[66] In *Evangelium Vitae*, John Paul II says the contraceptive mentality demeans children, and strengthens the temptation to abort undesired pregnancies.[67] A range of commentators, conservative and liberal, acknowledge truth in these predictions. Of course, marital infidelity, objectification of women, and child abuse have been pervasive prior to invention of modern contraceptives!

62. Even for infertile couples, he insists all sexual acts remain ordered to procreation.

63. *Familiaris Consortio*, no. 32.

64. West, *Theology of the Body for Beginners*, 106; Smith, *Humanae Vitae*, 85, 92–93.

65. John Paul II, *Theology of the Body*, 407–10.

66. *Humanae Vitae*, no. 17.

67. *Evangelium Vitae*, no. 13.

CRITICAL ANALYSIS

Despite consensus that contraceptives can be abused, there's disagreement about whether using them is *always* immoral. One might draw a comparison between contraceptives and credit cards. Undoubtedly, people can abuse the practice of purchasing on credit. Proliferation of credit cards exacerbates temptations to greed and materialism; powerful corporations profit by feeding these vices. The result is an impoverished objectification of happiness. Poor stewardship of credit can lead to bankruptcy and strain marriages. Young people can get over their heads in debt. As the "credit mentality" makes people accustomed to *having* things without the ability to *pay* for them, people may, in extreme cases, "separate" these two "natural aspects" of property ownership, and rationalize theft. Despite these risks, Catholicism doesn't consider credit card use intrinsically immoral—although for centuries, loaning money at interest was condemned as forcefully as contraception is condemned today.[68] The Church came to recognize a difference between exploitive, selfish use of credit, and that which manifests wise stewardship. This is the very sort of distinction which the majority of the papal birth control commission articulated.

Likewise, conservative and liberal theologians agree sexual body language can function sacramentally as a sign of God's grace, a symbolic re-exchange of marriage vows, and so on. Yet, some Catholics, who agree the unitive and procreative dimensions of marriage and sex mustn't be severed, also think contraception can be used in a morally acceptable way. They interpret "openness to procreation in each and every sexual act" as a rejection of abortion, rather than a ban on contraception for spouses committed to caring for any child they conceive, even when pregnancy is unplanned. (Here, "contraception" means methods without mechanisms that might impede implantation of an early embryo in the endometrium.)[69] The connection between unitive and procreative di-

---

68. John Noonan, *Can and Cannot Change.*

69. For a defense of this approach, see Genovesi, *In Pursuit of Love*, chapter 6. Since research doesn't yet answer all serious ethical questions about the impact of hormonal birth control on the endometrium, it would be most charitable for married couples who use contraceptives to err on the side of caution, following the advice of the papal birth control committee, and choose methods which do not "give serious grounds for suspecting that they are abortive." Though the abortifacient potential of hormonal methods may be statistically small for each woman, the issue is significant when one considers the millions of women who use them, often for many years. To err on the

mensions of marital intercourse is objectively broken by abortion; it is a direct, irrevocable separation between a procreative event (=a child conceived) and the sexual union from which it originated. Contraception, by contrast, affects the likelihood of potential procreation, but doesn't make actual procreation impossible. This is true not only because it isn't foolproof in preventing conception (honest sexual communication demands couples accept this reality). It's also true because contraceptives (those which cannot prevent implantation) do nothing to prevent any child conceived from being born. Couples who adopt this approach insist every sexual act remains open to procreation, both subjectively and objectively (assuming conception is physiologically possible).[70]

It's true that people affected by a contraceptive mentality can subjectively sever the link between sexual/marital union and procreation. Some people think they're entitled to an abortion if their contraceptive fails to prevent conception, or that people with no intention of marrying are justified in having sex so long as they use contraception. Catholics from across the theological spectrum can agree that such sexual communication is dishonest, demeaning of human dignity, and a grave misinterpretation of God's intentions. But, it doesn't follow that *all* contraceptive use distorts sexual/marital communication by overlaying it with objectively contradictory language incompatible with self-giving. All communication, particularly body language, has subjective, contextual, culture-bound elements. Language is never purely objective. The subjective element of sexual communication is exhibited if one compares testimonials by NFP enthusiasts and reluctant rhythm-method users in the Crowley study. All have practiced fertility control through periodic abstinence; some have subjectively experienced the method as optimally conducive to self-giving, but others have had a very different experience. Having researched testimonials of NFP and contraception

---

side of caution would be to adopt a charitable approach not unlike the decision of 150+ countries to forego the use of landmines, rather than risk using military devices which can be predicted to injure civilians on occasion (even if this isn't the intended purpose of the weapons). See the website of the International Campaign to Ban Land Mines, http://www.icbl.org/.

70. One might reasonably argue that a couple who uses, say, a barrier contraceptive during a woman's fertile period, knowing the method is not 100 percent reliable, and consciously willing to accept any child who may be conceived, is both objectively and subjectively more open to procreation than a couple who, through NFP, uses utmost caution to avoid procreation, say by limiting intercourse to the last week of the woman's menstrual cycle.

practitioners, Julie Rubio finds both groups experience their respective forms of sexual communication as promoting similar goods: self-giving, intimacy, mutuality, sexual pleasure, respect for women, and a connection between sexual and spiritual life.[71] This data doesn't support the assertion that contraception and NFP yield objectively incompatible types of communication. If the meaning of sexual body language is objective and immutable, in the *exact* manner theology of the body enthusiasts contend, it's curious that Catholicism took so long to appreciate the unitive purpose of marital sexuality, and to officially admit that spouses might legitimately have sex without intending to procreate.

Even if we agree there's no inherent contradiction between unitive and procreative dimensions of sexual intercourse within marriage, is it self-evident that difficulties experienced with periodic abstinence always arise from concupiscence and lust? Might these conflicts sometimes be a reflection of our finitude, which is morally neutral in itself? Reacting to theology of the body, Luke Timothy Johnson quips, "How many of us would welcome a dose of concupiscence, when the grinding realities of sickness and need have drained the body of all its sap and sweetness, just as a reminder of being sentient!"[72] Rick Gaillardetz, father of four boys, says, "The period of abstinence, if one includes the period when a woman is menstruating (a time when many couples prefer to abstain from sexual relations anyway) can range from eleven to sixteen days in a monthly reproductive cycle. This is a significant period of time for many couples who, if they have children, are often struggling as it is to keep sexual intimacy alive in their marriage. Factor in the circumstances in which one or the other of the spouses has a job requiring travel for extended periods of time and the demands of periodic abstinence can be transformed from 'an opportunity to find other ways to express their love' into a major obstacle in the marriage relationship."[73]

71. Rubio, "Beyond the Liberal/Conservative Divide."

72. Johnson, "Disembodied," 16.

73. Gaillardetz, *Daring Promise*, 110. Despite this critique, Gaillardetz says, "Natural Family Planning has much to commend it. It is a method that allows the couple to work in harmony with the woman's natural reproductive cycle rather than relying on intrusive artificial methods, many of which do harm to a woman's health. NFP also requires communication and cooperation between the husband and wife, rather than foisting responsibility on one of the parties to take a pill or use a condom. While the method does require periodic abstinence each month, these periods can be opportunities to explore other ways of expressing their love for one another. For all these reasons,

Spouses share a multi-dimensional vocation wherein both are dedicated in open-ended availability to serve many people's needs. Among couples who have determined that, at least temporarily, they shouldn't conceive more children, some may find that making room for regular sexual relations in the limited windows of opportunity NFP provides means arranging other commitments around their sex life. This strikes me as an inversion of vocational priorities, in effect, an idolatry of sex.

One weakness in the theology of the body is that its best-known devotees elevate certain parts of the "selves" spouses give each other—especially our potential fertility—and diminish or ignore others—perhaps most importantly, our complex vocational commitments. What does a "total gift of self" mean? If I include not simply my actual self, but my potential self as well, the possibilities are infinite. But I am a finite creature. I cannot actualize all the potential latent in me, for in pursuing some possibilities, I inevitably forego others. In my case, the "self" I have to give isn't simply my identity as a mother of four, who could potentially be a mother of five or more. It's just as much my identity as a teacher, who wishes to make commitments to my students, and to the institution where I teach. It's also my identity as a scholar, who would like to fulfill her commitment to write a new textbook for a university ministry program, and my identity as a daughter-in-law, who committed to relocate a few blocks from my infirm in-laws, intending to be available to them as needed. The "self" my husband has to offer likewise includes his identity as development director for a religious order, who has committed to raise several million dollars annually to fund many worthy ministries. Fulfilling these commitments is an incredible juggling act. We must be ready to shift plans at short notice as various people call upon us.

Presuming my husband and I have conscientiously discerned that we have all the kids we can handle, responsible parenthood, as understood by theology of the body enthusiasts, obliges us to confine sexual relations to infertile times. This presumes, implicitly, that others support us in that obligation. Let's do a reality check—bearing in mind that both my husband and I work for Catholic institutions, which presumably accommodate the NFP lifestyle better than other employers would. What

---

it is regrettable that the teaching of Pope Paul VI has been simply ignored by millions of Catholics. However, not everyone who disagrees with the papal teaching has simply ignored it.... These [dissenting] voices are too many to simply be dismissed as faithless and disobedient malcontents. The concerns they raise are real" (108–9).

would be the reaction if, when he receives the next unexpected phone call from a major donor who wants to meet him for dinner that very night, my husband responded, "Gee, I'd love to, but you know, my wife's almost done with her infertile phase for this menstrual cycle, and we had plans to give ourselves totally to each other, if you know what I mean . . ."? Or, what if I looked ahead to the week of final exams in December (when I normally spend every available waking moment doing school-work) and saw it would fall during my infertile time, and so I told my administration, "I may not be able to make the deadline for submitting grades . . . it would be a shame to let that week go by without taking some much-deserved time to symbolically renew my marriage vows"? Imagine this scene on the average Monday morning: "Sorry there's no milk for breakfast, kids. I didn't notice we needed it till 9:30 last night. It so happened the timing was perfect for a 'date night' for me and Dad. I had enough energy for that or a trip to the grocery, but not both. Maybe next time we're out of milk, the timing will be more convenient."

There are limits in giving my finite "self" to various people I'm committed to, in actualizing potentialities that exist in me. What criteria should govern my discernment? I could decide that a top priority is to take full advantage of opportunities for sexual intimacy my NFP chart provides, and address other priorities as time permits. In response to concern that NFP requires too much abstinence, the U.S. Catholic Bishops' NFP website insists that couples who have sex on all available infertile days will enjoy sex almost twice as often as the average couple.[74] To me, this argument misses the point. I don't think a married couple's sex life should be in the top tier of their vocational commitments. Sex should be prioritized in relation to "the total project of married life." The "selves" a husband and wife have to offer shouldn't be given only to each other. Yes, NFP can be a lifestyle choice that fosters unselfishness. But, if contraception makes it easier for some busy married couples

---

74. See http://www.usccb.org/prolife/issues/nfp/myths.shtml. The website's data hardly proves that NFP couples do, in reality, have sex twice as often as average couples; it only demonstrates that this is theoretically possible. According to the website's (uncited) data, average American couples, who presumably use contraceptives or sterilization and thus feel freer to have sex at any convenient time, in reality can find the time and energy for sex only eight or nine times per month (for couples 44 years and younger). If so, does it seem likely that an NFP couple seeking to avoid pregnancy, who had seven to ten fewer days per month available for sex, would in reality find time and energy for sex more often than other couples?

to squeeze in occasional sexual intimacy while generously fulfilling all their primary vocational commitments, the case can be made that contraception is likewise being used virtuously, to foster unselfishness by different means. NFP enthusiasts may not be troubled by the challenge of scheduling multiple commitments and still finding time for sex, but much depends on specifics of each couple's vocational commitments.

Catholic teaching challenges Christian families, as domestic churches, to generously share the church's mission, expanding their circle of care beyond themselves.[75] Catholic teaching on work challenges us to pursue service-oriented professions; these tend not to adhere to predictable schedules. Married couples may find contraception provides flexibility and peace of mind conducive to making outwardly-focused commitments, both short-term and long-term. One could argue that contraception can be used judiciously in a manner parallel to the gift of voluntary celibacy, which can enable people to forego actualizing their procreative potential so as to more freely serve God's kingdom. The case can be made that both NFP and contraception can assist the "total self-giving"—to each other and to the broader community— which Christian spouses strive to perfect in their multi-dimensional vocations.

Whatever method of family planning is used, responsible parenthood means considering the number and spacing of children, in relation to other vocational pursuits. Are our motives for having (or delaying/ not having) children prudent and altruistic? Should we adopt children rather than (or in addition to) conceiving our own? If we don't conceive or adopt, will we seek a comparable outlet of hospitality and service? The Catholic community has devoted boundless energy to analyzing family planning *methods*. There remains a need to reflect on our *motives* in family planning, and on stewardship of fertility entrusted to spouses in their complex vocations.

BIBLIOGRAPHY

Bourg, Florence Caffrey. "The Dual Vocation of Parenthood and Professional Theology." *Horizons* 32 (2005) 26–52.

———. *Where Two or Three Are Gathered*. Notre Dame, IN: University of Notre Dame Press, 2004.

Cahill, Lisa Sowle. *Between the Sexes*. Philadelphia: Fortress, 1984.

75. See Bourg, *Where Two or Three Are Gathered*, chapter 12, and Rubio, *Marriage and Family*, especially chapters 5 and 10.

"Celibacy." *New Advent Catholic Encyclopedia* (1917). Online: http://www.newadvent .org/cathen/03481a.htm.

Center for Applied Research in the Apostolate. *Marriage in the Catholic Church.* Georgetown University, 2007. Online: http://www.usccb.org/laity/marriage/ marriage_report.pdf.

Clark, Elizabeth, ed. *St. Augustine on Marriage and Sexuality.* Washington, DC: Catholic University of America Press, 1996.

Creighton University Center for Marriage and Family. *Time, Sex, and Money: The First Five Years of Marriage.* Omaha: Creighton University Press, 2000.

D'Antonio, William, et al. *American Catholics Today.* Lanham, MD: Rowman & Littlefield, 2007.

Ditewig, William T. "Married and Ordained." *America* (July 20, 2009). Online: http:// www.americamagazine.org/content/article.cfm?article_id=11771.

Gaillardetz, Richard. *A Daring Promise.* New York: Crossroad, 2002.

Genovesi, Vincent J. *In Pursuit of Love.* 2nd ed. Collegeville, MN: Liturgical, 1996.

Hochschild, Arlie. *The Second Shift.* 2nd ed. New York: Penguin, 2003.

———. *The Time Bind.* New York: Metropolitan, 1997.

Hoge, Dean. "The Current State of the Priesthood." Church in the 21st Century, Boston College, 2005. Online: http://bcm.bc.edu/issues/summer_2005/c21_hoge.html.

John Paul II, Pope. *The Theology of the Body.* Boston: Pauline Books and Media, 1997.

Johnson, Luke Timothy. "A Disembodied 'Theology of the Body.'" *Commonweal* (January 26, 2001) 11–17.

Kilner, John, et al., editors. "Bioethical Decisions When Essential Scientific Information is in Dispute: A Debate on Whether or Not the Birth Control Pill Causes Abortions." In *The Reproduction Revolution: A Christian Appraisal of Sexuality, Reproductive Technologies, and the Family,* edited by John F. Kilner et al., 177–201. Grand Rapids: Eerdmans, 2000.

Kowalski, Anthony. *Married Catholic Priests.* New York: Crossroad, 2004.

Larimore and Stanford. "Postfertilization Effects of Oral Contraceptives and their Relationship to Informed Consent." *Archives of Family Medicine,* 9 (2000) 126–33.

"Letter to Diognetus," Online: http://www.vatican.va/spirit/documents/spirit_20010522_ diogneto_en.html.

Liebard, Odile, editor. *Official Catholic Teachings: Love and Marriage.* Wilmington: McGrath, 1978.

Martos, Joseph. *Doors to the Sacred: A Historical Introduction to Sacraments in the Catholic Church.* Rev. ed. St. Louis: Liguori/Triumph, 2001.

McBrien, Richard. "Benedict XVI and Saint-Making." *The Tidings* (June 30, 2006). Online: http://the-tidings.com/2006/0630/essays.htm.

McCormick, Patrick. "Catholicism and Sexuality: The Sounds of Silence." *Horizons* 30 (2003) 191–207.

McLemore, Bonnie Miller. *Also a Mother: Work and Family as Theological Dilemma.* Nashville: Abingdon, 1994.

National Marriage Project. "State of Our Unions 2006: Life Without Children." Online: http://marriage.rutgers.edu/.

Noonan, John. *A Church that Can and Cannot Change.* Notre Dame, IN: University of Notre Dame Press, 2005.

O'Malley, John. "Some Basics About Celibacy." *America* (October 28, 2002). Online: http://www.americamagazine.org/gettext.cfm?textID=2564&articleTypeID=1&U UID=5708&issueID=409.

Payer, Pierre. *Sex and the Penitentials: The Development of a Sexual Code, 550–1150.* Toronto: University of Toronto Press, 1984.

Pennock, Michael. *This is Our Church.* Notre Dame, IN: Ave Maria, 2007.

Pew Forum on Religion in Public Life. *Faith in Flux* (April 27, 2009). Online: http://pewforum.org/docs/?DocID=411.

Portier, William. "Here Come the Evangelical Catholics." *Communio* 31 (2004). Online: http://communio-icr.com/articles/PDF/portier31-1.pdf.

Romanowski, William. "Take Your Girlie to the Movies." In *Religion, Feminism, and the Family,* edited by Anne Carr and Mary Stewart Van Leeuwen, 197–222. Louisville: Westminster John Knox, 1996.

Rubio, Julie Hanlon. "Beyond the Liberal/Conservative Divide on Contraception." *Horizons* 32 (2005) 270–94.

———. *A Christian Theology of Marriage and Family.* New York: Paulist, 2003.

Salzman, Todd, and Michael Lawler. *The Sexual Person: Toward a Renewed Catholic Anthropology.* Washington, DC: Georgetown University Press, 2008.

Schor, Juliet B. *The Overworked American: The Unexpected Decline of Leisure.* New York: Basic, 1991.

Smith, Janet. *Humanae Vitae: A Generation Later.* Washington, DC: Catholic University of America Press, 1991.

Weschler, Toni. *Taking Charge of Your Fertility.* San Francisco: Harper Collins, 1995.

West, Christopher. "A Response to Luke Timothy Johnson's Critique of John Paul II's Theology of the Body." Online: http://www.theologyofthebody.net/index.php?option=com_content&task=view&id=27&Itemid=48.

———. *Theology of the Body for Beginners.* West Chester, PA: Ascension, 2004.

Whitehead, Barbara Dafoe, and David Popenoe. "Who Wants to Marry a Soul Mate?: National Marriage Project, *The State of Our Unions* 2001." Online: http://marriage.rutgers.edu/Publications/SOOU/TEXTSOOU2001.htm.

Williams, Joan. *Unbending Gender.* New York: Oxford University Press, 2000.

Wogaman, Philip, and Douglas Strong, editors. *Readings in Christian Ethics.* Louisville: Westminster John Knox, 1996.

8

The Practice of Responsible Parenthood, NFP, and the Covenantal Unity of Spouses

Michel Therrien

IN WHAT FOLLOWS I would like to address the topic of Natural Family Planning (henceforth, NFP) and the Catholic Church's teaching on "responsible parenthood" from a perspective that has received little scholarly attention in the many works that promote or defend this teaching.[1] Few moral theologians discuss the subject from the perspective of virtue ethics, and in particular from the approach to virtue ethics that originates in the work of the philosopher Alasdair MacIntyre. My approach here is influenced especially by MacIntyre's theory of practices and their place within his virtue theory.

Along these lines, I would like to consider *Humanae vitae's* understanding of "responsible parenthood" as a *practice* within marriage, the successful mastery of which presupposes certain virtues and requires the command of certain skills and techniques.[2] Furthermore, I present my observations both as a moral theologian and as a practitioner of NFP. I will proceed first by explaining why I believe Pope Paul VI's description of "responsible parenthood" fits MacIntyre's definition of a *practice*. Second, I will discuss the virtues that *Humanae vitae* identifies as essential to the practice of responsible parenthood. Finally, I would

---

1. I am assuming that the reader is familiar with the conventional arguments for the Catholic Church's teaching on responsible parenthood already. See, for example, Grisez et al, "Every Marital Act"; May, "Contraception"; Quay, "Contraception and Marital Love"; Smith, *Why Humanae Vitae Was Right*.

2. Paul VI, *Humanae vitae* (trans. Smith), no. 10.

like to present the differences between NFP and artificial contraception in light of MacIntyre's theory of practices. In approaching the subject of "family planning" from this perspective, it is my hope that the reader will appreciate how the Church's teaching on responsible parenthood is more clearly grasped when we view it as a practice within the tradition of marriage covenant making and renewal.

SOME NECESSARY BACKGROUND

At the heart of the Church's teaching on conjugal love, human life is presented as a gift that God entrusts to spouses.[3] The word *life* in this context denotes something complex and multifaceted, for the good of human life is not merely physical or biological. As the late Pope John Paul II wrote, "Fatherhood and motherhood represent a responsibility which is not simply physical but spiritual in nature; indeed, through these realities there passes the genealogy of the person, which has its eternal beginning in God and which must lead back to him."[4] From a Christian perspective the loving response to this gift of *life* is to be faithful stewards of a sacred trust. Human life is commended to spouses as something their love is to receive from the creator and to direct toward the beatitude for which every human person is created. It is this sacred trust which stands as the great challenge of *Humanae vitae's* teaching on responsible parenthood.

Because the notion of *responsible parenthood* is so vital to my reflections here, it is worthwhile to quote the entire text of *Humanae vitae* where the concept is first presented:

> [C]onjugal love requires that spouses be fully aware of their mission of responsible parenthood. Today's society calls for responsible parenthood; thus it is important that it be rightly understood. Consequently, we must consider the various legitimate and interconnected dimensions of parenthood. If we consider biological processes first, responsible parenthood means that one knows and honors the responsibilities involved in these processes. Human reason has discovered that there are biological laws in the power of procreating life that pertain to the human person. If then we look to the innate impulses and inclinations of the soul, responsible parenthood asserts that it is necessary

3. John Paul II, *Gratissimam Sane*, no. 11.
4. Ibid.

that reason and will exercise mastery over these impulses and inclinations of the soul. If we look further to physical, economic, psychological, and social conditions, responsible parenthood is exercised by those who, guided by prudent consideration and generosity, elect to accept many children. Those are also to be considered responsible who, for serious reasons and with due respect for moral precepts, decide not to have another child for either a definite or an indefinite amount of time. The responsible parenthood of which we speak here has another intrinsic foundation of utmost importance: it is rooted in the objective moral order established by God—and only an upright conscience can be a true interpreter of this order. For which reason, the mission of responsible parenthood requires that spouses recognize their duties toward God, toward themselves, toward the family, and toward human society, as they maintain a correct set of priorities. For this reason, in regard to the mission of transmitting human life, it is not right for spouses to act in accord with their own arbitrary judgment, as if it were permissible for them to define altogether subjectively and willfully what is right for them to do. On the contrary, they must accommodate their behavior to the plan of God the Creator, a plan made manifest both by the very nature of marriage and its acts and also by the constant teaching of the Church.[5]

Since the encyclical's promulgation in 1968, the general response of Catholics to this teaching has been negative. The reason for this, however, does not actually appear until paragraph 14 of the encyclical, where a rather uncomfortable challenge confronts even the most well-meaning Catholic couples. It is here that Pope Paul VI explains that, in the spacing of their children, spouses may not use contraception but must practice methods of periodic abstinence.

At the time of the encyclical's promulgation, a grave concern among Catholic couples who were struggling with or rejecting this teaching was their experience of the only available method of "natural" child spacing, the Rhythm Method. This method determined the time of ovulation on the basis of statistical averages of women's menstrual cycles. Lamentably, the lived experience of many couples using the Rhythm Method was akin to playing Russian roulette. Many found it not very effective and, in combination with decreases in infant mortality rates, increased health standards, and so forth, the average family size had increased noticeably

---

5. Paul VI, *Humanae vitae*, no. 10.

over the past century or so, and not necessarily because couples were be-ing "guided by prudent consideration and generosity . . . to accept many children."[6] The challenges of *Humanae vitae* notwithstanding, however, the encyclical's presentation of responsible parenthood was and remains absolutely credible and important, as I hope to demonstrate below. And now that couples have recourse to newer natural family planning prac-tices that enable them to realize successfully the *whole* of the Church's teaching on responsible parenthood—including the reasonable post-ponement of pregnancy—Pope Paul VI's description of responsible parenthood has even greater significance.

For those unfamiliar with NFP, it would be good to provide a brief overview.[7] At present, NFP comprises three methods for either postpon-ing or achieving pregnancy in accordance with an individual woman's natural cycles of fertility. Through observations that monitor indicative bodily signs of fertility, such as fluctuations in body temperature, the changing position of the cervix, and the presence of mucus near the cer-vix and in the vaginal canal, a woman can accurately determine when she is ovulating. The spouses can then monitor these bodily indications so as to determine the best times to have intercourse for the sake of ei-ther achieving or avoiding pregnancy. One of the tremendous virtues of NFP, in fact, is its potential for overcoming infertility. It posts much higher rates of success than in-vitro fertilization and is much healthier for mother and child than fertility drugs. It is also far less expensive and does not involve the destruction of human embryos.[8] I should also men-

6. To be fair to the Church in this claim, I should point out that in the post WWII period doctors were discouraging mothers from breast feeding their children, which is an important technique in the natural spacing of children. This led invariably to much shorter intervals of time between pregnancies. Furthermore, most of the scientific re-search done at the time was focused on chemical based solutions to child spacing, as the contraceptive pill was being developed, meaning that natural methods were not given a fair shake in being perfected by means of further research. The vast improvements to natural methods developed as a reaction against the introduction of the pill in the 1960's.

7. The three methods of NFP are the Sympto-Thermal Method, the Creighton Method, and the Billings Ovulation Method. For a detailed and scientific presentation of these methods see Billings, Billings Method; Hilgers, NaPro Technology; Kippley, Art of Natural Family Planning. For online resources, go to www.woomb.org/bom/index .html or www.creightonmodel.com/index.html.

8. For statistical data on this, go to the Pope Paul VI Center's website at www.pope-paulvi.com.

tion the importance of breastfeeding as an integral component of NFP in the nourishing and spacing of children.[9]

NFP is called "natural" family planning, however, not because the methods evade any intervention of technology in the regulation of birth but because they help a couple to plan their family while also respecting and anticipating the natural cycles of fertility within a woman's body, and without attempting to alter, manipulate or suppress this cycle in any way. Technology and science are used to understand the unique and particular fertility of each woman rather than to approach fertility as a negative condition to be "treated" by some form of drug/chemical therapy or a barrier method. According to many studies, if practiced assiduously, NFP is as effective as any other method for avoiding pregnancy.[10]

But despite the many benefits of practicing NFP,[11] many if not most Catholic couples are disinclined to embrace the Church's teaching on responsible parenthood (henceforth a practice that I assume is coextensive with the use of NFP). Cultural influences notwithstanding, many Catholic couples, if they even hear of it, find NFP too challenging or unreasonable—even despite its vast improvement over the Rhythm Method. The principal objections arise either from the need for a couple to abstain from marital relations during periods of fertility—the time when a couple most naturally and intensely desire to engage in intercourse—or from the fear that the method will not work. The requirement of abstinence seems an unnatural and unnecessary suppression of

9. Sheila Kippley, *Breastfeeding and Natural Child Spacing*; *Breastfeeding and Catholic Motherhood*.

10. One reason many couples hesitate to use NFP is due to an understandable fear of getting pregnant at an inopportune time. This fear originates in a lack of confidence in the method due mostly to ignorance of how effective NFP is for postponing pregnancy or to a couple's self-determination that they are unable to practice the method competently. For studies demonstrating the usefulness of NFP in avoiding pregnancy, see Frank-Herrmann et al, "Effectiveness of a Fertility Awareness Based Method"; Ecochard et al. "Natural Family Planning Failures"; Hilgers and Stanford, "Creighton Model"; Howard and Stanford, "Pregnancy Probabilities." For an online source see BBC News, "Natural Contraception 'Effective.'" For descriptions on the practicability and benefits of using NFP, see Kippley, *Art of Natural Family Planning*.

11. These benefits would include the following: it is healthy and safe for women's bodies and psychological well-being, inexpensive by comparison to contraception, character building due to the exercise of virtues such as patience, temperance, and mutual trust; it is also relationship building in that planning a family responsibly requires team work, personal sacrifice and good communication between spouses. See Kippley, *Art of Natural Family Planning*.

sexual desire. In my opinion the aversion to NFP is accentuated because the moral differences between NFP and contraception are not self-evident and, quite honestly, difficult for most people to grasp conceptually; at least this has been my experience in discussing and teaching couples NFP. It is for this reason especially that my consideration of responsible parenthood as a *practice* might illuminate the Church's teaching on the differences between NFP and the use of contraception.

RESPONSIBLE PARENTHOOD AS A PRACTICE

Now that we have some background on NFP and its reception as a method of avoiding or achieving pregnancy, I need to explain how I am using the term *practice* in reference to responsible parenthood. In his book, *After Virtue*, Alasdair MacIntyre presents some excellent insights into the nature of practices, especially in their relationship to virtue.[12] MacIntyre defines a *practice* as

> any coherent and complex form of socially established cooperative human activity through which goods internal to that form of activity are realized in the course of trying to achieve those standards of excellence which are appropriate to, and partially definitive of, that form of activity, with the result that human powers to achieve excellence, and human conceptions of the ends and goods involved, are systematically extended.[13]

Admittedly, this definition is rather technical; but we can grasp his explanation of a practice more easily by the examples he provides: "Tic-tac-toe is not an example of a practice in this sense, nor is throwing a football with skill; but the game of football is, and so is chess. Bricklaying is not a practice; architecture is. Planting turnips is not a practice; farming is. So are the enquiries of physics, chemistry and biology, and so is the work of the historian, and so are painting and music."[14] And, I would add, so is responsible parenthood.

How does this definition correlate with *Humane vitae's* definition of responsible parenthood? Several things stand out in MacIntyre's description of a practice. The first part of the definition to unpack is that a practice is a "coherent and complex form of socially established coop-

---

12. MacIntyre, *After Virtue*, chapter 14.

13. Ibid., 175.

14. Ibid.

erative human activity." It should go without saying that the practice of responsible parenthood is a *cooperative human activity*.[15] To understand responsible parenthood in this way, one must have a deep sense of its *cooperative* nature, both among the parents and between the parents and the community. The cooperative and communal nature of responsible parenthood is affirmed in *Humanae vitae's* appeal to the spouse's duty toward God, themselves, the family, and society. And the appeal to justice here also demonstrates that responsible parenthood is a "socially established" human activity. It would be false to see parenthood as a merely private enterprise, for the broader social implications of not raising enough children to a fully integral human existence are evident in the increasing number of social ills that currently trouble our society—e.g. suicide rates, substance abuses, rapid depopulation, emotional, psychological and physical health problems in children, etc.

Moving on then, *Humanae vitae's* description certainly indicates that responsible parenthood is a *complex* activity as evidenced by its various "interconnected dimensions"—e.g., the biological, physical, economic, psychological, and social conditions of parenting. Furthermore, Paul VI's intention to associate responsible parenthood with reason, laws and precepts, self-mastery, prudence, generosity, moral order, duty, right judgment, and God's plan shows that it is also a *coherent* activity as well. In other words, we cannot accurately describe responsible parenthood as following sexual impulses in order to propagate the species as animals do. Of course, this also suggests that the conjugal act itself is not a practice; and nor is the mere use of periodic abstinence for that matter.

A second noteworthy aspect of MacIntyre's definition of a practice concerns whether responsible parenthood is ordered to "goods internal to that form of activity." To see this, however, it is helpful to take a quick look at the internal and external goods of any practice. MacIntyre argues that the *internal* goods of a practice are those goals (one could say) that are *intrinsic* to the activity. For example, a musician practices the art of music for the sake of making excellent music. Excellent music is

15. As Pope John Paul II affirms: "The family has always been considered as the first and basic expression of man's social nature. Even today this way of looking at things remains unchanged. Nowadays, however, emphasis tends to be laid on how much the family, as the smallest and most basic human community, owes to the personal contribution of a man and a woman. The family is in fact a community of persons whose proper way of existing and living together is *communion: communion personarum*" (*Gratissimam*, no. 7).

the internal good and the musician is deemed successful if he or she can achieve this good by playing up to or beyond the standard of excellence which the musical tradition proposes as the measure of the musician's competency. The *external* goods of a practice are those ends one might achieve accidently in virtue of being an excellent practitioner. In the case of music, this might be honor or fame, etc. I am mostly interested here with the *internal* goods of responsible parenthood. While certainly not an exhaustive list, *Humanae vitae* proposes the following as internal goods of the practice of responsible parenthood: 1) the covenantal unity of the spouses; 2) the achievement of pregnancy by means of a deliberate decision to conceive out of the generosity of the couples' love as well as the postponement of pregnancy when there are responsible reasons for doing so; and 3) the dignity of the woman *qua* wife and mother.[16]

MacIntyre goes on to state that these internal goods are "realized in the course of trying to achieve those standards of excellence which are appropriate to, and partially definitive of, that form of activity." This is an important part of his analysis insofar as he explains that any practice, and one's mastery of it, must stand up to the standard which the community and its tradition present as criteria for excellence:

> A practice involves standards of excellence and obedience to rules as well as the achievement of goods. To enter into a practice is to accept the authority of those standards and the inadequacy of my own performance as judged by them. It is to subject my own attitudes, choices, preferences and tastes to the standards which currently and partially define the practice.[17]

In other words, to say that one has achieved excellence in some practice, he or she must be able to achieve the internal goods of that practice according to the standards of excellence which the tradition proposes. He goes on to state that the standard of excellence for any practice requires the mastery of certain technical skills integral to the practice.[18]

16. The reader might notice that two of the internal goods I have listed here are closely related to what *Humanae vitae* refers to as the "finality" or end of the conjugal act. See Paul VI, *Humanae vitae*, nos. 8, 9, 11–13. The third good is not a "finality" of marriage but clearly referenced by the encyclical as a good to be protected (nos. 17).

17. MacIntyre, *After Virtue*, 177.

18. Ibid.: "What is distinctive of a practice is in part the way in which conceptions of the relevant goods and ends which the technical skills serve—and every practice does require the exercise of technical skills—are transformed and enriched by these extensions of human powers and by that regard for its own internal goods which are partially definitive of each particular practice or type of practice."

Pope Paul VI affirms that there are standards of excellence when insisting that responsible parenthood rests upon what he calls an intrinsic foundation: "[responsible parenthood] is rooted in the objective moral order established by God.... For which reason, the mission of responsible parenthood requires that spouses recognize their duties toward God, toward themselves, toward the family, and toward human society, as they maintain a correct set of priorities."[19] The objective moral order that Paul VI identifies closely with the virtue of justice provides spouses with a clearly defined measure of [at least moral] competency for the practice of responsible parenthood. But allow me to side-step this delicate matter for the time being, as I will discuss this "standard of excellence" in greater detail below.

What MacIntyre says about "standards of excellence" also offers a marvelous corroboration with Pope Paul VI's claim that "it is not right for spouses to act in accord with their own arbitrary judgment, as if it were permissible for them to define altogether subjectively and willfully what is right for them to do. On the contrary, they must accommodate their behavior to the plan of God the Creator, a plan made manifest both by the very nature of marriage and its acts and also by the constant teaching of the Church." If "responsible parenthood" is a practice according to MacIntyre's definition, it would follow that this activity ought to be evaluated according to those standards of excellence that define this practice. Here Pope Paul VI's appeal to God's plan, the nature of marriage, and the constant teaching of the Church lays out the sources according to which the Christian tradition of marriage defines "excellence" in the practice of responsible parenthood.

This observation raises a key question about any practice, namely, how are we able to identify the goods internal to a practice? MacIntyre states in another well known work that a person acquires the ability to identify these goods by having his or her character formed in the course of learning the practice. In other words, one must be a practitioner in order to judge for oneself what excellence is:

> Just as an apprenticeship in sculpture or architecture is required in order to recognize what excellent performance in these arts consists in . . . so a capacity for identifying and ordering goods of the good of life, the achievement of which involves the ordering of all these other sets of goods, requires a training of character

19. Paul VI, *Humanae vitae*, no. 10 as quoted in full above.

in and into those excellences, a type of training whose point emerges only in the course of training. Learning of this kind, as of other kinds, is what the uneducated, left to themselves, do not and cannot want.[20]

If we take seriously what MacIntyre is saying here, we should appreciate the meaning of Pope Paul VI's claim that, "only an upright conscience can be a true interpreter of this [objective moral] order." What this suggests is that those who have acquired the moral character that indeed develops from having practiced responsible parenthood are able to "recognize better what excellent performance" is in this practice. MacIntyre's point, and mine for that matter, is not intended to be elitist, as if one had to be an artist to appreciate a work of art or, in the practice before us, a married person practicing responsible parenthood in order to recognize excellent parenting, say in a child's good behavior in public. Rather, MacIntyre's point is that one cannot recognize the standard of excellence for *practicing* some art unless one has experience in the practice. Analogously, Paul VI is saying that it is those who have embraced Christian moral living (i.e., an upright conscience) that are best able to judge what the goods of responsible parenthood are and how to achieve them.

However, I believe the necessity of practice indicated above also demonstrates perfectly why the virtue of obedience is so critical to this practice. It is precisely when we conform ourselves to the "objective moral order," which the Christian tradition puts before us as the "standard of excellence" for responsible parenthood, that we are able "through an upright conscience" to identify the goods which the practice of responsible parenthood is to achieve.

The final element of MacIntyre's definition of a *practice* states that the result of entering into a practice successfully is that "human powers to achieve excellence, and human conceptions of the ends and goods involved, are systematically extended." Thus, practices have an intergenerational component to them; they are intrinsically ordered to further developing and passing on excellence and by so doing preserving the goods that are constitutive of the tradition which the practice cultivates. Obviously, the practice of responsible parenthood aims to extend the excellence of marriage and family life as well as the good of the persons that marriage and family life serve. Note, then, how the pope opens

---

20. MacIntyre, *Whose Justice? Which Rationality?* 110. I am grateful to Stanley Hauerwas for citing this text in his recent work, *State of the University*, 116.

the paragraph on responsible parenthood: "[C]onjugal love requires that spouses be fully aware of their *mission* of responsible parenthood. Today's society *calls* for responsible parenthood."[21] The words *mission* and *call* here commission spouses to practice responsible parenthood in such a manner that the excellence of family life and the ends and goods involved be extended. In the Christian sense of this term, to be entrusted with a *mission* is to be "sent out" to build the Kingdom of God in some manner by giving witness to the love of God. The practice of responsible parenthood witnesses to the goods of spousal love and human life, both of which are integral signs of God's love.[22]

PRACTICES AND VIRTUE

By this point, I hope I have sufficiently shown the reader that *Humanae vitae's* understanding of "responsible parenthood" fits quite comfortably into MacIntyre's definition of a practice. We now need to look at a final aspect of MacIntyre's theory of practices: how practices relate to virtue. MacIntyre's approach to virtue ethics is useful because he distills what is common to all understandings of virtue in the history of thought. As he explains toward the climax of the book, "virtue is an acquired human quality the possession and exercise of which tends to enable us to achieve those goods which are internal to practices and the lack of which effectively prevents us from achieving any such goods"[23] In this explanation, we should note how MacIntyre defines virtue as a *quality* associated with the achievement of certain goods internal to a practice. Thus, for example, a warrior society understands the virtue of courage principally within the practice and art of war, while by contrast, a Christian community understands and esteems courage in quite a different way, preeminently in the witness of Christian discipleship and martyrdom.[24]

---

21. Emphasis mine.

22. For the best discussion on the "mission" of a married couple in regard to human life, see Smith, "*Munus* of Transmitting Human Life."

23. MacIntyre, *After Virtue*, 178.

24. An important point of clarification, however, is that MacIntyre avoids a relativistic view of virtue by advocating toward the end of the work for a unifying understanding of the human good, a *telos* of human fulfillment, against which any account of virtue ultimately stands or falls. Nevertheless, he guards earnestly the idea that one's quest for the human good and thus of the virtuous life is inevitably conditioned by and bound up with a moral tradition and one's life in a community (chapter 15).

The important point here is that the achievement of the internal goods of a practice—as defined by a tradition's standard of excellence—is indicative of a person's virtue. Consider what he says in the following passage:

> It belongs to the concept of a practice ... that its goods can only be achieved by subordinating ourselves to the best standards so far achieved. . . . We have to learn to recognize what is due to whom; we have to be prepared to take whatever self-endangering risks are demanded along the way; and we have to listen carefully to what we are told about our own inadequacies and to reply with the same carefulness for the facts. In other words, we have to accept as necessary components of any practice with internal goods and standards of excellence the virtues of justice, courage and honesty.[25]

Stated otherwise, virtues are necessary dispositions that enable us to achieve the internal goods of a practice.

So what are the most important virtues by which a couple can achieve the internal goods of responsible parenthood? *Humane vitae* points to three essential virtues: justice, prudence, and charity. As we have seen already, the document refers to the virtue of justice by reminding spouses of their "duty" toward God, themselves, the family, and society. It is the recognition and fulfillment of what they owe to whom, in fact, that enables spouses to fulfill their *mission* as responsible parents. To God, couples owe their fealty to his law, both natural and divine.[26] To each other, spouses owe their fidelity and exclusivity in the area of conjugal intimacy and the complete sharing of their lives. To the best of their ability, they also owe each other the fruitfulness of their bodies and the mutual gratification that accompanies conjugal love.[27] To the family, spouses owe all that is necessary for the proper development of each person within the family in the fullness of his or her dignity. What this means is that parents are enjoined to provide for each other and their children's physical, practical, psychological, moral, and spiritual needs to the best of their ability. This may also indicate that what is owed to the family is a limit to its size, something to be determined by the prayer-

25. MacIntyre, *After Virtue*, 178.

26. Paul VI, *Humanae vitae*, no. 10–13.

27. Ibid., no. 9. This is what St. Paul means incidentally when he speaks about the right that a man and woman have over each other's bodies (1 Cor 7:3–4).

ful discernment of the spouses. Finally, to society, the spouses owe the fulfillment of all the above obligations. Insofar as the family is the first cell of society, every society is affected deeply by the spouses' ability and right to fulfill their mission of responsible parenthood and to pass this practice on to their children.[28]

Prudence is the second virtue essential to achieving the goods internal to responsible parenthood. In his explanation of the natural inclinations of human nature, Thomas Aquinas reminds us that the human being is inclined not only to the begetting, but also to the *raising* of offspring.[29] According to the Church's teaching on responsible parenthood, this twofold orientation of the procreative inclination provides the basis for not only a couple's obligation to transmit new human life, but also to space out the birth of their children when just reasons require it.[30] As *Humanae vitae* makes explicit, while every act of intercourse must be open *per se* to procreation, not every act of intercourse must result in conception.[31] In other words, in seeking to fulfill the requirements of responsible parenthood, the Church affirms throughout her teachings that a couple should be open to new life but should also give prudent consideration to supplying, from their limited resources as a couple, the necessary provisions that the existing family requires (including the spouses themselves) in order to attain a full and integral human life.[32]

Finally, it should be obvious that the virtue of charity is the most essential virtue for achieving the goods of responsible parenthood. On this matter *Humanae vitae* is quite profound:

> God the Creator wisely and providently established marriage with the intent that He might achieve His own design of love through Men. Therefore, through mutual self giving, which is unique and exclusive to them, spouses seek a communion of

28. Paul VI, *Humanae vitae*, no. 17.

29. *Summa theologiae* I–II, 94.2. *Humanae vitae* refers to this two-fold inclination in par. 8.

30. This, by the way, is another reason that NFP is so crucial to the practice of responsible parenthood. NFP is effective in both the achievement and avoidance of pregnancy and in a manner that conforms to the requirements of justice and prudence which the Christian tradition upholds.

31. Paul VI, *Humanae vitae*, no. 11.

32. In addition to *Humanae vitae*, no. 10 referenced above, see also no. 16; *Gaudium et spes*, no. 50–51; John Paul II, *Familiaris consortio*, no. 28; *Gratissimam sane*, no. 16; *Catechism of the Catholic Church*, no. 2368.

persons. Through this communication, the spouses perfect each other so that they might share with God the task of procreating and educating new living beings.[33]

It is clear from this text that the successful practice of responsible parenthood is motivated above all by charity and that it has its very reason for being from charity. But what exactly does it mean to say that charity is essential to achieving the internal goods of responsible parenthood? In a culture that identifies "love" so closely with self-fulfillment and romantic sentimentalism, it is worthwhile pausing to reflect a moment longer on the sublimity of the Church's teaching about conjugal love.

To help us see how vital charity is to achieving the internal goods of responsible parenthood, let us return briefly to Thomas Aquinas who presents us with an insightful understanding of charity as the right ordering of love within the soul. In what he calls the "order of charity," he provides a useful schematic for how we are to love in charity:

> The order of those four things we have to love out of charity is expressed in Holy Writ. For when we are commanded to love God with our "whole heart," we are given to understand that we must love Him above all things. When we are commanded to love our neighbor "as ourselves," the love of self is set before love of our neighbor. In like manner where we are commanded (1 Jn 3:16) "to lay down our souls," i.e., the life of our bodies, "for the brethren," we are given to understand that a man ought to love his neighbor more than his own body; and again when we are commanded (Gal 6:10) to "work good . . . especially to those who are of the household of the faith," and when a man is blamed (1 Tim 5:8) if he "have not care of his own, and especially of those of his house," it means that we ought to love most those of our neighbors who are more virtuous or more closely united to us.[34]

In short, the right ordering of love in charity emerges as the just response to and affirmation of the intrinsic value of the beloved, and also as the proper sense of responsibility for the beloved.

If we take what Aquinas says about the order of charity to heart, we can assume that achieving the goods internal to the practice of responsible parenthood depends very much upon the integrity of spouses in the right ordering of their love. I use the term *integrity* here to refer to the

---

33. Paul VI, *Humanae vitae*, no. 8.
34. ST II–II, 44.8 ad 2.

requisite order of love spouses need in order to achieve the full measure of their covenantal unity, the begetting and proper development of children, the dignity of women, etc. The point here is that in charity conjugal love is rightly ordered to the goods internal to responsible parenthood, such that we can say charity is the origin of their covenantal unity and the wellspring of their intention to fulfill their mission as responsible parents. To put an even finer point on it, the integrity of the spouses' love in charity is the *animus* of their unity; it is also the fountainhead for not merely their desire to conceive new life, but even more importantly, to realize the proper development of the children they conceive. Spouses are not called merely to be affectionately "close" to each other in their love, but to be in covenant with each other, which is something more fundamental to their relationship to each other and to their children (more below). Nor are they merely passing on biological life to their children, but rather the full integrity of human existence which they are to enjoy as husband and wife in their love for each other. In a lucid passage from his apostolic exhortation, *Familiaris consortio*, Pope John Paul II describes how much responsible parenting is bound up with the right ordering of love:

> The task of giving education is rooted in the primary vocation of married couples to participate in God's creativity: by begetting in love and for love a new person who has within himself or herself the vocation to growth and development, parents by that very fact take on the task of helping that person effectively to live a fully human life. . . . Their role as educators is so decisive that scarcely anything can compensate for their failure in it. For it devolves on parents to create a family atmosphere so animated with love and reverence for God and others that a well-rounded personal and social development will be fostered among the children. Hence, the family is the first school of those social virtues which every society needs. . . . In addition to these characteristics, it cannot be forgotten that the most basic element, so basic that it qualifies the educational role of parents, is parental love, *which finds fulfillment in the task of education as it completes and perfects its service to life: as well as being a source, the parent's love is also the animating principle and therefore the norm inspiring and guiding all concrete educational activity*, enriching it with the values of kindness, constancy, goodness, service, disinterestedness and self sacrifice that are most precious fruits of love.[35]

35. John Paul II, *Familiaris Consortio*, No. 36.

The truth of John Paul II's claim here is most evident when we look at this relationship between the virtue of charity and achieving the goods of responsible parenthood negatively. Today more than ever, we ought to notice how the disintegration of conjugal love so often leads to the tragedy of divorce and the disintegration of children's lives—even their complete annihilation in abortion. We could also say that the total and complete communion that charity realizes for spouses draws from within its own depth the efficacy to bring to fruition the fullness of life which belongs to marriage by nature. It is for these reasons that the virtue of charity is indispensible to achieving the internal goods of responsible parenthood.

Let me now sum up: on the basis of MacIntyre's definition of a practice, I have shown that responsible parenthood is a practice with its own set of internal goods and standards of excellence. Furthermore, I have shown that the standards of excellence for the successful achievement of these internal goods is determined by the moral criterion the Christian tradition sets forth for the practice of responsible parenthood and depends upon the requisite virtues of justice, prudence, and especially charity.[36]

What I will do next is show what the Christian tradition determines to be essential if spouses are to achieve the most fundamental internal good of responsible parenthood, their covenantal unity. In seeing this, my hope is that it will become clear why the use of NFP is integral to the practice of responsible parenthood. As we proceed, it should also be easier (I hope) to grasp why the use of artificial contraception inhibits spouses from achieving the full extent of their covenantal unity.

THE PRACTICE OF RESPONSIBLE PARENTHOOD AND ACHIEVING THE GOOD OF COVENANTAL UNITY

The first internal good of responsible parenthood I mentioned above is the covenantal unity of the spouses. For the remainder of this discussion, I would like to focus principally on this good, especially because it seems

---

36. In the remainder of this paper I am only going to discuss the virtues of justice and charity. I would thus reiterate at this time that the virtue of prudence is indispensible in determining whether a couple should postpone pregnancy—something NFP is indispensible for—and in regard to how the goods of family life are to be identified and ordered.

to figure so prominently in the debates surrounding *Humanae vitae's* teaching on responsible parenthood. I would suggest right off that, of the two ends of marriage, the covenantal unity of the spouses is more fundamental than the transmission and education of human life. The latter good proceeds as the *fruit* of covenantal unity. It is true that magisterial teaching assigns a primacy to the procreative end of marriage, but let us not be mistaken about what this means.[37] I have found that a helpful way to think about the primacy of ends within marriage is in terms of the common goods in which the spouses participate by means of their love.

The covenantal unity of the spouses is an *intrinsic* common good; that is, a good common to both spouses that we can describe as the *intrinsic* ordering of their relationship as husband and wife in charity, as we saw above.[38] The transmission and education of human life is the *extrinsic* common good to which this covenantal unity is naturally ordered, as to its fruit. Pope John Paul II expresses this with some noticeable sublimity:

> The words of consent define the common good of the couple and of the family. First, the common good of the spouses: love, fidelity, honor, the permanence of their union until death—"all the days of my life." The good of both, which is at the same time the good of each, must become the good of the children. The common good, by its very nature, both unites individual persons and ensures the true good of each. . . . In the newborn child is realized the common good of the family. Just as the common good of spouses is fulfilled in conjugal love, ever ready to give and receive new life, so too the common good of the family is fulfilled through the same spousal love, as embodied in the newborn child.[39]

37. *Gaudium et spes*, no. 50: "Marriage and married love are by nature ordered to the procreation and education of children. Indeed, children are the supreme gift of marriage and greatly contribute to the good of the parents' themselves."

38. This use of *intrinsic* here is not to be confused with the word *internal* as in the internal goods of the practice of responsible parenthood, even though they are related as we shall see.

39. John Paul II, *Gratissimam*, no 10–11. The *Catechism of the Catholic Church*, no 2366, also expresses this truth by saying that, "Fecundity is a gift, an *end of marriage*, for conjugal love naturally tends to be fruitful. A child does not come from outside as something added on to the mutual love of the spouses, but springs from the very heart of that mutual giving, as its fruit and fulfillment."

The common good of covenantal unity is fulfilled or completed, we might say, in the husband and wife becoming one flesh in their mutual consent to become parents together, a point I will explain more fully below.

Hence, insofar as it is the order of things that new life ought to proceed from the covenantal unity of spouses, there is a primacy to the covenantal unity of spouses. Yet because this covenantal unity achieves its complete fulfillment in new human life, in this way, the procreative end enjoys primacy as well, but in a different manner. The two common goods here are bound up with each other as well, for only in the full unity of covenantal love does a child have a chance of achieving his or her full human potential; and to the extent to which the unity of covenantal love disintegrates, so too do we see the child experience unnecessary and often tragic difficulties in their life.[40] Thus, it seems fitting to focus principally upon the covenantal unity of the spouses, since the good of human life in all its dimensions depends foremost upon this unity.

In reflecting upon covenantal unity as the most fundamental internal good of responsible parenthood, one might think of this unity mostly in terms of the closeness spouses experience when giving themselves to each other in marriage, especially through the marital act. Indeed, it is easy to suppose that covenantal unity refers merely to the emotional bond which both forms and is sustained by marital intimacy. It is this more psychological view is sometimes equated with the notion of the communion of persons through the gift of self that originates in Christian Personalism, especially Pope John Paul II's theology of the body.[41] While bonds of affection and a sense of closeness are certainly vital aspects of covenantal unity, I would suggest this is not the primary sense of this unity as the Christian tradition understands it. More specifically, for a proper understanding of unity as a good *internal* to the practice of responsible parenthood, we need to look at the Christian tradition of marriage and where it originates. It is this tradition that puts before us those "standards of excellence" by which we can determine how and if this good is achieved or not.

---

40. John Paul II, *Gratissimam*, no 10. "The question about children and their education is profoundly linked to marital consent, with its solemn promise of love, conjugal respect, and fidelity until death. The acceptance and education of children—two of the primary ends of the family—are conditioned by how that commitment will be fulfilled."

41. John Paul II, *Theology of the Body*.

Up to this point I have assumed that in the Christian tradition marriage is a covenantal relationship between two persons; but what does this mean exactly? To understand the essence of covenantal unity, it is helpful to have a clear grasp of what a *covenant* is.[42] Part of the difficulty today is that we are predisposed to understanding marital unity according to a narrative tradition inherited from a culture of individualism that couches the unitive dimension of marriage first and foremost in terms of personal fulfillment. In this context, we might understand a covenant to be no more than a legal contract situated culturally within a religious setting. But as such, the covenantal significance of marital unity loses the inner meaning which the Christian tradition of covenant making assigns it.

In the biblical tradition a covenant establishes a familial bond of kinship between two consenting parties who are otherwise not related to each other. A covenant is established by the swearing of an oath before God as witness and binds the parties to certain *familial* rights and obligations as indicated in the oath sworn. As the biblical scholar Frank Moore Cross explains, a covenant "is . . . a widespread legal means by which duties and privileges of kinship may be extended to another individual or group, including aliens."[43] Biblical covenants were also established by oath signs like "non-imprecatory speech acts or other rituals," such as sacrifice.[44]

To grasp better the ritual form of covenant making in the Judeo-Christian tradition, let us look at one of the clearest illustrations. At Mount Sinai, God entered into a covenant with the people of Israel with this oath, "Now therefore, if you will obey my voice and keep my covenant, you shall be my own possession among all peoples . . . and you shall be to me a kingdom of priests and a holy nation" (Ex 19:5).[45] Israel responded to God by swearing an oath to follow God's commandments: "And the people answered together and said, 'All the words which the Lord has spoken we will do'" (Ex 19:8). This covenant was then consummated by a ritual sacrifice and the sprinkling of sac-

42. For the most recent and comprehensive study on covenant theology, see Hahn, *Kinship by Covenant*.

43. Cross, "Kinship and Covenant in Ancient Israel," 8. Also Hahn, "Covenant in the Old and New Testaments," 264.

44. Hahn, "Covenant in the Old and New Testaments," 266.

45. Biblical quotations are from the RSV.

rificial blood upon the people: The text states, "And Moses took the blood and threw it upon the people, and said, 'Behold the blood of the covenant which the Lord has made with you in accordance with all these words'" (Deut 24:8). The significance of blood sprinkling here as a symbolic oath act of covenant ratification is that the blood represents the familial bond that now exists between God and Israel in virtue of the covenant. The two parties now become one flesh, as it were; they are kinsfolk as symbolized by the blood. In the new covenant that Christ established, we see that he brought about the fulfillment of the covenant kinship between God and humanity by the paschal mystery of his flesh and blood sacrifice, making us his bride and brothers and sisters to each other (Hebrews 8; Ephesians 5).[46]

The biblical tradition of covenant making is relevant because marriage is the first covenant described in scripture and the paradigm for all subsequent covenants.[47] According to the narrative tradition captured in Genesis, the first man and woman are joined together as husband and wife (spousal kin) to become one flesh (Gen 2:24). Indeed, the marriage covenant was understood to be the primordial covenant of the natural order and, as with all covenant making, it established a special type of kinship by means of a speech act (oath swearing) and a performative act, both of which are represented by the symbol of blood. Referencing the work of Gordon Paul Hugenberger, Scott Hahn states that, "In the case of marriage, solemn declarations (*verba solemnia*) and sexual union [a non-imprecatory 'oath sign'] were acts of covenant ratification."[48]

Between Adam and Eve, the text of Genesis indicates this ratification in a partial way by Adam's exclamation, "This at last is bone of my

46. John Paul II, *Gratissimam*, no. 19: "The confirmation and *fulfillment* of the spousal relationship between God and his people are realized in Christ, in the New Covenant. Christ assures us that the Bridegroom is with us (cf. Mt. 9:15). He is with all of us; he is with the Church. The Church becomes a Bride, the Bride of Christ. This Bride . . . is present in each of the baptized and is like one who presents herself before her Bridegroom. 'Christ loved the Church and gave himself up for her . . . , that he might present the Church to himself in splendor . . .'"

47. See Dell, "Covenant and Creation." See also what John Paul II says in *Gratissimam sane*, no. 7: "The family, as a community of persons, is thus the first human 'society.' It arises whenever there comes into being the conjugal covenant of marriage, which opens the spouses to a lasting communion of love and of life, and it is brought to completion in a full and specific way with the procreation of children: the "communion of the spouses gives rise to the "community" of the family."

48. Hahn, "Covenant in the Old and New Testaments," 266 [brackets are mine].

bones and flesh of my flesh" (Gen 2:23), which would imply a covenant speech act (an oath), as suggested by the conclusion to Adam's proclamation: "Therefore, a man leaves his father and mother and clings to his wife, and they become one flesh" (Gen 3:24). The covenant ratification is also implied when the text tells us that Adam "knew his wife and she conceived and bore Cain" (Gen 4:1), the act wherein their becoming one flesh is consummated. Although it is not explicit in the text of Genesis, the symbol of blood is also present in the consummation of this primordial covenant of nature by the flow of blood that issues from the woman with the first experience of intercourse and also by the flow of blood at the birth of the child.

The initial insight this give us is that, by its natural and primordial structure, the covenantal unity of marriage is created by 1) the sworn oath of the man and woman by which they freely consent to belong entirely to each other as spousal partners, 2) the union of their bodies in the marital act, which consummates this particular form of total self-giving, and 3) the sacrificial blood that symbolizes the "one-fleshness" the spouses now enjoy in virtue of their covenant. Pope John Paul II expresses this ritual form of the marriage covenant in personalist terms and more eloquently in the following text:

> By its very nature the gift of the person must be lasting and irrevocable. The indissolubility of marriage flows in the first place from the very essence of that gift: the gift of one person to another person. This reciprocal giving of self reveals the spousal nature of love. In their marital consent the bride and groom call each other by name: "I . . . take you . . . as my wife (as my husband) and I promise to be true to you . . . for all the days of my life." A gift such as this involves an obligation much more serious and profound than anything which might be "purchased" in any way and at any price. Kneeling before the Father, from whom all fatherhood and motherhood come, the future parents come to realize that they have been "redeemed." They have been purchased at great cost, by the price of the most sincere gift of all, the blood of Christ of which they partake through the Sacrament. The liturgical crowning of the marriage rite is the Eucharist, the sacrifice of that "Body which has been given up" and that "Blood which has been shed," which in a certain way finds expression in the consent of the spouses.[49]

49 John Paul II, *Gratissimam sane*, No. 11. He goes on to state, "When a man and woman in marriage give and receive each other in the unity of 'one flesh', the logic of the

As a way to bring into clearer focus the implication of how marriage covenants are established within the Christian tradition, it is helpful to observe what is often overlooked in the narrative of Genesis—Adam and Eve were kin to each other prior to this covenant, but in a different way. Presumably, they were son and daughter to the Father and thus brother and sister to each other. Yet something new is realized in their marriage covenant—a unity that was not present until they gave themselves to each other specifically through the oath and act proper to marriage. From then on they were husband and wife—i.e., covenantally united in the common consent to transmit human life in cooperation with the Creator, which is an activity that being merely brother and sister does not commission a man and woman do. But Adam and Eve were no longer meant to be merely brother and sister as God's command to be fruitful and multiply suggests.[50]

Now that we have considered the biblical roots of the tradition, let us turn briefly to the Church's legal tradition and consider what the *Code of Canon Law* says about the ritual form of the marriage covenant.[51] I would suggest that only in light of the biblical tradition are we able to understand fully the meaning of the following canons:

> (1057) Marriage is brought about through consent of the parties, legitimately manifested between persons who are capable according to law of giving consent; no human power can replace this consent. Matrimonial consent is an act of the will by which a man and a woman, through an irrevocable covenant, mutually give and accept each other in order to establish marriage. (1061) A valid marriage between baptized persons is called ratified only

sincere gift of self becomes part of their life. Without this, marriage would be empty; whereas a communion of persons, built on this logic, becomes a communion of parents. When they transmit life to the child, a new human 'thou' becomes part of the horizon of the 'we' of the spouses, a person whom they will call by a new name: 'our son ...; our daughter ...' 'I have gotten a man with the help of the Lord' (Gen. 4:1), says Eve."

50. John Paul II alludes to this in *Gratissimam sane*, no. 8, when he states: "The Book of Genesis, in speaking of a man who leaves father and mother in order to cleave to his wife (cf. Gen. 2:24), highlights the conscious and free choice which gives rise to marriage, making the son of a family a husband, and the daughter of a family a wife." He goes on to state, "When the Church asks 'Are you willing?', she is reminding the bride and groom that they stand before the creative power off God. They are called to become parents, to cooperate with the creator in giving life. Cooperating with God to call new human beings into existence means contributing to the transmission of that divine image and likeness which everyone 'born of a woman' is bearer."

51. Coriden, *Code of Canon Law*.

if it has not been consummated; it is called ratified and consummated if the parties have performed between themselves in a human manner the conjugal act which is per se suitable for the generation of children, to which marriage is ordered by its very nature and by which the spouses become one flesh.

The first canon concerns the speech act that ratifies the covenant; the second one concerns the performative act that consummates the covenant. We should now be able to see clearly the correlation between *Canon Law's* definition of the marriage covenant and the biblical tradition of covenant kinship. Although I have assumed this all along, I would further suggest that every subsequent conjugal act throughout the course of marriage has the same covenantal meaning. Every conjugal act is a commemorative act for the spouses, in which their covenantal unity is renewed and memorialized.[52]

So where does this get us if we seek to better understand how to achieve the good of covenantal unity from the perspective of those "standards of excellence" by which the Christian tradition measures the successful practice of responsible parenthood? Contrary to what might be a more popular take on the unitive dimension of marriage, the Christian tradition holds up covenantal unity primarily as a good that is achieved by a very specific form of self-giving in which spouses embody by means of the conjugal act their consent to be lifelong partners in the transmission and education of human life. What this means, I would suggest, is that the unitive and the procreative goods of marriage are not like two links of a chain that may or may not be severed. Rather, they are flip sides of the same covenantal reality.

In effect, the full measure of covenantal unity is realized when a man and woman declare verbally and bodily to each other, "I give myself to you in *this* way, that I might become father or mother to your children." This is the ultimate reason why the Church maintains that these two aspects of conjugal love cannot be separated. The Church is not implying merely that a couple *may not* separate these two goods, but rather that these goods cannot be severed because they are, in truth, one reality. The opposite of this, of course, would be for a man and a woman to seek in the other, not a partner in the transmission and education of human life, but an object of sexual gratification, as in the acts of

---

52. This is true in the same way that celebrating the Eucharist is a memorial of the Lord's death and thereby a renewal of the New Covenant.

fornication and adultery. This kind of "giving oneself over to the other" is not ontologically spousal (or covenantally unifying) in nature—even if sexually gratifying—because it seeks only mutual self-gratification. To put this briefly into a virtue perspective, such love is not charitable or just, but intemperate and concupiscible.[53]

This truth about the unitive dimension of the marriage covenant, however, might be more palatable if we consider marriage in its sacramental dimension. We learn from Paul's letter to the Ephesians, chapter 5, that the marriage covenant signifies the great mystery of Christ's union with the Church. Paul tells us that this sacramental signification is especially evident in the way spouses are to be "subject" to one another. Wives are to be under the mission of (or submissive to) their husbands in all things *as to the Lord*, while husbands are to love their wives as their own bodies, *as Christ loved the Church*. These words echo back to Adam's words, "at last bone of my bone . . ." Paul goes on to state: "He who loves his wife loves himself. For no man ever hates his own flesh, but nourishes and cherishes it, *as Christ does the Church* [e.g., eucharistically] . . . . 'For

---

53. In this regard, it is interesting to observe the growing trend and cultural acceptance of cohabitation as a legitimate form of sexual unity. The legal significance of "free unions" has to do primarily with money, property, insurance or other such things, and not with an indissoluble bond of kinship that exists as a partnership for the mission of transmitting and educating human life. It would seem that the more our culture views sexual partnership in terms of mutual self-gratification the less people see a need to be "married." I would suggest, however, that the underlying factor in the culture of cohabitation, especially in its lack of permanence, is the various personal risks that naturally accompany this view of sexual partnership. And thus this trend of avoiding marriage reveals how much marriage as an institution is actually bound up with the successful practice of responsible parenthood. Generally speaking, if in coming together sexually a couple is not expressing their will to be spouses to each other in the act of intercourse (i.e. to at least potentially fulfill the mission of parenthood) there seems little need to acknowledge their union as having any covenantal meaning. Quite frankly, in this kind of culture the risk of abandonment by the other is too great—so why have children? But this is to put the cart before the horse; *self fulfillment is not the reason to get married, but what results when one does so for the right reason.* The pervasiveness of divorce in our culture is indicative of the same problem; it is much easier for a couple to part ways in disappointment when the primary motive for coming together in the first place is mutual self-gratification. In saying all of this, however, in no way am I trying to diminish the vital importance of self-fulfillment and personal happiness within marriage. The difference, however, is that in the Christian tradition of marriage self-fulfillment and personal happiness are the fruits of a very particular form of self-giving proper to people joined together covenantally as spouses. The practice of responsible parenthood, therefore, cultivates the kind of self-giving that leads to authentic self-fulfillment and marital bliss.

this reason a man shall leave his father and mother and be joined to his wife, and the two shall become one flesh'" (Eph 5:28–32). By such admonitions, Paul clearly has conjugal love in mind. What he seems to be driving at is that, from a Christian perspective, the exemplar of conjugal love is the love of Christ, a love that in its complete self-giving is fruitful and life-giving.

The implication here is that for a man and woman to love one another spousally, by giving themselves to each other in a manner that actually makes them one flesh, they not only become a sign of but they actually participate in the great mystery of Christ's covenantal union with his Bride, the Church. Pope John Paul II explains this in a passage from his Wednesday catecheses:

> This invitation, which the Apostle addresses to Christian spouses, has its full motivation inasmuch as, through marriage as a sacrament, they participate in the salvific love of Christ, which at the same time expresses itself as his spousal love for the Church. In the light of Ephesians—precisely *through participation in this salvific love of Christ—marriage is confirmed and simultaneously renewed as the sacrament of the human "beginning,"* that is, as the sacrament in which man and woman, called to become "one flesh," share in the creative love of God himself. They share in it both by the fact that, created in the image of God, they have been called in virtue of the image to a particular union (*communion personarum*, the communion of persons), and because this union has itself been blessed from the beginning with the blessing of fruitfulness (see Gen. 1:28)[54]

I would infer from this passage and from Paul that it is in the light of the great mystery of Christ's covenantal union with the Church—which is established by his sacrificial gift of self on the cross—that we are able to grasp why the practice of responsible parenthood is so critical for achieving covenantal unity.

Let us consider this more closely. While this may sound restrictive initially, I would suggest that to achieve the full measure of covenantal unity spouses must consent to give each other their distinct biological genealogies in the marital act, even if biological realities such as natural infertility or old age prevent conception from occurring.[55] It is this gift

54. John Paul II, *Theology of the Body*, Catechesis 102.2 (emphasis is the pope's).

55. By the qualifier *full measure* I am referring to a completeness of covenantal unity. From what we have already discussed, consent alone brings a man and women

which is distinctively *spousal* in nature. In other words, to be "one flesh" with each other, it is decisive for each spouse to hand over to the other—as a supreme gift of self—his or her generative power, fertility, blood line, and so forth. This very "embodied" intention to give oneself to the other is what makes the conjugal act consummatory or memorializing of the spousal kinship the man and woman have established by their verbal consent.[56] To put this in terms of the practice of responsible parenthood, it is this particular gift of self in charity—unique to the marriage covenant—that enables the spouses' to achieve the full measure of their covenantal unity. Consider this text from John Paul II, which I believe makes the same point:

> In particular, responsible fatherhood and motherhood directly concern the moment in which a man and woman, uniting themselves in one flesh, can become parents. This is a moment of special value both for their interpersonal relationship and for their service to life: they can become parents—father and mother—by communicating life to a new human being. The two dimensions of conjugal union cannot be artificially separated without damaging the deepest truth of the conjugal act itself.[57]

The important condition for achieving the full measure of covenantal unity, however, is not that a new life is actually conceived by this act, or even that the spouses intend to conceive, but that the act is performed precisely *as* a consummation or commemoration of (i.e., a complete actualization of) their *spousal* covenant—i.e., their commitment to be cooperators with God in the transmission and education of human life. This is why the "consenting" acts of fornication or adultery do not express spousal kinship between a man and a woman, even if a child is conceived by the act. Covenant consummation and renewal requires

---

into covenantal unity. Nevertheless, the conjugal act consummates or brings to its full measure the covenantal unity that the spouses share in virtue of their vows.

56. I do not mean to suggest here that the physical dimension of conjugal love exhausts the meaning of the conjugal act. The conjugal act is a sign that expresses the will of the spouses to fulfill the vows they have sworn to share the whole of life together as husband and wife, and all that this entails. Yet it is precisely the gift of themselves in the mingling of their fertility that gives the vows sworn some real teeth. This act expresses their commitment to the mission of parenthood, if the act brings forth a new life. But this also implies that simply "doing the deed" is insufficient if in "doing it" a couple also negates their generative potential. I'll discuss what this means momentarily.

57. John Paul II, *Gratissimam sane*, no. 12.

that the spouses perform the conjugal act in such manner that their gift to each other expresses their actual intention to be *spouses* in the sharing of their whole lives with each other for the sake of this sacred mission. The symbol of blood here is indispensible because it represents the fusion of their two genealogies into a potentially new genealogy.

But let us now put this into what is perhaps a more familiar terminology. What we have been considering thus far about covenant consummation and renewal suggests that for a marriage covenant to be fully consummated or commemorated the conjugal act must be "ordered *per se* [through itself] to the procreation of human life."[58] Likewise, in the theological view presented here, this may also help us grasp why *Canon Law* declares the marriage covenant consummated only "*if* the parties have performed between themselves in a human manner the conjugal act *which is per se suitable for the generation of children . . .*"[59] If read in light of the biblical tradition of covenant making this statement would seem to suggest that any manner of performing the marital act that includes the decision by one or both spouses to directly cause one's own infertility would result in a failure to achieve the full measure of covenantal unity the act is supposed to express.

But the question that remains is what exactly makes a conjugal act "ordered *per se*" to procreation? Although I have just hinted at it, in all honesty, I find this to be the most difficult aspect of the Church's teaching on the practice of responsible parenthood to grasp conceptually, especially when a couple may decide to avoid pregnancy by means of practicing NFP. What is the real difference between the practice of NFP and the use of artificial contraception? Since the promulgation of *Humanae vitae*, moral theologians have given several (often) philosophical answers to this question. It is my hope that the difference between them will be made clearer by comparing these two practices in the light of what we have discussed above about covenant making and renewal in the Christian tradition of marriage.

---

58. See Paul VI, *Humanae vitae*, no. 11.

59. I state this as a theological opinion—but one with substantial support I believe—*only* because the commentary on this canon states that it is a "theological issue" whether contraception "impedes the sexual act as an effective sign of the complete gift of one spouse to the other." Coriden, *Code of Canon Law*, 745. However, the gloss should not be taken to mean that contraception is thus morally licit.

THE USE OF ARTIFICIAL CONTRACEPTION
AND THE PRACTICE OF NFP

Returning to *Humanae vitae's* teaching on responsible parenthood, Pope Paul VI describes a contraceptive act as an act whereby "spouses impede the order of generation from completing its own natural processes."[60] What is essential to the pope's description of a contraceptive act, it seems, is the *decision* to impede the natural processes of generation. If we interpret this statement in the light of what we now know about the biblical tradition of covenant making and renewal, we can see that the practice of responsible parenthood necessitates the man and woman's *consent* to give themselves to each other in a very specific way, as spouses, even if nature itself has rendered the couple infertile. The point here is not that spouses are forbidden to avoid pregnancy, but that the decision to make oneself infertile in doing so prevents the act of intercourse from being fully a covenantally unifying act. In this covenantal perspective, we should recognize that a deliberately contraceptive act of intercourse is a logical contradiction insofar as spouses declare their consent to refuse to each other the very gift that expresses their covenantal union. In the practice of responsible parenthood, this form of self-giving is a vital "standard of excellence" which the Christian tradition holds up as a criteria for successfully achieving the full measure of the good of covenantal unity. It is not the biological dimension alone that counts but the intention to love the other in *this* way. And I would also add that this is an essential gift of self which the virtues of justice and charity enable a couple to give each other.

If we now compare the use of artificial contraception to the practice of NFP, hopefully we can see the difference between them more clearly. When a couple practices NFP to avoid pregnancy—and for just reasons only—they are not acting so as to impede the order of generation from "completing its own natural processes." But how is this so? To put it in the most simple way I can imagine, the practice of NFP does not involve a decision to render either spouse infertile. When spouses perform the marital act during a naturally infertile time, the cause of infertility is the woman's own biological processes, as would be the case with an elderly woman. Or we might say that the self-gift of one's fertility in the act of intercourse is not withheld by a free decision *within* the act

---

60. *Humanae vitae*, no. 16.

of intercourse itself. And so, if spouses abstain during naturally fertile times, the spouses are still participating by their embodied consent in the order of generation and thereby consummating or commemorating their covenant. From this point of view, let us consider what Richard J. Fehring and William Kurz, S.J., say in their article on the anthropological differences between contraception and NFP:

> A broader definition of natural family planning includes what is often referred to as the NFP lifestyle, a lifestyle in which men and women learn to live with, understand, and appreciate their fertility. Fertility is fully integrated into their relationship and a way of living. This integration of fertility is what provides NFP with its holistic nature. One key to NFP is that it values the integral meaning of sexual intercourse between a man and woman. NFP allows the sexual act to retain its integrity, in that its procreative nature (i.e., the natural fertile potential of the act) remains, along with its unitive or bonding nature. With NFP nothing is done to interfere with fertility or with the reproductive system, an integrated biological organism that is vital for the propagation of humankind. . . . Contraception, which is often referred to as birth control, is the prevention of the fertilization of the ovum. Contraception works either by suppressing, blocking, or destroying fertility. Unlike natural family planning, which works by understanding and monitoring the reproductive system, contraception (by its very name) takes action against conception and the human reproductive system.[61]

It is the differences described here that help us to understand how the practice of NFP allows the conjugal act to remain *per se* [through itself] ordered to procreation, even if spouses do not consent to conceive at this or that time. What this means covenantally is that the conjugal act within the practice of NFP retains its character as a complete giving of self that consummates or renews the marriage covenant. Indeed, because of how a couple in giving themselves to each other so completely regard and treat their fertility as a good to be shared, they are still expressing fully their covenantal unity. Perhaps this is why the Church calls this practice *responsible* parenthood.

But, admittedly, this is difficult to embrace today; and so it may be a good time to remind us what MacIntyre says about participation in a practice: "To enter into a practice is to accept the authority of those stan-

---

61. See Fehring and Kurz, "Anthropological Differences," 239–40.

dards and the inadequacy of my own performance as judged by them. It is to subject my own attitudes, choices, preferences and tastes to the standards which currently and partially define the practice." The conjugal act is ensconced within the tradition of marriage covenant making and renewal; and this tradition is not subject to the spouses' authority as parties to the covenant.[62] In fact, these conditions are inscribed already into the nature of what the marriage covenant is ontologically and the form of how marriage covenants are made and commemorated.

To bring this reflection to a consideration of virtue, allow me to say a word or two about justice and charity in regard to the practice of responsible parenthood and NFP. In terms of what spouses owe in justice to God, to each other, to their children, and to society, it is easy to see how justice and charity relate to each other within the context of the marriage covenant. If we were to ask, what specifically do spouses "owe" all these parties, we would discover that what they owe is their total gift of self in a specifically *spousal* way. Ironically, the virtue of justice in marriage is realized by means of a conjugal love that is ordered by charity, that is, by the complete gift of self proper to spouses and which results in that "communion of persons" Scripture refers to as becoming "one flesh." It should be no surprise, then, that couples who lack these virtues will quite naturally find themselves in a compromised state of affairs as evident in the tragedy of divorce. Here I should point out that spouses who faithfully "practice" NFP have significantly lower rates of divorce (under 5 percent) and greater marital satisfaction than those who use contraception.[63] This would suggest that those who faithfully embrace

62. See what Pius XI says in *Casti conubii*, no. 6: "This freedom, however, regards only the question whether the contracting parties really wish to enter upon matrimony or to marry this particular person; but the nature of matrimony is entirely independent of the free will of man, so that if one has once contracted matrimony he is thereby subject to its divinely made laws and its essential properties." And again in *Gaudium et spes*, no. 48: "The intimate partnership of life and the love which constitutes the married state has been established by the creator and endowed by him with its own proper laws. . . . For God himself is the author of marriage and has endowed it with various benefits and with various ends in view. . . . By its very nature the institution of marriage and married love is ordered to the procreation and education of offspring and it is in them that it finds its crowning glory. Thus the man and woman who 'are no longer two but one' (Mt 19:6), help and serve each other by their marriage partnership; they become conscious of their unity and experience it more deeply from day to day. The intimate union of marriage, as a mutual giving of two persons, and the good of children demand total fidelity from the spouses and require an unbreakable unity between them."

63. Fehring and Kurz, "Anthropological Differences," 245–57; Wilson, "Practice of

the practice of responsible parenthood possess those qualities (i.e., the virtues of this practice) that allow them to achieve the internal goods of the practice, the most fundamental being their covenantal unity. Because the practice of NFP respects the covenantal structure of marriage, it follows that the spouses that practice it achieve greater communion.

To conclude this comparison between the practice of NFP and the use of artificial contraception I have proposed that we best understand the unitive dimension of conjugal love within the biblical tradition of covenant making and renewal. Because the consummation and renewal of the marriage covenant requires the couples' consent to give themselves to each other in a specifically spousal manner, such that each act of intercourse remain *per se* ordered to procreation, a deliberately contraceptive act of intercourse prevents a couple from achieving the full measure of their covenantal unity. Contrary to this, NFP functions such that spouses can postpone pregnancy in a way that respects the covenantal character of the conjugal act. The covenantal integrity of NFP also works to the benefit of the spouses union in charity and justice such that they are able to enjoy more fully the communion of persons which the marriage covenant realizes. We could even say that, because of how NFP respects the gift of fertility, it is an indispensable technique, the mastery of which enables spouses to practice responsible parenthood successfully.

With all that has been said in this essay—and there has been much said—I would like to attempt a final and simple conclusion, namely, that to comprehend *Humanae vitae's* teaching on responsible parenthood, it is helpful to understand responsible parenthood as a *practice* within the biblical tradition of marriage covenant making, a tradition that presents us with certain standards of excellence that determine the measure of success for this most sacred practice. Here we can see that the practice of NFP honors the ritual form of covenant making and renewal, while the use of artificial contraception does not. Moreover, the virtues of justice and charity enable a couple to act so as to achieve covenantal unity precisely because they dispose the spouses to express their conjugal love to each other in a manner that fully embodies the oaths they have sworn to each other as husband and wife.

Natural Family Planning." For a study that does not arrive at conclusive evidence, see Edgar and Daughtry, "Marital Satisfaction." Admittedly, more studies would need to be done on this in order to garner the kind of empirical data that would prove this beyond a shadow of a doubt.

BIBLIOGRAPHY

BBC News "Natural Contraception 'Effective,'" (February 21, 2007). Online: http://news .bbc.co.uk/2/hi/health/6375261.stm.

Billings, Evelyn, and A. Westmore. *The Billings Method: Controlling Fertility without Drugs or Devices.* Niagara Falls, NY: Life Cycle, 2000.

Coriden, James A., et al., editors. *The Code of Canon Law: A Text and Commentary.* New York: Paulist, 1985.

Cross, Frank Moore. "Kinship and Covenant in Ancient Israel." In *From Epic to Canon: History and Literature in Ancient Israel,* 3–21. Baltimore: The John Hopkins University Press, 1998.

Dell, Katherine J. "Covenant and Creation in Relationship." In *Covenant as Context: Essays in Honour of E.W. Nicholson,* edited by A. D. H Mayes and R. B. Salters, 111–34. Oxford: Oxford University Press, 2003.

Ecochard, R., et al. "Analysis of Natural Family Planning Failures: In 7007 Cycles of Use." *Fertilite Contraception Sexualite* 26 (1998) 291–96.

Edgar, Marta, and Donald Daughtry. "Marital Satisfaction and Family Planning Practices." Ann Arbor, MI: University Microfilms, a paper delivered at the American Psychological Association, August 18–21, 2005.

Fehring, Richard J., and Willliam Kurz, S.J. "Anthropological Differences between Contraception and Natural Family Planning." *Life and Learning X: Proceedings of the Tenth University Faculty for Life Conference,* 239–57. Washington DC: University Faculty for Life, 2000.

Frank-Herrmann, P., et al. "The effectiveness of a Fertility Awareness Based Method to Avoid Pregnancy in Relation to a Couple's Sexual Behaviour during the Fertile Time: A Prospective Longitudinal Study," *Human Reproduction* 22 (2007) 1310–19.

Grisez, Germain, et al. "Every Marital Act Ought to Be Open to New Life: Toward a Clearer Understanding." *The Thomist* 52 (1988) 365–426.

Hahn, Scott. "Covenant in the Old and New Testaments: Some Current Research (1994-2004)." *Currents in Biblical Research* 3 (2005) 263–92.

Scott Hahn, *Kinship by Covenant: A Covenantal Approach to the Fulfillment of God's Saving Promises.* New Haven: Yale University Press, 2009.

Hauerwas, Stanley. *The State of the University: Academic Knowledges and the Knowledge of God.* Oxford: Blackwell, 2007.

Hilgers, Thomas W. *The Medical and Surgical Practice of NaPro Technology.* Omaha: Pope Paul VI Institute, 2004.

Hilgers, T. W., and J. B. Stanford. "Creighton Model NaProEducation Technology for Avoiding Pregnancy: Use effectiveness." *Journal of Reproductive Medicine* 43 (1998) 495–502.

Howard, M. P., and J. B. Stanford. "Pregnancy Probabilities During Use of the Creighton Model Fertility Care System." *Archives of Family Medicine* 8 (1999) 391–402.

John Paul II, Pope. *Familiaris consortio* (The Role of the Christian Family in the Modern World) (1981).

———. *Gratissimam Sane* (Letter to Families)(1994).

———. *Man and Woman He Created Them: A Theology of the Body,* trans. Michael Waldstein. Boston: Pauline, 2006.

Kippley, Sheila. *Breastfeeding and Catholic Motherhood: God's Plan for You and Your Baby.* Manchester, NH: Sophia Institute, 2005.

———. *Breastfeeding and Natural Child Spacing.* Raleigh, NC: Lulu, 2008.

————. *The Seven Standards of Ecological Breastfeeding: The Frequency Factor.* Raleigh, NC: Lulu, 2008.

Kippley, John and Sheila. *The Art of Natural Family Planning Student Guide.* Cincinnati: Couple to Couple League International, 2007.

MacIntyre, Alasdair. *After Virtue: A Study in Moral Theory.* Notre Dame, IN: University of Notre Dame Press, 1981.

————. *Whose Justice? Which Rationality?* Notre Dame, IN: University of Notre Dame Press, 1988.

May, William. "Contraception, Gateway to the Culture of Death." *Faith* 33:4 (2001) 7–15.

Paul VI, Pope. *Humanae vitae* (1968). Translated by Janet E. Smith. New Hope, KY: New Hope.

Quay, Paul. "Contraception and Marital Love." *Theological Studies* 22 (1961) 18–40.

Smith, Janet. "The *Munus* of Transmitting Human Life: A New Approach to *Humanae Vitae.*" *The Thomist* 54 (1990) 385–427.

Smith, Janet, editor. *Why Humanae Vitae Was Right: A Reader.* San Francisco: Ignatius, 1993.

Wilson, Mercedes Arzú. "The Practice of Natural Family Planning versus the Use of Artificial Birth Control: Family, Sexual and Moral Issues." *The Catholic Social Science Review* 7 (2002) 1–30.

9

Bodies Poured Out in Christ:
Marriage Beyond the Theology of the Body

DAVID CLOUTIER & WILLIAM C. MATTISON III

THE INCARNATION, THE WORD of God become flesh, is at the center of Christianity. Though there are many theologies of the incarnation, all agree that the Incarnation is the first and last reason to reject all versions of Christianity that are "Gnostic" or "dualist"—that is, which refuse to identify the real presence of the living God in material creation. The Gnostic temptation has, according to many thinkers over the last centuries, particularly infected Catholic sexual ethics. In response to this, all recent Catholic moral theology has moved in what can be called a "more positive" direction, more fully emphasizing the goodness of sexuality and the body in general.

But how positive? Ecstatic? Transcendent? Glorious? Perhaps. We might ask: toward what end does the incarnation press? Of course, the ultimate promise contained in the incarnation is that of the resurrection of the body. The glorified body of Christ appears only once in the Gospels before his death: in the story of the Transfiguration. In that story, Jesus is depicted conversing with Moses and Elijah, who represent the law and the prophets of Israel, a tradition of which Jesus is the culmination.[1] In this essay, we use the story of the transfiguration to make two arguments. First, we suggest that in rightly praising the positive potential of the human body, some Catholic sexual ethics fails to provide the kind of prophetic challenge to ordinary life represented by Moses

1. See, for instance Johnson, *Gospel of Luke*, 153–56.

and Elijah, the prophetic tradition of Israel. Such a tradition ought to challenge the "Pharaohs" of any age, the false idols, by recalling people to the Law. An alternative to these approaches, Pope John Paul II's "theology of the body" (henceforth, TOB) in many ways serves this prophetic purpose quite well, while affirming the goodness of the body and sexuality. Second, we argue that while TOB succeeds in offering a *both* positive *and* prophetic account of the potential of the body, it too fails because of its desire to, like Peter, build houses on the glorious mountaintop, rather than descend into the world that has not yet been glorified. In this is it still not prophetic enough. We argue that TOB's failure to be prophetic with regard to certain cultural idols leaves it unfortunately with much more in common with them than one might think.

In treating TOB in this article, we are particularly concerned with its *reception* in the American context. In a church notorious for its views on sex as a series of *thou shalt nots*, the growing popularity of TOB and its radically positive approach to human sexuality shows signs of validating George Weigel's prediction that John Paul has presented us with a "theological time bomb" that is set to go off.[2] So in the article, we draw on not only the Pope's text itself, but also the work of its most prominent popularizer, Christopher West. While West's interpretation has sparked considerable controversy of late, its prominence and popularity are indicative of both the strengths and weaknesses of TOB as a pastoral program guiding the Church's teaching on sexuality.[3]

---

2. Weigel, *Witness to Hope*, 343.

3. On the controversy, see especially Schindler, "Christopher West's Theology of the Body." While we generally agree with such critiques, we cannot but help recognize the dominance and even major ecclesial support West's work, in person and in books, has achieved. West's more outrageous language, we believe, is certainly not used by the pope, but it is also a fair extension of some of TOB's basic claims about the apparently pristine redemption wrought by Christ, and the privileged access to the divine via the human body. Thus, our treatment of West and TOB here is not meant as a claim that West necessarily "gets John Paul II right," but rather that West's reading of the Pope is (a) not an unreasonable interpretation of the Pope's work (including possible weaknesses), and (b) especially likely to be a common means of "receiving" TOB in the Church, since few laypeople are likely to slug through the 600 pages of talks.

THEOLOGY OF THE BODY: A VISION BOTH POSITIVE
AND PROPHETIC

One of the perceived deficiencies of pre-Vatican II Catholic sexual ethics was its "negative" attitude toward marriage and sex. This is perhaps
less apt with regard to marriage, though surely marriage was commonly regarded as a less elevated state than celibacy. But the perception
is certainly true with regard to sex. With sex viewed suspiciously at
best (and at worst as dirty, shameful, and a result of human sinfulness), Catholic guidance on such matters primarily concerned when
it was permissible, even excusable. Besides reflecting a deficient view
of moral theology as focused on obligation and obedience to norms,
there was lacking in this approach any understanding of sexuality as a
"positive" part of the moral life.[4]

Responding to this deficient view of sex is central to many post-Vatican II works in Catholic sexual ethics. For example, Joan Timmerman's
The Mardi Gras Syndrome castigates the tradition for all the fences it
builds around sexual love. Timmerman, argues that medieval norms like
limiting morally acceptable times for sex within marriage (Tuesdays were
OK) reveal a suspicion of sexuality that mars much Church teaching on
sexuality into the twentieth century.[5] She calls for a vision of sexuality that is cleansed of this distrust. Similarly, Christine Gudorf begins
her text by summarizing all the voices calling for "the development of a
sexual theology which would reject body/soul dualism and do justice to
the Incarnation."[6] Margaret Farley's recent book also targets "anthropological dualism" and "an emphasis on sin and shame" that has infected
Christian thought on human sexuality.[7] Many other examples could be
cited. But as Bernard Cooke says when summarizing the trajectory of
the magisterial teaching tradition, the entire tradition moves toward a

---

4. On the deficiencies of the "morality of obligation" approach of pre-Vatican
II moral theology, see Pinckaers, *Sources of Christian Ethics*. Of course, the tradition
identified "procreation" as a positive part of the moral life, but, as writers such as the
ones cited below have shown, the tendency was to extol the end while being highly
suspicious of the means.

5. Timmerman, *Mardi Gras Syndrome*.

6. Gudorf, *Body, Sex, and Pleasure*, 1.

7. Farley, *Just Love*, 11.

"positive estimation" of human sexuality that is eventually presented fully in *Gaudium et Spes*.[8]

The general agreement about this trend toward a more positive assessment of human sexuality, however, left open significant questions. Culturally, views about sex as "fulfilling" were generally left unspecified, and tended toward a permissiveness that seemed excessive. So how was this revised Catholic view of the positive potential of human sexuality to be given specificity? For many authors, scientific views and personal experience were crucial. Gudorf, for example, insists on "beginning with sexuality, not the Christian sexual tradition," trying "to understand as best we can human sexuality itself, and this means consulting both biological and social science, as well as the experience of human individuals and communities."[9] In these cases, "science" often meant a great deal of psychology. Some of the leading Catholic writers of the era, like Andre Guindon and Eugene Kennedy, were psychologists by training.[10] For this whole range of authors, the way forward for Catholic sexual ethics was to try to integrate the best current psychological knowledge with recoverable insights from the tradition, especially ones about interpersonal communion and the expression of love. Articulating sex as "natural" meant affirming it as an expression of love.

In addition to this primary theme of interpersonal communion, understood primarily through modern psychology, two other specifications run throughout the literature: justice, and experiences of the sacred or transcendent. Especially in the work of many female writers, both religious and lay, the importance of recovering justice in the face of patriarchal domination was highlighted.[11] And some work, in various ways, began to develop theologically a narrative of sex as an ecstatic, transcendent, or sacred experience.[12]

8. Cooke, "*Casti Connubii* to *Gaudium et Spes*," 113.

9. Gudorf, *Body, Sex, and Pleasure*, 3.

10. See, for example, Kennedy, *What a Modern Catholic Believes*. After an initial chapter entitled "there were no good old days," the entire rest of the book is organized via the developmental narrative of the psychology of the period.

11. For Farley, "justice in love, and the actions which flow from love" form the basis for her entire ethic. See *Just Love*, 207. But Timmerman, who is more focused on reviving the "personal" significance sense, also spends an entire chapter establishing her ethic in "a social justice context." See *Mardi Gras Syndrome*, 50.

12. Timmerman does this by developing a very broad notion of "sacramentality," starting her entire book with the assertion that "sex is a sacramental reality," and ex-

The problem with all three of these specifications—interpersonal love, justice, and transcending ecstasy—was that rarely did authors say anything about sex that was distinctively Christian. These affirmations accorded with generalized cultural ideals about sex. Andre Guindon goes so far as to state:

> It is possible to speak of a sexual revolution today. It seems to us, however, that the meaning of this phenomenon is quite the opposite of what people using this expression often have in mind. Sexual relationships today are generally of a much higher human quality than they have ever been in this history of mankind for the simple reason that, for the first time, two human beings are able to have an adult dialogue.[13]

He tries to temper this exalted evaluation of the 1970s by referencing the "meaningless permissiveness" of the times. However, such permissiveness, according to Guindon, "quite naturally accompanies this ongoing transformation."[14] It is assumed that the permissiveness is merely a short phase, through which civilization will pass, on its way to mature intimacy. Such a reading of "the signs of the times" is likely to seem to us today as far too optimistic. Surely Catholic reflection on sex and marriage should reflect "the joys and the hopes" of all people, but it also must address their "griefs and anxieties."[15] Like *Gaudium et Spes* itself, Catholic reflection, while overcoming its own flawed past (i.e., dualism), must provide some means of discernment—or better, prophetic challenge!—for living out the mission of Christ in the world.

This narrative sets the stage for the entrance of TOB, and can help explain its popularity among a significant number of (particularly younger) Catholics today. In reaction against the negative assessment of sex and the body in earlier Catholic ethics (and beyond), Catholic ethicists have offered insufficiently critical positive assessments of the beauty

---

plaining that "a sacramental reality . . . is that delivers to us the experience of God's presence or places us in touch with the basic mystery—the mystery that we are loved by God." See *Mardi Gras Syndrome*, 1–2. Even this first chapter, however, ends with Abraham Maslow, and then proceeds to social scientific research in chapter 2. Gudorf naming sexual pleasure as "grace and gift," rooting in the notion of the "inclusive love" revealed in the gospels, of which sexual experiences can be a sort of parable. See *Body, Sex, and Pleasure*, 81–138, esp. 116–19.

13. Guindon, *Sexual Language*, 112.

14. Ibid.

15. *Gaudium et Spes*, no. 1.

and importance of sex in our lives. Both this positive assessment, and the lack of a sufficiently substantive theological vision about the meaning and purpose of sex apart from extremely flexible generalities, made it nearly impossible to articulate and substantiate a *prophetic* vision regarding sex and marriage, which might function to critique problematic aspects of the wider culture's positive stance toward sex. As a result many (particularly young) people found themselves without any burdensome restrictions on their sex lives, *but also* without any rich account of the meaning of sexuality to substantiate specific practices whereby they could live out their sexuality in honor of that meaning.

Theologians of the body don't make this same mistake. They recognize the situation today is *not the same one* faced by the authors cited above: a body-hating church and a body-affirming culture. Rather, TOB proponents see themselves as trying to cope with an *irrelevant* church and a *deeply confused* culture. As Christopher West remarks, the problem is not that our culture says sex is *too good*, but that it doesn't really know *how good sex is*. In other words, critics of the broader culture get it wrong when they complain that it overemphasizes the importance of sex. As West argues, the culture's focus on sex is not misplaced—it's the culture's account of sexuality's meaning that comes up short. By offering a sexual ethic that is theologically grounded, attractive, and challenging, proponents of TOB "up the ante" on the culture's notions of sexuality's meaning. It not only affirms the turn to the positive, but also offers a vision that helps discern the good and the bad in the wider culture, a thickly theological understanding of the prophetic value of sexual norms.

Like the aforementioned approaches (and perhaps even surpassing them), the theology of the body offers a glowing assessment of the body and human sexuality. Yet they do so in the context of a far more substantive story, namely, the Christian story. For the TOB, the sum of the Christian story is self-giving love. Such love is the very essence of God ("God is love"), who is a Triune communion of persons. This love is the very point of the story of salvation history, in which God creates all from nothing out of love. Humanity is created in the *imago Dei*, uniquely capable of such love and invited to a destiny of union with God and other in self-giving love. Despite human sinfulness, which is at root a human rejection of God's invitation to a life of self-giving love in preference for living on our own self-serving terms, God continually reaches out to humanity to reconcile humanity to himself. This culminates of course in God's becoming man in the person Jesus Christ, the Incarnate Son sent by the Father to reconcile humanity with God (John 3:16) and enable us to "share in the divine nature" in the communion of saints. This love, seen most obviously in the greatest commandment, is also the way of discipleship, the way of beginning to participate in that divine nature, even in this life.

What has any of this to do with sex? For TOB, the self-giving love that is the point of the story is no spiritualized love. It is in-carnate, and not simply in the person of Jesus Christ. TOB proponents claim that the meaning of life—self-giving, as opposed to self-gratifying, love—is "written on our very bodies." As John Paul II argues, "the consciousness of the meaning of the body derived from this [gift]—in particular the consciousness of the spousal meaning of the body—constitutes the fundamental component of human existence in the world."[16] This is a strong claim. But what *is* the "spousal meaning" of the body? John Paul refers to the human body's "*power to express love: precisely that love in which the human person becomes a gift* and—through this gift—fulfills the very meaning of his being and existence."[17] This is the original condition of the body. As he writes, "This is *the body: a witness* to creation as a fundamental gift, and therefore a witness *to Love as the source from which this same giving springs.*"[18]

In our culture, the body mediates various "stories." It can be a display of power or a commercial come-on. It can be an arena of anxiety given the massive display of "ideal" bodies which make one's own body seem inadequate. But even the positive assessments of the human body found in the broader culture pale in comparison to the glorified account of the body offered by TOB. A witness to a loving Creator, and a gift to be passed on in love? This is positive indeed! John Paul II says that "[t]he body, in fact, and only the body, is capable of making visible what is invisible: the spiritual and the divine. It has been created to transfer into the visible reality of the world the mystery hidden from eternity in God, and thus to be a sign of it."[19] One can begin to understand how the message is liberating in comparison to many cultural stories about the body.

16. John Paul II, *Man and Woman*, 189.
17. Ibid., 185–86, emphasis in original.
18. Ibid., 183, emphasis in original.
19. Ibid., 203.

This context allows for not only a positive but also a thoroughly theological account of marriage and sexuality. TOB's exaltation of self-giving love as the meaning and purpose of life focuses on marriage and sexuality as unique access points to the story of salvation history and a particularly important way of "embodying" this story. It enables TOB enthusiasts to use discussions of marriage and sexuality to draw in listeners to the central mysteries of the Christian story. For example, in his books and lectures, Christopher West stresses that Scripture both begins and ends with marriage. "Everything that God wants to tell us on earth about who he is, who we are, the meaning of life, the reason he created us, how we are to live, and even our ultimate destiny is contained somehow in the truth and meaning of marriage and sexuality," West writes.[20] It is hard to imagine a more dazzling, glorified view of marriage and sexuality. It is also one that functions effectively as a catechesis for an under-catechized generation. As robustly theological rather than blandly positive, TOB offers not only a rich meaning of human sexuality, but also substantiates practices and norms for living out one's sexuality in a truly life-giving, self-giving manner. It makes sexuality into discipleship, and teaches discipleship through sexuality.

TOB thus positions itself for a successful critique and revision of the Catholic tradition's own propensity to regard sex and marriage as carnal and substandard. At the same time, in contrast to other accounts that do so by mimicking the broader cultural changes, it provides a radical, prophetic alternative to the bland visions of sex in the culture, which are unable to give specific guidance and "rules" for differentiating life-giving from destructive sexual relationships. Not only does TOB provide a more theological vision, but that vision also "cashes out" with more specific guidance, which may be challenging for some, but a challenge which can be experienced as liberating, rather than oppressive. TOB's account of human sinfulness, and specifically "lust" with regard to sexuality, provides what a simply "positive" account of sexuality cannot. Given the connotations of "lust" as a pre-Vatican II term that reflects an inherent suspicion toward the body and sex, TOB proponents often use the term *instrumentalization*. Sex that uses, or instrumentalizes, another person solely for one's own good is a corruption of the divine gift of sexuality, which is always meant to be an arena of self-gift. As to what constitutes chaste (self-giving) sex versus

20. West, *Good News*, 19.

lustful (instrumentalizing) sex, TOB proponents rely on an embodied understanding of sex as uniquely capable of both engendering new life and unifying people into one flesh in order to generate practices and norms that reflect this exalted view of the meaning/purpose of sex. The content of these norms is nearly indistinguishable from those old, negative, pre-Vatican II rules. They are no doubt challenging, and demand the disciplining of our sex lives. But this is a challenge consistent with Israel's prophets, calling people with a hopeful vision of renewal via return to fidelity to the covenant, even if they had strayed. For many, this theological grounding and promise of meaning and fulfillment inspires rather than daunts and cows.

Is such a challenging vision present in other "positive" postconciliar Catholic sexual ethics? We fear not. Many end up "lowering the bar," hoping to persuade young people to avoid the worst excesses of our sexual culture—or at least to avoid getting hurt. In our teaching experience at Catholic colleges, we know that our students are eager for a challenge, for something truly life-giving and life-sustaining. They are quite "experienced" and toughened by the sexual culture already, and they hunger for a vision of something better, one that speaks to the possibility of redemption and conversion. Their deepest need is not to hear that sexuality "is not so bad," but that "it's time for a change," uttered not in tones of eternal condemnation (as in the past) but in tones of invitation.

This is West's tack. He insists that "the pope imposes nothing and wags a finger at no one."[21] Rather, the pope is merely reflecting on human experience in light of Scripture and inviting others to do the same. When it comes to sexuality, "it doesn't matter how often we've settled for something less," West says. "This is a message of sexual healing and redemption, not condemnation."[22] Young people have not heard enough of this from the church in the past or present, West contends, and they are longing for a message that sex can be beautiful and deeply meaningful. The pope's theology aims at precisely such a vision. It is a vision presented like a prophet, pointing the way to a new day, beyond the conflicts and injustices of the present age.

21. West, *For Beginners*, 16.
22. Ibid.

THEOLOGY OF THE BODY: NOT POSITIVE
AND PROPHETIC ENOUGH

Though we applaud the commitment of TOB to offer not only a more *positive* but also a more fully *theological* account of sex and marriage (or at least of sex and marriage vows), we worry that TOB feeds cultural sexual paradigms that endanger the practice and stability of sacramental marriage. After all, while the previous section presented TOB as responding to a cultural longing for a richer meaning of sexuality and marriage, the underspecified longing in the broader culture is not completely unspecified. The exalted understanding of marriage for which so many long is aptly described in a report of the National Marriage Project as a "SuperRelationship." What characterizes this Holy Grail of relationships is its intensity and privacy. The "SuperRelationship [is] an intensely private spiritualized union. . . . Indeed, this intimate couple relationship pretty much defines the sum total of marriage."[23] The report further indicates that such a marriage is not seen as a public institution, nor as a religious one—only 42 percent believed that their "soul mate" had to share their religious views. Given the implicit content of this cultural longing, and tendencies in TOB's own understanding of what characterizes fully self-giving sex and marriage, we fear that TOB reinforces the SuperRelationship ideal, and is thus marked by problems attendant to it. Ironically, TOB may therefore contribute to the destabilization of marriage in ways similar to the corrosive impact of the SuperRelationship ideal. Thus, in this section, we want to explain the ways in which TOB may be insufficiently prophetic and theological in challenging certain aspects of the broader culture, and in identifying marriage as a path of discipleship. Marriage characterized by true self-gift may be even more glorious than TOB describes, but that is because real self-gift in a fallen world does not remain with the glorious "SuperRelationship" on the mountain, but rather descends into the world in radical service.

The main strategy for TOB in guiding people to holy marriage and sex is eradicating the lust that is antithetical to self-gift, and espousing a state of chaste purity absent the interior disintegration endemic to our postlapsarian condition. But in its enthusiasm for the purity of pre-Fall Adam and Eve, it forgets that we are not them, and that as Christians *we are not called to be them.* We cannot be them, for we do not dwell in Eden,

---

23. Whitehead and Popenoe, "The State of Our Unions," 6–14.

even in our own homes. And thus expounding such a limited vision of marriage and sex can set people up for failure. TOB's myopic fixation on eradicating sexual lust in order to preserve pure, selfless sexual union is not only an incomplete view of the nature and scope of embodied self-giving love, but is also dangerous in undermining what it laudably attempts to buttress, particularly in the American cultural context.

What do we mean by "myopic fixation" on purity and lust? One example appears very early in TOB. John Paul is describing the "original" (i.e., pre-Fall) discovery of the man and woman of their bodies, and their sexuality. They are "interiorly free" or "free with the freedom of the gift," able to give themselves to one another "in the full freedom from all constraint of the body and [its] sex."[24] What might that "constraint of the body and of sex" be? The Pope explains, "Here we mean above all freedom as self-mastery (self dominion)."[25] John Paul II is referring to the freedom for self-gift that is only possible in the absence of the disordered and disintegrated desires that constitute human sinfulness.

Further on, John Paul returns to this "original" state when discussing redemption in Christ, and in particular Christ's reference to "the beginning" in the gospels. Christ's reference, John Paul writes, "can be justified only by the reality of the redemption; outside of it there would, in fact, remain only the threefold concupiscence or that 'slavery of corruption' about which the Apostle Paul writes (Rom 8:21)."[26] In discussing redeemed life in Christ, John Paul's immediate emphasis is on the similarity of such graced life to the purity of the original state, where people exhibited mastery over themselves before the tainting of sin.

What is the problem here? Of course part of life in Christ is having well-ordered desires to keep us from being wracked by lust. It is true that redeemed life in Christ shares much in common with the original state of purity. In our broken condition after the fall, humanity does indeed need to be called back to lives of self-gift rather than (at least in sexuality and marriage) lives of lust. But people are rarely very good at simply turning away from bad desires. They far more often turn *toward* something they see or are starting to see as more life-giving. What TOB offers one to turn toward is a life of purity, claiming that marriage and sex in such a life are far better than anything offered by the broader culture. But in this life,

24. *Man and Woman*, 185, 187.

25. Ibid., 186.

26. Ibid., 323.

even for those living a graced life in Christ, the punishment (if not the fault) of original sin remains.[27] In other words, we do not and cannot live the lives of purity possible before the Fall. To the extent that God's grace enables our desires to be healed and directed toward self-giving love rather than lustful instrumentalization, there are important points of commonality between pre-Fall lives of purity and redeemed lives in Christ. Yet note how even the use of "healed" in the previous sentence marks a difference in those loving desires. Like the post-Resurrection flesh of Christ, which bears the marks of the crucifixion even in its glory, people who are redeemed by God's grace have desires that are healed, but bear the scars of sinfulness. And the world where they are called to give themselves away in self-giving love is very much scarred and all too often still wounded.

Thus, the emphasis on the purity of interior motivations, we contend, is an importantly inadequate account of a life of mutual self-gift, one that misses the mark of the self-sacrificial character and real challenges of redeemed Christian love. One of the best ways to demonstrate how the vision of purity lauded by TOB is importantly different from redeemed life in Christ as understood here is examining the occasions held up by TOB as paradigms of self-giving embodied love. All too often these are ecstatic occasions of intense intimacy. They are transcendent, liminal moments, such as sexual intercourse or wedding vows. Yet we learn from the gospels that while a life of discipleship may indeed contain transcendent/ecstatic moments—akin to what the disciples experienced on the Mount of the Transfiguration—the life of discipleship is primarily about coming down from that mountain, taking up one's cross, and serving others precisely in their need. This true Christian discipleship is a life that may be "ec-static" in the truest sense of "going outside" one's self, but such self-giving ecstasy, far from being transcendent and pure, is embodied and messy. Christ's call to fullness of life, even in married life, is not marked primarily by private and intense romantic intimacy.

Consider two narratives that help illustrate the difference described here. The first is an example taken from West's writings. He describes

27. For more on the distinction between experiencing the evil of punishment for sin even as distinct from the evil of fault, see Thomas Aquinas, *Summa Theologiae* III 15 on the defects of Christ's soul, esp. III 15,6 ad.3. Since even Christ, like us in all things but sin, experienced the suffering that originated in human sinfulness, surely even those who are redeemed by God's grace in this life can expect also to continue to suffer similarly.

how his father-in-law wept at Mass the day after his wedding, and when asked why, he responded, "For the first time in my life, I understood the meaning of Christ's words, 'This is my body, given for you.'"[28] The context makes clear he is referring to wedding night sex. The point of this story is that Christian sex is not simply something "permitted," but that it is an important part of the embodied, self-giving love that is the hallmark of married life in Christ. Sex is sacramental in this telling, even to the point of being linked to the Eucharist.

But this story is about sex, wedding-night sex, which is not marriage. Is it really plausible to imagine that *one* night of sex allows us to "truly understand" the meaning of Christ's bodily self-giving love? Consider another story. It comes (surprisingly enough) from far-from-pure television series *Sex and the City*. Near the end of the series, after the characters Miranda and Steve, who have an infant son, have finally married, Steve's mother (a nasty woman) becomes demented, and they move her into their home. One day while Steve is at work the mother wanders off, and Miranda goes looking for her in a panic, eventually finding her entirely disoriented, eating out of a garbage can. We then see Miranda gently bathing her mother-in-law's aged, ugly body. Magda, Miranda's Eastern European (and very traditional) cleaning lady, spies them. As Magda leaves for the day, she sneaks up to Miranda with a smile and tells her, with a nod to the bathroom, "What you did there, *that* is love." Ever-cynical Miranda actually asks Magda to forget it and not tell Steve, since "it will upset him." Here we have someone not only exemplifying a true marital act of self-gift in an embodied and broken world, but also someone who so loves her spouse that she prefers her deed be unknown to him rather than let him be upset by a disturbing image of his mother.

West's story narrates in theological terms the romantic bliss of wedding-night sex. But this is not the heart of marriage, let alone self-giving love in general. The Gospels, our most important stories, tell us that Magda is right. The example of Jesus in the Gospels isn't one that focuses on intensely private intimate moments, such as sexual intercourse untainted by lust. Rather, the in-breaking grace of God's Kingdom is seen more clearly in stories like Miranda's than in stories of wedding-night sex. Christ himself is present when we are involved in the works of mercy, as broken bodies serving broken bodies. *These* are the para-

28. West, *For Beginners*, 10.

digmatic acts of embodied self-giving love, a love Jesus practiced every day of his ministry (as opposed to sexual self-giving, which he did not practice!).

Ironically, in this comparison of two stories West's pious example serves to obscure what in this instance the dreaded "culture" makes clear, hinting that perhaps we have more to learn from the culture than TOB lets on, if only we have the right lens (Jesus) with which to view it. (It may also suggest that TOB trades on an oversimplified account of the culture, where God's grace is ever at work mysteriously.) *Sex and the City* helps us recognize that Miranda and Steve's married bodies aren't just bodies that have (chaste or unchaste) sex and (pure or impure) desires. Their bodies have histories, where God's grace has to work in more extended and murkier occasions than moments of ecstatic sexual love. For Miranda and Steve's marriage, Miranda's ability and willingness to give bodily care to Steve's mother may tell us much more about their self-giving love, their marriage, and its function as an analogy to God's love for us, than any *sexual* encounter would.

West would applaud this work of mercy, of course, but where is the description of this sort of bodily generosity in his work? He makes the challenge of embodied self-giving love too easy, reducing the problem of sin to a matter of sexual selfishness vs. self-giving, and presenting the life-giving alternative to sin as intense and private ecstatic moments. The lifelong practice of self-giving love involves struggle and pain and sacrifice that is not simply about controlling (in West's favorite phrase) "the urge to merge." Sexual lust is not the primary problem; our real challenge is loving the people we find around us in all their embodied brokenness.

In this way, we believe that TOB is insufficiently prophetic in its challenge to the privatized "SuperRelationship" ideal of the culture. Our objection is *not* informed by pessimism about the possibilities of sexual self-giving, nor is it an attempt to dismiss the teaching of *Humanae vitae.*[29] Rather, the myopic fixation on sexual purity is an importantly

29. We take Luke Timothy Johnson's well-known critique, "Disembodied," to be one that, while paying some attention to issues of experience, ends up with a primary focus on opposing TOB due to its reinforcing (poorly, he believes) the teaching against birth control. While our argument is somewhat sympathetic to Johnson's concerns about actual experience, we think his claim that "none of [love's] grandeur or giddiness" (112) appears in these talks misses the real problem of privatizing romantic love. And besides, West's work shows how the pope's "purity" can be made all too "grand"!

incomplete *story* of married discipleship and the challenges to it in contemporary culture. Yes, it is a strong antidote to the culture of "lust," and
in particular bodily objectification. But though redeemed life in Christ is
indeed marked by a healing of our disintegrated and lustful desires that
frees us to give of ourselves, that self-giving love is exemplified not primarily in ecstatic/transcendent moments such as sex or wedding vows
but in the service to each other in our brokenness that Christ exemplified and called his disciples to do the same.

The goal of a perfected interiority seems "unrealistic," not in the
sense of "difficult," but in the sense of an artificial description of spousal love and its challenges. Let us once again recall the story of the
Transfiguration: TOB's fixation on sexual purity suggests a model of
discipleship akin to seeing the glorious body of Jesus transfigured on
the mountain. But this moment of glory, while beautiful, is not the essence of living the gospel in this life. Jesus reveals that the grace of the
Kingdom is found not primarily on the mountain, but in coming down
the mountain to serve the world and its broken bodies. TOB's presentation of Christian sacramental marriage as a return to innocence actually
damages people by failing to focus them on the more painful, but also
more beautiful, reality of graced married life in all its facets. TOB tends
to replicate the culture's own fixation on sexual chemistry and magic
(i.e., that private and intense romantic intimacy) as the essence of faithful married love. This romanticism creates an unmerited expectation
from spouses (particularly concerning sex), and instead of serving as an
antidote to divorce culture, may even feed into it.

Does this romanticism actually feed divorce? Studies suggest up to
70 percent of American divorces happen in "low-tension" marriages, defined as marriages where there is no serious fighting, abuse, or drug use.[30]
Couldn't these marriages with low-level but persistent discontent work?
The vast majority of our students view staying in such an "unhappy
marriage" as only slightly preferably to the lower circles of Hell. Their
romanticism about marriage, or—in the case of those seeing it through
TOB—their seeming piety toward marriage, makes them believe that
less-than-ideal marriages are lifetime prison sentences. Thus the heart
of the divorce culture may very well be our transcendent expectations of
marriage, expectations TOB inevitably feeds, since glorified expectations

---

30. See Amato and Booth, *Generation at Risk*, 220.

can lead people to conclude a marriage has failed much too quickly.[31] In focusing on the grace palpable in transcendent moments (like wedding-night sex or the transfiguration), TOB actually shortchanges the work of God's grace by obscuring what St. Paul calls its greatest glory, its ability to show itself precisely in and through our weakness and brokenness.

On the face of it, this seems a paradoxical claim: that a glorified view of marriage feeds a divorce culture. But let us borrow a page from West's repertoire and say it is not that West has *too* exalted a view of graced married life; it is not exalted enough! Stories such as West's father's wedding are indeed important reminders of how marriage and sex are taken up into a theological rich account of Christian discipleship. The first section of this chapter argued what TOB has done this better than certain other alternatives. But it is still importantly deficient.

How can this deficiency be overcome? We argue that redemption instead can (and should) be seen as the in-corporating of brokenness into Christ's healing body, the Church, through the shared life and mission of a marriage. This is the fully-developed, Christ-like understanding of total self-gift in a life that is not pre-Fall and yet not yet fully glorified. Such love may have moments of intense and private intimacy. But just as the Christ depicted in the gospels is no isolated mystic, but instead the wandering, suffering servant, so too his model of service ought to be the tie that binds together couples in Christ.

This re-focusing or re-visioning of true love can be done in two (related) ways. First, we can look at where true self-giving happens within spousal and familial relationships. Holding up a model of intense private intimacy shortchanges the real miracle of graced marriage by focusing the attention of spouses to ecstatic, transcendent moments as paradigmatic of their marriage. TOB's narration of graced marriage focuses on the liminal, transcendent moments, and thus offers no account of the ordinary and healing presence of God's transformative grace in the countless everyday occasions where spouses practice the corporal and spiritual works of mercy toward one another and those in their families. We need to recall Miranda's act is as intimate and self-giving and embodied (though clearly different!) as marital sex with Steve. So one way we enjoin TOB to expand its scope and offer an even greater vision of marriage is by narrating these stories as well.

---

31. For a fuller articulation of this danger in the present culture, see Whitehead, *Divorce Culture*.

A second way the scope of TOB's vision of marriage must be expanded is beyond the spouses and even nuclear family. Miranda's story is a start here since it involves her mother-in-law, but even it is limited in scope (although it does involve Magda in shared reflection on the goods of marriage). Graced married life is also about embodied self-giving love to the world, and especially the poor. In fact it seems the greatest challenge for sacramental marriage in our contemporary American context is building a relationship in which this bodily intertwining is put in mercy-filled service to the broken world Christ has redeemed. This service is extended to one's spouse, and further to the neighbor, in ways that go far beyond lust-less sex. Such bodily availability and service, especially to the poor, is a crucial arena where God's grace sustains marriages.

David McCarthy, in his book *Sex and Love in the Home* describes such family life as an "open household."[32] In the open household, members do not simply love one another (a love which always threatens to become suffocation), but they open their (nuclear) family to the disruptive but ultimately Christ-bearing presence of others, especially others in need: extended family, neighbors, strangers, and the poor. In this way, the united bodies of a married couple are not simply looking at each other, but they assume the position of Christ's body in the world. They are not simply ministers to one another at the wedding, but become ministers of Christ in and through their sacramental calling: living out one's marriage as a vocation in service to the world. Marriage creates a "little church," in the Vatican II sense of the Church as the sacrament of Christ to the world.[33] Being a "domestic church" does not simply mean having another locale for devotional practices. Being such a church must include embodied service beyond the family, making the couple and their children vulnerable to the suffering of those around them when the cultural impulse is to shut such suffering out of the "happy home." Such a mission of mercy and service lies at the center of the common life of a truly sacramental Christian marriage, at least as much as sexual self-giving.

32. McCarthy, *Sex and Love in the Home*, 85–108. The chapter is now anthologized in Curran and Rubio, *Marriage*, 211–37.

33. Jana Bennett describes this "sacramental expansion of the household" in terms of overcoming the public/private distinction. See *Water is Thicker Than Blood*, 136. The book also offers an excellent background on the notion of "little" or "domestic church."

Sadly, this sort of work is nowhere to be found in West's TOB.[34] Because of the absence of any articulation of the social mission of the Christian family, West's presentation further supports the inward-looking, consumption-oriented, privatized practice of marriage already dominant in most American households. He would do well to attend to the lengthy and substantial presentation of this social mission provided by John Paul himself in his 1980 exhortation *Familiaris Consortio* and 1994's Letter to Families. In these works, the call to love other bodies through the works of mercy moves beyond the family circle. Unfortunately these themes are not incorporated into the Pope's own *Theology of the Body*, and thus West's presentation is a very plausible way of reading these particular texts. When the social mission is omitted, TOB makes couples think they can live a closed, consumer lifestyle to the hilt, for example—so long as their sex life conforms to the views of the church. A full presentation of John Paul's own theology of marriage would lead West to a less privatized view of marriage, where the shared mission and social bonds formed in the community would serve as supports to the couple, as well as a calling to them in the life of their marriage. This would be a truly prophetic call in a culture of consumerism. But perhaps such a call is avoided because it would prove so "unpopular" among West's intended audiences, who may share the culture's highly privatized, "closed" version of the household.

When Jesus shows his glory on the mount of the transfiguration, Peter (whom the gospels tell us was so overwhelmed he didn't know what he was saying) wants to stay and even build houses to dwell on the mountain. But Christians are not allowed to dwell on the mountain, nor in Eden. With its focus on sexual self-giving and purity, TOB threatens to leave its audience on the mount of the transfiguration rather exhorting them to follow Christ down the mountain to serve the broken bodies of the world, even to the point of death. Christ's own example reveals that Christian discipleship is more about laying down one's life in embodied self-giving love than it is about the peak experiences. We worry that TOB's audience will be left disillusioned and ill-prepared for sacramental marriage. They may find themselves in marriages where

34. It should be noted that a more recent popularized exposition of TOB by Anderson and Granados, *Called to Love*, concludes with a rousing chapter integrating John Paul's writings on the social mission of the family into his TOB work. It is noteworthy, however, that the chapter contains not a single reference to TOB itself!

self-giving embodied love within the family is understood too narrowly, and furthermore fails to extend beyond the family itself to the world outside.

In defining embodied self-giving love so narrowly, TOB risks giving us the perishable bread of the culture, which we eat but which does not ultimately satisfy, rather than the real bread of Christ's Body which does not perish. That real eucharist consists of seeing our mutual donation of our bodies to each other in marriage as a commitment not just in the bedroom, but in the entire common life of the marriage. We give our bodies to our spouses not simply for the spouse, but in order to become more fully Christ's Body. That Body is not one that gives to others and to the world primarily through sex, but rather through pouring itself out in radical service typified in the works of mercy. TOB's fixation on the body solely in the bedroom is like a fixation on the Body solely at the consecration: crucial, but incomplete on its own.

BIBLIOGRAPHY

Amato, Paul R., and Alan Booth. *A Generation at Risk: Growing Up in an Era of Family Upheaval*. Cambridge: Harvard University Press, 1997.

Anderson, Carl, and Jose Granados. *Called to Love*. New York: Doubleday, 2009.

Bennett, Jana Marguerite. *Water is Thicker Than Blood: An Augustianian Theology of Marriage and Singleness*. New York: Oxford University Press, 2008.

Cooke, Bernard. "*Casti Connubii* to *Gaudium et Spes*: The Shifting Views of Christian Marriage." In *Marriage and the Catholic Tradition: Scripture, Tradition, and Experience*, edited by Todd A. Salzman, Thomas M. Kelly, and John J. O'Keefe, 109–14. New York: Crossroad, 2004.

Curran, Charles E., and Julie Hanlon Rubio, editors. *Marriage (Readings in Moral Theology, no. 15)*. New York: Paulist, 2009.

Farley, Margaret. *Just Love: A Framework for Christian Sexual Ethics*. New York: Continuum, 2006.

Gudorf, Christine E. *Body, Sex, and Pleasure: Reconstructing Christian Sexual Ethics*. Cleveland: Pilgrim, 1994.

Guindon, Andre. *The Sexual Language*. Toronto: University of Ottawa Press, 1977.

John Paul II, Pope. *Man and Woman He Created Them: A Theology of the Body*. Translated by Michael Waldstein. Boston: Pauline, 2006.

Johnson, Luke Timothy. "A Disembodied 'Theology of the Body.'" *Commonweal* 128:2 (2001) 11–17.

———. *Gospel of Luke (Sacra Pagina)*. Collegeville, MN: Liturgical, 1991.

Kennedy, Eugene. *What a Modern Catholic Believes About Sex*. Chicago: Thomas More, 1971.

McCarthy, David Matzko. *Sex and Love in the Home*. London: SCM, 2001.

Pinckaers, OP, Servais. *The Sources of Christian Ethics*, trans. Sr. Mary Thomas Noble, OP. Washington, DC: Catholic University of America Press, 1995.

Schindler, David L. "Christopher West's Theology of the Body." Online: http://www .headlinebistro.com/hb/en/news/west_schindler2.html.

Timmerman, Joan. *The Mardi Gras Syndrome: Rethinking Christian Sexuality*. New York: Crossroad, 1984.

Weigel, George. *Witness to Hope*. New York: Cliff Street, 1999.

West, Christopher. *Good News about Sex and Marriage*. Cincinnati: Servant, 2000.

———. *Theology of the Body For Beginners*. West Chester, PA: Ascension, 2004.

Whitehead, Barbara Dafoe. *The Divorce Culture*. New York: Knopf, 1997.

Whitehead Barbara Dafoe, and David Popenoe, "The State of Our Unions: The Social Health of Marriage in America 2001." Online: http://marriage.rutgers.edu/ Publications/SOOU/NMPAR2001.pdf.

10

The Practice of Sex in Christian Marriage[1]

JULIE HANLON RUBIO

I WANT TO BEGIN with a story that will help us consider the differences between younger and older generations of Catholics and determine how theology might respond to the concerns of the present generation about good sex. Several years ago, a senior colleague told me how excited he was to find an old copy of *Modern Youth and Chastity* in a second hand piece of furniture he had bought.[2] Dismayed when I told him I had not read it, he immediately copied it for me and placed it in my mailbox. This document—a theologically significant work written by prominent moral theologian Gerald Kelly, S.J.—was an influential part of the pre-Vatican II popular communication of traditional Catholic sexual morality, prominent in high school and college religion classrooms. *Modern Youth and Chastity* makes a rational case against premarital sex (and other acts which may bring one to the near occasion of sin), and is, in the main, representative of the pre-Vatican II approach to sexual ethics.[3] It devotes its energy to convincing Catholics to avoid sexual sin, while giv-

---

1. In this essay, excerpts from chapter 4, pp. 97–127, of Julie Hanlon Rubio, *Family Ethics: Practices for Christians*, copyright © 2010, Georgetown University Press, are reprinted with permission. www.press.georgetown.edu.

2. Gerald Kelly, S.J., *Modern Youth and Chastity*. It was designed "to give to young men and women of approximately college age a clear, adequate presentation of the Catholic moral teaching on chastity" (3).

3. Among others, John S. Grabowski criticizes the legalism of Catholic sexual ethics in *Sex and Virtue*, 14–19.

ing little attention to what constitutes good sex.[4] While Kelly makes sure to say that sex is good within its proper confines, this is a minor concern compared to the dominant focus on stopping sexual sins of unchastity by limiting sex to marriage.[5]

Because my early religious formation took place in the 1970s and 80s, this approach to sex was not one I recognized. I can remember no strong messages against premarital sex from Catholic school religion classes or from the liberal house church community in which I was reared. At home, my parents, while not in agreement with the more extreme practices of some of their married friends, consciously raised me and my two brothers to reject the strongly negative sexual messages dominant in their youth. If we did not hear this message clearly enough from them, we got it from free access to television shows like "Love: American Style," "Three's Company," "Love Boat," and the like. Though they advised us to save sex for marriage, my parents did not want their children growing up thinking that avoiding sexual sin was the "be-all and end-all" of Christian life.

The sexual theology I came to read in graduate school provided rational argumentation for the approach I first learned at home. Liberal theologians reared in the same subcultures as my parents devoted a great deal of time to arguing that Catholics had a right to dissent from Catholic teaching on contraception.[6] They took for granted the idea that sex is directed to *both* love and procreation, and looked to real-life experience to discover the many meanings of sex.[7] Putting the baggage of

4. The core of *Modern Youth and Chastity* is chapters ten and eleven, which describe in great detail the practical moral principles toward which the whole text leads.

5. Chastity is defined near the end of *Modern Youth and Chastity* as, "The habit of regulating the use of the generative faculty according to the principles of reason and of faith" (52). The three chapters on chastity focus on developing the virtue in order to control the sexual appetite and avoid mortal sin. Only in the last of these chapters is an attempt made to speak of chastity as "the most practical expression of sincere love for Christ" (97).

6. See, for instance, Shannon, *Lively Debate*; Keane, *Sexual Morality*; Kosnik et al., *Human Sexuality*; Mahoney, *Making of Moral Theology*.

7. An important move of the Council fathers was their decision to leave behind the traditional ranking of the ends of sex, which placed procreation over loving union between husband and wife, in order to affirm the equal importance of both (*Gaudium et spes*, no. 50). Among the most significant works by liberal theologians are the following: Selling, *Embracing Sexuality*; Dominian, *Let's Make Love*; Whitehead, *Marrying Well*; Gudorf, *Body, Sex, and Pleasure*; Jung with Coray, *Sexual Diversity and Catholicism*; Cahill, *Sex, Gender*; Farley, *Just Love*; Scott and Horell, *Human Sexuality*; Moore, O.P.,

sex's connection to sin behind them, they explored the spirituality of sex and argued for the importance of sexual pleasure. Conservative theologians, on the other hand, argued decisively for the inseparable connection of union and procreation in all sexual acts, but they, too, wrote more of the significance of sex in a marriage, of legitimate pleasure that could be distinguished from lust, and of the spiritual potential of holy sex.[8] Post-Vatican II theologians of all persuasions wanted to say more about the tradition's "yes" to sex rather than focusing on its many "no's."

While at first, younger theologians stayed away from the issue that dominated post-Vatican II moral theology, they have now begun to approach sexual ethics, and they do so in ways that differ from those of their elders. They seek first to affirm the tradition rather than questioning it. Instead of focusing on the goodness and spiritual depths of sex, younger theologians are more likely to speak of the ordinariness of sex, question romance, and extol self-sacrifice.[9] The more recent sexual theology is influenced by the work of John Paul II who characterized sex as a ritual enactment of the total self-giving that lies at the center of Christian life.[10] Some younger theologians follow his lead by emphasizing the gift of fertility as central to the self that is only fully given in covenant marriage. Others think of self-gift as something offered to one's spouse over a lifetime of shared discipleship. All offer a more distinctively Christian understanding of what sex is about, an alternative to a cultural ethos that says sex is good when it feels good, physically and emotionally, as long as it is just.

Perhaps, given the cultural saturation of sex without limits, there is little need to talk about the goodness of sex.[11] It may be time for theologians to give more sustained attention to how the practice of sex can further growth in self-sacrificial love. However, it seems right to pause for a moment and ask, "Is this the direction in which the new Catholic sexual ethics ought to be heading?"

Body in Context; Lawler and Salzman, *Sexual Person*.

8. Among the most significant conservative works are: Grabowski, *Sex and Virtue*; Shivanadan, *Crossing the Threshold of Love*; McCarthy, *Sex and Love in the Home*; Cloutier, *Love, Reason, and God's Story*.

9. See especially McCarthy, *Sex and Love in the Home* and Cloutier, *Love, Reason, and God's Story*.

10. John Paul II, *Familiaris Consortio*, no. 11.

11. See Wilson, "Sex Without Intimacy."

In one sense, the new direction seems exactly right. If Christianity can say little more about sex than sex is good, as long as it is between people who respect and value one another in some way, something is wrong. We now have a plethora of sexual guides written by Catholics and Protestants that promote sex using familiar language of romance and pleasure.[12] Surely, Christians ought to have something distinctive to say about what sex means what two people who are married engage in it and about why they ought to engage in the practice of sex at all. What does sex have to do with a life of discipleship? This is a question worth pursuing.

However, I am hesitant to go further down this path, for two reasons. First, I am not certain that Christians of this generation are convinced of the goodness, let alone the holiness, of sex. I offer a few illustrative examples. At a recent undergraduate conference on marriage at St. Louis University, a student giving a paper asserted that adolescents need to hear more than "sex is bad." When asked by a professor if this message is really still current, the student replied that even when adults said, "sex is good," they nonetheless communicated to students that it was bad, because they spoke so much of the importance of avoiding it. When I first began asking students in my Sexual Ethics class to attend a performance of the *Vagina Monologues,* I suspected that many would find the message of sexual freedom redundant and unnecessary; few did. Rather, they were shocked and pleasantly surprised to see sex discussed in such an open and affirming way.[13] And every semester, when I try to engage students in class discussions about why sex is holy, I am struck by how few readings I have to choose from and by how novel students find the concept.

One of my own adolescent sons once listed for me his top twenty questions about Christian faith, and among them was, "Why is sex so terrible?" Stunned, I asked him if he remembered that we had taught him that sex between married people is good. He said he did, sort of, but more real for him were the more recent exposures to sex education centered on avoiding sexual disease, pregnancy, and sexual predators.

---

12. See, for instance, Popcak, *Holy Sex.* A recent *Time* magazine story, Van Biema, "And God Said, 'Just Do It,'" notes the increase of seminars on good sex in Christian churches.

13. This is not to say that they agree with everything in the play. Many note the absence of healthy, committed sexual relationships.

Moreover, those he hears speaking frequently and openly about sex are mostly people whose values he questions, while good, respectable people he knows well do not talk about sex the way they talk about books, politics, or religion. "If sex is so good," he asked, "why are people so ashamed of it?"

Contemporary Christians may be able to say, "sex is good," but we are far from knowing what we mean. While we have left *Modern Youth and Chastity* behind, we are not yet ready to discard post-Vatican II discussions linking sexual pleasure to the holy. And yet, we also stand in need of an alternative to the purely romantic or hedonistic approaches to sex prevalent in popular culture. In this chapter, I attempt to follow the lead of John Paul II and younger theologians by locating the goodness of sex in authentic self-giving. However, in doing so, I will not speak of self-gift as a key dimension of sex while neglecting other aspects of sex that are probably more recognizable for most people. While I will avoid speaking of pleasure as if it were all sex has to offer, I will suggest that pleasure is central to sex's deeper meaning. *My suspicion is that pleasure and self-gift are not really two separate dimensions of sex at all. Rather, it is in and through sexual pleasure that self-gift occurs.* With this in mind, I will argue as follows: (1) Though fertility is an important part of self-gift for some at all times, and for many at particular times, in the main the self-gift of married sex is personal and requires vulnerability, self-sacrifice, and bodily belonging; (2) Self-gift of this kind is directly linked to the giving and receiving of pleasure; (3) Good sex in marriage necessitates a commitment to an ongoing practice oriented to self-giving love through the pursuit of pleasure for oneself and one's spouse. My hope is that turning our gaze on the goodness of sex will allow us to move from a negative focus on sexual sin or an amoral separation of sex from faith to a positive discussion of how good sex in marriage might be pursued.

1. WHAT DOES IT MEAN TO GIVE YOURSELF TO A SPOUSE?

When John Paul II describes sex, he speaks of the mutual self-giving between spouses as its core. Truly human sex "by means of which man and woman give themselves to one another ... is by no means something purely biological, but concerns the innermost being of the human person as such."[14] Although the importance of self-giving is clear, its substance is less so. What, after all, does it mean to give one's "innermost being" to another in a particular act? For the pope, self-giving is not simply giving one's love, because certain forms of sex between people who love each other are not fully giving. Sex between partners who are unmarried cannot be fully self-giving, because only a commitment to lifelong marriage bespeaks total, irrevocable self-gift.[15] Likewise, contraception impedes self-gift because a part of the self—one's fertility—is held back.[16] Furthermore, if a spouse could fail to give the temporal or fertile dimensions of him or herself, it seems that the spouse could also err by failing to give another part of the self.

Fertility

Is fertility the heart of self-gift? Numerous accounts of couples who forgo contraception in favor of NFP support the centrality of fertility attested to by John Paul II.[17] John Grabowski holds that John Paul II sees fertility not simply as "a biological part of the person that can be altered at his or her discretion," but "an existential reality . . . pertain[ing] to the person as a whole."[18] Most theologians writing about sexual ethics, however, see fertility as possible gift that is only rarely brought forward over the long course of married life.[19] They do not understand themselves as failing to give when they hold back that possibility, or when that possibility is nullified by age. They do not feel used or betrayed by a spouse in these situations, as they would if one of them engaged in sex without love, because fertility is not understood by most as integral to the self at all times.

14. John Paul II, *Familiaris consortio*, no. 11.

15. Ibid.: "The total physical self-giving [between unmarried persons] would be a lie if it were not the sign and fruit of total personal self-giving, in which the whole person, including the temporal dimension, is present."

16. Ibid.: "[When couples use contraception they] 'manipulate' and 'degrade' human sexuality and with it themselves and their married partner by altering its value of 'total' self-giving."

17. Rubio, "Beyond the Liberal/Conservative Divide on Contraception," 279–80.

18. Grabowski, *Sex and Virtue*, 131. He notes that the Pope finds this understanding of fertility or "sexual union as embodied self-giving" in the Genesis account of creation.

19. Rubio, "Beyond the Liberal/Conservative Divide on Contraception," 280–81. See also Salzman and Lawler, *Sexual Person*, 73.

Despite this continuing disagreement, both groups would agree that there is much more to self-giving than fertility. Grabowski, for instance, speaks eloquently to potential of sex to be "a recollection and enactment of a couple's marriage promise to one another," "a bodily gesture of self-offering."[20] Margaret Farley suggests that sex can be "openness to the other in the intimacy of embodied selves."[21] Both are reaching for language that expresses the personal self-gift that works through two sexually-engaged bodies. Both are deeply concerned with the personal dimension of sexual self-gift.

However, some married theologians have raised concerns about the implications of total self-gift as an ethical norm, noting that it seems all but impossible to give one's whole self to one's spouse in any one sexual act,[22] and worrying that the language may unhelpfully imply "two halves who need to become one whole," which "suggests a form of self-sacrifice that has never been good, especially for women."[23] Grabowski counters that married spouses can give themselves as they are without fearing they are not living up to romantic ideals of passionate love in each moment, for the "'objective' meaning of the bodily language they speak may or may not be fully assimilated in the couple's 'subjective' experience at any given moment."[24] This seems a healthy realism, but, as Grabowski realizes, we need to further our understanding of how sex can be "a dialogue of love."[25] If we cannot talk about how sex in marriage can be less or more self-giving on a personal level, the norm of self-gift seems relatively empty.

It seems necessary, then, to put aside for the moment disputes about the necessity of giving one's fertility in each and every sexual act and acknowledge that personal union is the primary intention, action, consequence, and experience of most married sexual encounters. Unity is the reason most couples make room for sex in their lives over time. Therefore, the primary location of self-gift is here. This does not mean that the giving of one's fertility—especially with the hope and intention of conceiving a child, is not a particularly significant moment of self-

20. Salzman and Lawler, *Sexual Person*, 68.

21. Farley, *Just Love*, 173.

22. McCarthy, *Sex and Love in the Home*, 43–48.

23. Ibid., 266.

24. McCarthy, *Sex and Love in the Home*, 69.

25. Ibid., 142.

giving sex in marriage.[26] It does not deny that the willingness to accept a child (while having sex at such a time or in such a way that the possibility of conception is severely restricted) is a genuine instance self-gift. It does suggest the larger significance of personal self-gift in the sexual lives of married couples, as well as the need to think more about what the personal dimension of self-gift entails so that the term can function not just as an ethical limit but as an ethical ideal for married couples seeking good sex. What, then, does self-gift mean on a personal level?

Vulnerability

Self-giving entails vulnerability, the willingness to risk bringing one's true self and one's desires to another person. Good sex that is self-giving involves the vulnerability of self-exposure that is symbolized by nakedness but also involves the emotions. There is a certain risk not only in physically baring oneself but in seeking or longing for another person's embrace. Enda McDonagh speaks movingly of the vulnerability in married sexual friendship, within which spouses "reveal and cherish more of each other's distinctiveness, strangeness and otherness. All of this is heightened by their sexual otherness, the desire it kindles and the fear it may provoke in its very strangeness."[27] Vulnerability means acknowledging that one's own needs cannot be met by oneself alone; we each stand in need of another. To be vulnerable is an ongoing task that allows two persons to bring more and more of "innermost being" to each other.

It is the vulnerability of sex that causes most contemporary theologians to argue that sex belongs in committed relationships, usually marriage. Karen Lebacqz's short essay, "Appropriate Vulnerability," argues that there is too much risk in sex with those who are not mutually committed:

> Sexuality has to do with vulnerability. Eros, the desire for another, the passion that accompanies the wish for sexual expression, makes one vulnerable. It creates possibilities for greater joy but also for greater suffering. To desire another, to feel passion, is to be vulnerable, capable of being wounded.[28]

26. Traina, "Papal Ideals and Marital Realities: One View From the Ground," 273–74.

27. McDonaugh, *Vulnerable to the Holy*, 91.

28. Karen Lebacqz, "Appropriate Vulnerability," 258. Donna Freitas's book, *Sex & the Soul* vividly showcases the lack of vulnerability in the sex lives of most college students who substitute pleasure for intimacy.

Lebacqz finds appropriate vulnerability in the lack of shame Adam and Eve feel despite their nakedness and advises that it can most often be found in marriage because of the safety commitment brings.[29] Her claims resonate because many know the sting of inappropriate vulnerability and the security and satisfaction of committed relationships that allow room for risk and growth.

Though one can engage in sex without vulnerability, surely it is less than ideal. As Christine Gudorf writes, "Going through the motions of sex, without having first gone through the struggle to understand, disclose, and compromise around differences is sex without symbolic meaning."[30] It is sex without vulnerability. If sex outside of marriage is a lie because it does not express the joining that bodies speak, sex without vulnerability is not fully truthful either, even when partners are married. The tradition has often spoken of desire in physical terms only, as if it were given. The only ethical challenge was controlling it. Contemporary writers speak from experience of desire as risk, as struggle, as something many try to avoid. We can now say that the vulnerability of self-exposure—including desire—is a good to be pursued.

Sex within marriage, then, ought to be appropriately vulnerable. In marriage, partners are able to risk exposure and failure "in a mutually vulnerable and mutually committed relationship."[31] Couples who consistently work to open themselves to each other, to reveal more and more of their "innermost being" and their love for their partner, are training themselves in intimacy. A sexual relationship like this "becomes a school for love. It teaches us that when we bare our full selves, not only our bodies but our feelings, desires, fears, and commitments and offer ourselves to the loved spouse who loves us, that we are rewarded with intimacy that offers us closeness, communion, stimulation, and companionship."[32] While self-exposure within marriage is far less risky than casual sex, if taken seriously, it can be far more demanding. Mutual, personal vulner-

---

29. Lebacqz, "Appropriate Vulnerability," 259–60. Lebacqz does not rule out the possibility of appropriate vulnerability in other kinds of committed relationships.

30. Ibid., 259–60.

31. Ibid., 260.

32. Gudorf, "Why Sex Is Good for Your Marriage," 129. McDonagh goes further, claiming that vulnerability in marital friendship prepares us for vulnerability to the holy, *Vulnerable to the Holy*, 92.

ability is a crucial part of a sexual relationship that aims toward self-giving.

Sacrifice

Sacrifice is another part of self-giving, personally considered. The Christian tradition has rarely associated self-sacrifice with sexual relationships. Historically, marital sex has been associated with lust and pleasure, justified first only by procreation, later because it kept spouses from seeking sexual pleasure elsewhere, and later still because it promoted the union of the spouses. If sacrifice was involved, it was the sacrifice of spouse (usually the wife) who was encouraged to acknowledge the "marital right" of her husband to sex even if she was not interested.[33] Because sex involves pleasure, engaging in it was viewed as self-indulgence, not self-gift.

However, contemporary theologians affirm that good sex requires sacrifice and may develop the capacity to sacrifice. David Cloutier writes that practicing chastity within marriage means not "withholding the gift, but giving the gift only when it 'fits'... couples who use NFP have testified that the 'rhythm' of the method has actually brought them closer together."[34] Self-sacrifice is connected to self-giving and union. However, even those who do not use NFP attest to the import of sacrifice, because all sex involves surrendering to an intimate encounter with another person through which we find ourselves.[35] When two people are making love, they must free themselves of self-centeredness in order to enter more fully into the reality of their union. Sidney Callahan notes that this will sometimes be difficult, for "[j]ust as the mind flees God, the nonintegrated self evades full sexual focus on another by relapsing into rational thought, irrelevancies, or drifting into self-absorption," yet it is worth disciplining oneself, for "[a] collected, integrated self cannot only give

---

33. A good, brief overview of development in the tradition is Selling, "Meanings of Human Sexuality."

34. Cloutier, *Love, Reason, and God's Story*, 207.

35. See John Grabowski, who argues that all human beings "are created for love" and "fulfilled in the self-donation of love," *Sex and Virtue*, 125, or Christine Gudorf, who sees in orgasm a surrender of self-control, "a little death, a losing of oneself," that can potentially open people up to become more self-giving in all areas of their lives, *Body, Sex, and Pleasure*, 108–9.

more but can give more easily."[36] Giving oneself to one's spouse requires sacrifice, even if every act will not reach the heights of intentional, pure, and total self-giving.

Moreover, because sex involves two people with different sex drives, sexual histories, sexual preferences, and personalities, finding a practice that works for both of them requires self-giving on the part of both. There will be sacrifice when one chooses to be open to sex or to forgo sex in response to the other. As studies show that sexual frequency declines over time but high frequency is associated with sexual and marital satisfaction, this negotiation and sensitivity to changing needs and desires will need to continue over time.[37] Few theologians today would welcome a return to the language of marital rights; yet sex, when truly giving and not simply using the other person, requires self-sacrifice so that each can adequately recognize the needs of the other.[38] There is no one standard of frequency; couples need to find a balance that is right for them. However, the prevalence of sexual and marital dissatisfaction suggests that many look elsewhere for the attention they should be receiving from their spouses, whether physical or emotional. Couples have to find a regular sexual practice that is satisfying and meaningful to both. The sacrifice this entails (whether in having sex or giving it up) should not be avoided.

Some theologians have been critical of the emphasis of traditional Catholic theology on sacrifice. Mitch Finley, for instance, believes a lingering sense that couples can have too much self-indulgent sex is underneath the advocacy of Natural Family Planning. Instead, he argues that because sex is so personal and spiritual, couples should no more seek to avoid sex than avoid Mass.[39] In one sense, his caution seems correct: sex is not some dark pleasure that one is better off without. On the other hand, good sexual practice might sometimes call for a break from sex. If a full spiritual life involves regular Sunday Mass, it might also call for yoga, a walk, a prayer group, or meditation, depending on individual needs. Even if Mass has privileged status, all are paths to intimacy with God. Similarly, whether abstaining from sex because couples are respect-

36. Callahan, *Beyond Birth Control,* 140.

37. Call et al, "Incidence and Frequency of Marital Sex," 650.

38. See, for instance, Grabowski, *Sex and Virtue,* 125, and Gudorf, *Body, Sex, and Pleasure,* 119.

39. Finley, "Dark Side," 207.

ing the natural rhythm of a woman's cycle or because they need to do something else instead, they will sometimes have to sacrifice in order to deepen their sexual relationship.

Sacrifice is fundamental to a strong commitment to continue having sex over time, even when sex becomes routine. During many periods in a couple's marriage, there will be challenges to keeping up a regular sex life: pregnancy, illness, travel, children and parents requiring care, demanding jobs, personal difficulties, etc. Couples who nonetheless refuse to let their sexual practice die are seeking the sacred in the ordinary and affirming it, even when it might be easier not to. Though this is not the sort of sexual sacrifice traditionally upheld, the work of contemporary theologians reinforces the claim both having sex and forgoing it can be vital parts of self-giving love for married couples.

Bodily Belonging

Spouses do not simply seek greater emotional or spiritual union through sex; they also seek to be united in their bodies. The bodily union is not simply something they work at so that they can be more spiritually integrated. Through good sex, they become more self-giving and more strongly wedded bodily and spiritually.

Some theologians see each sexual act as a reenactment of a couple's marital vows. Drawing on John Paul II's theology of the body and canon law regarding the necessity of sex to seal the covenant promises of sacramental marriage, Grabowski holds that sex is "an activity that seals the covenant relationship between man and woman in marriage. As such, it has an anamnetic quality in that it is a recollection and enactment of what the couple promise in their vows to one another."[40] Grabowski invests sex with spiritual and relational significance that it has historically lacked by connecting the practice of sex to liturgy and highlighting its role in solidifying spousal bonds.

In this context, in which we have largely put behind us dualist thinking and suspicion of desire, the traditional marriage formula, "With my body, I thee wed," is more intelligible. Adrian Thatcher points out that Christians have turned to Trinitarian imagery to understand human beings as fundamentally relational and desire as the good impulse that draws us together. Desire is not a state of imperfection to be overcome,

---

40. Grabowski, *Sex and Virtue*, 47–48.

but is "what brings us out of ourselves, rescue[s] us from private self-hood, drive[s] us to seek the arms of our beloved, to reach out from ourselves, to learn to love."[41] Physical desire, in all its messiness then, is a reminder of human neediness and interconnection, and sexual union is an expression of both. It is a celebration of belonging.

Yet, it is important not to overstate the significance of any one sexual act. David McCarthy rightly criticizes the common claim that "[s]exual desire moves us toward a complete unity of selves."[42] He rightly notes that every sexual act cannot be all of this. "Not in an instant, but over time, we come to belong. . . . what we do today gains its meaning in relation to yesterday and what we will do tomorrow. For sex to have depth, it needs extended bodily communion over time."[43] Sex is ordinary—part of a bodily life lived in common in the context of the household. Yet, like all good practices, it also points toward the transcendent, precisely because the bodies of husbands and wives come together so many times during their common life.

In any sexual encounter, husbands and wives may recall moments of their sexual life together: their wedding night and honeymoon; those nights when they wanted to conceive a child; times when they came together after a long absence, difficult pregnancy, or period of estrangement; times when they sought comfort because of the illness or death of a family member or personal failures; the celebratory sex of anniversaries and good news. Their many sexual encounters fade into each other, yet as bodies change, children are born and grow, and commitments shift, still here is this practice, this ritual they enact again and again, extending their mutual belonging.

For married couples, sex that is good on a personal level requires the vulnerability of self-exposure, the sacrifice of attending to the needs of another over time, and the seeking of a bodily belonging that brings them together in a personal union marked in their bodies. This is what is means to give one's "innermost being" to a partner, not in one single act, but in a sexual relationship embedded in marriage that extends through time.

---

41. Adrian Thatcher, "Intimate Relationships and the Christian Way," 6.
42. McCarthy, *Sex and Love in the Home*, 43.
43. Ibid., 45–46.

2. SEXUAL SELF-GIFT IS DIRECTLY LINKED TO PLEASURE

Even if the most significant aspect of sexual self-giving is personal, it does not follow that pleasure is unimportant. Traditional Catholic accounts of sexuality downplay the significance of pleasure by naming procreation and union as the two inseparable ends, while considering pleasure to be a good and natural consequence of loving sex that is open to procreation. This is surely preferable to traditional writings offering only suspicion of sexual pleasure. However, pleasure is still viewed as something that results when couples do the more important work of personal self-giving. It is not something that a good Christian pursues, for to do so is to act selfishly or disrespect a spouse.[44] John Paul II's emphasis, before he became pope, on the beauty of simultaneous orgasm is representative of this approach. Many have remarked on the idealism of such as emphasis, but more significant in my view is the pope's ambivalence about the seeking of pleasure.[45] When both spouses experience pleasure at the same moment, both can be understood as primarily focused on giving the other pleasure, rather than receiving it. Popcak makes this point explicit in his book *Holy Sex* (an attempt to bring the pope's theology to a broader audience), arguing that it is better to always think of one's partner's pleasure.[46] Even if, paradoxically, this loving attitude will result in greater pleasure for oneself, this cannot be the focus. Pleasure is a consequence of personal self-giving, but not a legitimate pursuit.

However, my contention is that the active pursuit of sexual pleasure is intimately connected to the personal self-giving of good sex. In the previous section, I explored three aspects of that self-giving. In this section, I show how all three involve the active pursuit of sexual pleasure.

---

44. Though Gregory K. Popcak goes a long way toward expressing a healthy appreciation of pleasure in *Holy Sex*, he limits its significance by identifying what he calls the One Rule of Infallible Lovers, "a couple may do whatever they wish as long as both feel loved and respected and the marital act ends with the man climaxing inside the woman" (191). The demand to give one's fertility in every act overrides personal needs and desires that may draw the couple closer together at a deeper level.

45. Wojtyla, *Love and Responsibility*, 272–73.

46. Popcak, *Holy Sex*, 260. Infallible lovers, Popcak claims, "*focus* primarily on meeting the *other's* needs, trusting that their own needs will be met in turn. This way, each lover gets all of his or her needs met without having to be selfish or self-protective" (260).

Vulnerability

Vulnerability involves exposure not only of affections and weaknesses, but also of desires. There is vulnerability in sexual longing for another person. One acknowledges that one's own needs cannot be met by oneself alone. At times, physical and emotional desires can be overpowering. Admitting this and then allowing another person to be the one who tries to meet those desires is risky. Finding a satisfying practice for two different people is not always easy. Perhaps the desired spouse will not be equally desirous. Perhaps one will be uneasy with the other's sexual longing or with the ways in which the other wants to find sexual pleasure. Perhaps one will find the other's naked body or the depths of the other's desire unattractive. Perhaps one will grow frustrated with the process before the other. Speaking desire aloud is risky, even with a beloved spouse, who is always "other," even when deeply loved and deeply known. Popcak advises, "[w[hen your spouse asks you to expand your sexual repetoire beyond your immediate comfort zone, I encourage you to understand your spouse's desire as God's invitation to you to grow in new ways to express God's own complete, total, unreserved passion for your mate."[47] Though one might quarrel with the emphasis on novelty, there is wisdom in the idea that personally self-giving sex involves the risk of self-exposure that comes in seeking pleasure and responding to one's beloved.

Furthermore, personally self-giving sex involves the vulnerability of allowing oneself to give into a certain measure of abandon. While some measure of self-control or moderation is a necessary if one is to take one's partner's needs seriously, good sex also means letting go. Mary Pellauer writes frankly of the riskiness of acknowledging her own sexual desire, "The middle is often confusing. I often do not know exactly what I want or need at this time. This stage does not supply me or my partner with clear guidance about how to satisfy these deep undercurrents. Sometimes I flail around. But in the farther reaches of this phase, I would do anything to make this last forever."[48] Pellauer speaks to the longing, the frustration, the imperfection of sex in marriage. She describes, from a woman's perspective, the vulnerability of expressing desire, figuring out how to satisfy desire, and allowing desire to be met. "That my pleasure

---

47. Popcak, *Holy Sex*, 203.

48. Pellauer, "Moral Significance," 157.

was important to him, this was hard to accept, to let in. That he would refuse his own release till I had mine, that he was willing to persist in trying to bring my release/ecstasy, that he reveled in it: This shook me very deeply.... I experience it as grace, an instance of his vulnerability-to-me reaching out to meet my vulnerability to him."[49] The one who allows herself to be this vulnerable gives herself, her "innermost being," just as surely as the partner who tries so hard to answer her desires. The grace of which Pellauer speaks comes about because one spouse is willing to express desire, and the other is willing to answer that call.

The Christian tradition has been uncomfortable accepting pleasure because of the obvious excesses of hedonistic sex, so prevalent in our culture. This is particularly the case in this moment, when the rise of "hook-up culture" alerts us to the need to emphasize the goodness of self-giving love in committed relationships. And we should not fail to emphasize this good. However, it is important to also remember that within commitment, there is freedom to love and be loved, to give and receive, to ask and answer. It is not wrong to say, therefore, that good sexual practice that is self-giving involves acknowledging and speaking the way one wants to be loved. Part of being exposed to one's spouse is exposing one's sexual desires. To seek one's own pleasure in sex one must consider oneself worthy of receiving pleasure, worthy of being loved. This dimension of sex is crucial to self-gift. Theologian John Giles Milhaven recognizes the individual enjoyment in sex and yet shows how it results in spousal union that transcends individual selves. He describes the experience of falling asleep next to his wife in terms that sound almost hedonistic:

> ... as I slope down with Julie to sleep, thoughts float off. I don't think. I enjoy. I enjoy myself.... It's hard to describe since it lasts only seconds and I scarcely notice it happening. The bliss is not just in the losing of tension, concerns, thoughts, etc. Voluptuous fullness takes over me. I am filled by the pleasure of swelling desire and the pleasure of desire collapsing into sweet satisfaction. Gluttonous, needy, triumphant desire of the enveloping darkness.[50]

49. Ibid.

50. Milhaven, "Sleeping Like Spoons," 88. Milhaven claims he is reporting the experience of his friend Fergie, but it is at least arguable that he is speaking of his own experience.

His concern is with his own pleasure, but the context for his pursuit of joy is clearly a marriage in which both he and Julie are deeply known and loved.[51] Further, it is through his pursuit of his own pleasure that he becomes—unconsciously—a source of pleasure for his wife. Their union is not separate from but rooted in their own desires.

Affirming the pursuit of pleasure as a part of vulnerability in sexual relationships calls women and men to enter as fully into sex as they can and give as much of themselves as possible, not fearing but embracing the needy part of themselves.

Sacrifice

Conversely, the pursuit of sexual pleasure also involves sacrifice. For instance, self-control is needed for good sex that is a source of true pleasure for both men and women. NFP advocates note that times of abstinence involve a measure of self-mastery that is necessary for good sex. Sex when called for is then fully human because not driven by blind instinct.[52] Moreover, many women experience more pleasure with NFP, finding its rhythms closer to their own.[53] Others note that self-control is necessary to honor one's partner's need for pleasure. Christine Gudorf in particular calls men to greater self-control and persistence in helping their wives achieve orgasm.[54] John Paul II's advocacy of mutual, simultaneous orgasm also relies on the self-control of both spouses, particularly, as he notes, men.[55] In all of these cases, self-giving involves self-control related to the pursuit of pleasure. With a certain measure of sacrifice, more pleasure is possible, and so is more deeply personal sexual practice. We ought not worry that the pursuit of pleasure for oneself must result in the neglect of self-giving or of one's partner. The pursuit of pleasure involves self-sacrifice. It does not lead away from unitive sex but toward it.

51. Milhaven, "Sleeping Like Spoons," writes, "I don't think of Julie as I go off to sleep. She's not in my mind. But she's in my legs, torso, and arms. Not in my head. Without thinking of it, I know her there going to sleep like me. I know her knowing me the same way. This must be why that trust rises swiftly and fills us" (89).

52. Shivanadan, "Natural Family Planning and the Theology of the Body," 25.

53. Rubio, "Beyond the Liberal/Conservative Divide on Contraception," 292.

54. Gudorf, Body, Sex, and Pleasure, 85. Gudorf carefully distinguishes between control and repression.

55. Wojtyla, Love and Responsibility, 272–73.

Must sexual pleasure be actively pursued instead of gratefully received? Most theologians are willing to affirm the good of sexual pleasure for men and women in marriage, but "generally presume it to be … automatic."[56] However, Patricia Jung makes a strong case that cultural norms make it more difficult for women to experience pleasure.[57] She notes that 26 percent of women regularly do not experience climax, 32 percent report a lack of interest in sex, and 23 percent said sex is not pleasurable for them.[58] Certainly, more women today expect to experience sexual pleasure, but some are frustrated or content to let it go. Grabowski argues that even though the tradition has not paid a great deal of attention to this problem, "a case can be made that psychologically and theologically this sexual release within the context of bodily union is not unrelated to the gift of self that intercourse signifies."[59] Getting to the deeper involvement that Grabowski, following John Paul II, advocates may entail some sacrifice, as women move through pain or boredom to find what is pleasing to them, and as men confront the pain of not being able to satisfy their spouses, and take the focus off their own pleasure, but keep striving and giving of themselves to enable their wives' self-gift. The pursuit of pleasure may involve significant sacrifice, but it is a necessary part of a practice of sex that is truly self-giving for both.

Bodily Belonging

The seeking of pleasure is also central to bodily belonging, the third dimension of self-gift, for it is desire for pleasure that pulls couples into the practice of physical embrace that is necessary to belonging. There is a relationship between the capacity to seek and experience pleasure and the capacity to give of one's self and unite with a partner. Gudorf rightly notes the intermingling of self-love and other-love, showing that sex involves not a contest but a dance in which seeking pleasure for oneself gives pleasure to one's partner and experiencing the pleasure of one's partner cannot easily be separated from one's own physical pleasure.[60]

56. Jung, "Sanctifying Women's Pleasure," 81.

57. Ibid., 84–89.

58. All figures cited in Jung, "Sanctifying Women's Pleasure," 82, from the 1992 National Health and Social Life Survey.

59. Grabowski, *Sex and Virtue*, 141. Grabowski allows that this ideal may not always be realized.

60. Gudorf, *Body, Sex, and Pleasure*, 115–16.

The good of self and neighbor are so intertwined as to be inseparable. As Jung puts it, "[o]ur sexuality draws us into one another's arms—and consequently into an awareness of and concern about the needs of that other."[61] Giving a central place to the pursuit of sexual pleasure is crucial to a maintaining a sexual practice experienced as bodily belonging.

Bodily belonging is both sexual and the spiritual. William May claims that sex drive is not subhuman but "integrally personal," if ordered by chastity.[62] He posits that marriage is a "communion in being" and sex "is intended to foster this communion in being." Sex is how husbands and wives communicate and cement their communion.[63] With their bodies they speak their desire to live for each other, to belong to each other. This claim is helpful as long as desire is not spiritualized, but understood as it is experienced—as desire to experience pleasure and be pleasure for one's partner, to touch or be touched in ways that produce the greatest pleasure, to be inside or engulf the most intimate part of the other, to rest in intimate physical embrace. We should not run from the physicality of this desire, even as we know it is more than physical. Married couples know that they engage in this dance with their whole selves. It is in and through not just the joys but the struggles of their lives (through family arguments, job losses, the pain of seeing their children struggle, the deaths of parents and grandparents, dark times in their own relationship, etc.) that they want, connect, remember, and hold on. It is radically different than the pleasure experienced in a hook-up when desire is just desire. This is the bodily experience of belonging, the giving and receiving of one body to another over a lifetime.

Summing Up: Self-Gift and the Pursuit of Pleasure

What does pleasure have to do with self-gift? Everything. If we lose sight of this reality, we will spiritualize sex out of recognition. The tendency to say, "sex is good," and then go on to step over its physical reality to speak of its emotional and spiritual rewards, is still with us. It is necessary to keep reminding ourselves, sex as it is—as wanting one's own pleasure and the pleasure of one's partner—is what God gave human beings. These very physical drives scream out our neediness, our dependence,

61. Jung, "Sexual Fidelity," 94.
62. May, "Sexuality and Fidelity," 282–83.
63. Ibid., 286.

our creation for connection. These desires refuse to let us continue in the myth of independence. They point us squarely toward each other and pull us inside and around each other, lest we miss the message. Sex is all about self-gift because it involves vulnerability, self-sacrifice, and bodily belonging, but all of this takes place through the giving and receiving of pleasure. Sex involves a dance of hunger, feeding, and being fed, and celebrating, and it is because of these things and not apart from them that it is good.

3. TOWARD GOOD SEXUAL PRACTICE IN MARRIAGE

I began by discussing the present context, in which Christians hear all the time that sex is good, but fail to truly take in this good news because problems in the culture and the church. I located the heart of the problem in a reluctance to connect self-gift (praised whole-heartedly in the church and only partially in the culture) to pleasure (central in the culture, peripheral in the church). I set out to show that self-gift and pleasure are intimately connected, and to argue that Christian couples rightly pursue pleasure on the way to self-giving in their sexual relationships.

Some may argue that there are many other ways that couples give themselves to another, many of which are far more difficult and important than sex. They wonder if it is really appropriate to expend this much time and energy discussing a relatively minor part of married life. Isn't there far too much attention on sex already? Shouldn't we instead uphold the self-gift of spouses who care for sick partners, forgive spouses who cheat on them, or care for children while their spouse works far away from home, for example? Surely, it is good to remember that for an average married couple, sex accounts for just an hour or two of their week.[64] Often, it is probably not the most challenging task of the week, given other challenges.

However, I want to uphold sex as a crucial practice in marriage, a practice that is central to a Christian couple's efforts to live their marriage as discipleship, resisting the emptiness of a culture that prizes having over being.[65] What does sex have to do with resisting a materialist culture? Can sex be understood as a practice of resistance like prayer,

---

64. Call et al., "Incidence and Frequency of Marital Sex," 641.

65. John Paul II, *Solicitudo Rei Socialis*, no. 36.

fasting, or simplicity? Or, as one my students asked, "With sex, isn't it just yes or no?"

Though it may seem odd to think about sex in marriage as a fundamental practice of resistance, there are good reasons for doing so. I understand practice with Craig Dykstra and Dorothy Bass, as an intentional, shared action, situated in the context of a tradition, ordinary in outward appearances but transcendent in its association with fundamental human goods.[66] This understanding of practice allows for a different way of thinking about sex which allows us to ask what sort of sex life married couples *should* have, and ponder what goods they *ought* to seek. A practice of sex in marriage can be a powerful response to the culture of consumerism, a rejoinder to the loss of solidarity that is so distressingly common. But it can do this only if couples pursue sex as self-giving. Faithful sexual practice in marriage requires an ongoing, regular commitment to bring one's whole self into relationship with one's spouse. Only with this kind of commitment can spouses grow in the bodily and personal intimacy necessary for the kind of marriage John Paul II calls "communion," and prepare them for solidarity with others outside the home.[67]

A positive Christian sexual ethic assumes the potential of sex to speak the commitment of marriage vows, not in explicit promises or earth-shattering experiences, but in the very ordinary repetition over time of a bodily act that says, "I still want to be with you. I will always want to be with you." Such a practice ought to be attentive to three relational goods basic to sex, all of which are connected to the pursuit of pleasure. *Vulnerability* requires a disciplining of desires to a relationship, a reasonable limitation to free one's attention for one particular other. We say, in effect, "I'm not going to any place or to anyone else. I'll pour my relational energy into you." Thus committed, spouses are free to be increasingly vulnerable to one another over time and free to come forward with their desire to experience pleasure.

Good sexual practice also involves *self-sacrifice*. True self-giving love can only come about through the pursuit of pleasure that inspires a desire to sacrifice for its sake. If both spouses do not desire pleasure for

---

66. I am drawing on the rich discussion of practice in Dykstra and Bass, "A Theological Understanding of Christian Practices," 13–32. See also Bass, ed., *Practicing Our Faith*.

67. John Paul II, *Ecclesia in America*, nos. 42–52.

themselves, they are not fully loving themselves or connecting with their spouse. On the other hand, spouses who do not seek the pleasure of their partner fail to embrace a necessary measure of sacrifice that love requires. Binding myself to a changing other over time and committing to staying passionately engaged may sometimes require sacrifice. At times, retreating into myself would be the easier way, but self-gift is not always easy, and neither is self-giving sex, yet the good of marriage demands that we not stop trying to give, for self-giving and receiving involve the kind of risk that engenders deep relationship.

Finally, *bodily belonging* is perhaps the most significant aspect of self-giving married sex. Though couples share many bodily experiences, sex is unique to marital friendship and plays a key role in the development of one-flesh unity. If couples are faithfully committed to remaining connected, not just emotionally but physically, they will seek to maintain the sexual side of their life together. Honoring and nurturing sexual desire will bring them together bodily, emotionally, and spiritually. It will continue to open each spouse to the other, and that opening will not only nourish the communion of their married life together, it will prepare them to open themselves to others. Thus, sex is a foundational practice for Christian marriage, the first practice of resistance to which married couples committed to discipleship ought to be faithful.

BIBLIOGRAPHY

Bass, Dorothy C., editor. *Practicing Our Faith*. San Francisco: Jossey-Bass, 1997.

Cahill, Lisa Sowle. *Sex, Gender, and Christian Ethics*. Cambridge: Cambridge University Press, 1996.

Call, Vaughn, et al. "The Incidence and Frequency of Marital Sex in a National Sample." *Journal of Marriage and Family* 57 (1995) 639–52.

Callahan, Sidney. *Beyond Birth Control: The Christian Experience of Sex*. New York: Sheed & Ward, 1968.

Cloutier, David. *Love, Reason, and God's Story: An Introduction to Catholic Sexual Ethics*. Winona, MN: St. Mary's, 2008.

Dominian, Jack. *Let's Make Love: The Meaning of Sexual Intercourse*. London: Darton Longman & Todd, 2001.

Dykstra, Craig, and Dorothy C. Bass. "A Theological Understanding of Christian Practices." In *Practicing Theology: Beliefs and Practices in Christian Life*, edited by Miroslav Volf and Dorothy C. Bass, 13–32. Grand Rapids: Eerdmans, 2002.

Farley, Margaret A. *Just Love: A Framework for Christian Sexual Ethics*. New York: Continuum, 2006.

Finley, Mitch. "The Dark Side of Natural Family Planning." *America* 164 (February 23, 1991) 206–7.

Freitas, Donna. *Sex & the Soul: Juggling Sexuality, Spirituality, Romance, and Religion on America's College Campuses.* New York: Oxford University Press, 2008.

Grabowski, John. *Sex and Virtue: An Introduction to Sexual Ethics.* Washington, DC: Catholic University of America Press, 2003.

Gudorf, Christine E. *Body, Sex, and Pleasure: Reconstructing Christian Sexual Ethics.* Cleveland: Pilgrim, 1994.

———. "Why Sex Is Good for Your Marriage." In *Human Sexuality in the Catholic Tradition,* edited by Kieran Scott and Harold Daly Horell, 123–36. Lanham, MD: Rowman & Littlefield, 2007.

John Paul II, Pope. *Ecclesia in America.* Washington, DC: United States Catholic Conference, 1996.

———. *Familiaris Consortio.* Washington, DC: United States Catholic Conference, 1981.

———. *Solicitudo Rei Socialis.* Washington, DC: United States Catholic Conference, 1988.

Jung, Patricia Beattie. "A Case for Sexual Fidelity." *Word & World* 14:2 (1994) 115–24.

———. "Sanctifying Women's Pleasure." In *Good Sex: Feminist Perspectives from the World's Religions,* edited by Patricia Beattie Jung et al., 77–95. New Brunswick, NJ: Rutgers University Press, 2001.

Jung, Patricia Beattie, with Joseph Andrew Coray, eds. *Sexual Diversity and Catholicism: Toward the Development of Moral Theology.* Collegeville, MN: Liturgical, 2001.

Keane, Philip. *Sexual Morality: A Catholic Perspective.* New York: Paulist, 1977.

Kelly, SJ, Gerald. *Modern Youth and Chastity.* St. Louis: The Queen's Work, 1943. Kosnik, Anthony, et al. *Human Sexuality: New Directions in American Catholic Thought.* Garden City, NY: Doubleday, 1979.

Lawler, Michael, and Todd Salzman. *The Sexual Person: Toward a Renewed Catholic Anthropology.* Washington, DC: Georgetown University, 2008.

Lebacqz, Karen. "Appropriate Vulnerability." In *Sexuality and the Sacred,* edited by James B. Nelson and Sandra P. Longfellow, 256–61. Louisville: Westminster/John Knox Press, 1994.

Mahoney, John, SJ. *The Making of Moral Theology.* Oxford: Clarendon, 1987.

May, William E. "Sexuality and Fidelity in Marriage." *Communio* 5 (1978) 275–93.

McCarthy, David Matzko. *Sex and Love in the Home.* New ed. London: SCM, 2004.

McDonaugh, Enda. *Vulnerable to the Holy in Faith, Morality, and Art.* Dublin: The Columba Press, 2004.

Milhaven, John Giles. "Sleeping Like Spoons." In *Sexuality and the Sacred,* edited by James B. Nelson and Sandra P. Longfellow, 85–90. Louisville: Westminster John Knox, 1994.

Moore, O.P., Gareth. *The Body in Context: Sex and Catholicism.* New York: Continuum, 2001.

Pellauer, Mary. "The Moral Significance of Female Orgasm," In *Sexuality and the Sacred,* edited by James B. Nelson and Sandra P. Longfellow, 149–68. Louisville: Westminster John Knox, 1994.

Popcak, Gregory K. *Holy Sex: A Catholic Guide to Toe-Curling, Mind-Blowing, Infallible Loving.* New York: Crossroad, 2008.

Rubio, Julie Hanlon. "Beyond the Liberal/Conservative Divide on Contraception." *Horizons* 32 (2005) 270–94.

Scott, Kieran, and Harold Daly Horell, editors. *Human Sexuality in the Catholic Tradition.* Lanham, MD: Rowan & Littlefield, 2007.

Selling, Joseph A. *Embracing Sexuality: Authority and Experience in the Catholic Church.* Burlington, VT: Ashgate, 2001.

Selling, Joseph A. "The Meanings of Human Sexuality." *Louvain Studies* 23 (1998) 22–37.

Shannon, William, editor. *The Lively Debate: Responses to Humanae Vitae.* New York: Sheed & Ward, 1970.

Shivanadan, Mary. *Crossing the Threshold of Love: A New Vision of Marriage.* Washington, DC: Catholic University of America Press, 1999.

———. "Natural Family Planning and the Theology of the Body." *National Catholic Bioethics Quarterly* 3 (2003) 23–32.

Thatcher, Adrian. "Intimate Relationships and the Christian Way." *Modern Believing* 44 (2003) 5–14.

Traina, Cristina. "Papal Ideals, Marital Realities: One View From the Ground." In *Sexual Diversity and Catholicism*, edited by Patricia Beattie Jung, 269–88. Collegeville, MN: Liturgical, 2001.

Van Biema, David. "And God Said, 'Just Do It.'" *Time* (June 26, 2008).

Whitehead, Evelyn and James. *Marrying Well: Possibilities in Christian Marriage Today.* Garden City, NY: Doubleday, 1981.

Wilson, Brenda. "Sex Without Intimacy: No Dating, No Relationships." *NPR Morning Edition* (June 8, 2009).

Wojtyla, Karol. *Love and Responsibility.* Translated by H. T. Willetts. San Francisco: Ignatius, 1993.

11

A Theologically Premised Theory of Sexual Difference

Augustine, Barth, and Contemporary Revisionists

CHRISTOPHER C. ROBERTS

D OES THE DIFFERENCE BETWEEN male and female matter for marriage, and if so, how and why? Are there compelling theological
reasons for insisting that the two human protagonists in a marriage
should be sexually differentiated, or is marriage a more flexible covenant, which any two humans can keep, and for which sexual difference
is indifferent?

Answering these questions comprehensively requires many necessary and overlapping lines of inquiry. Biblical exegesis, systematic
theology, feminist philosophy, and so on—the relevant scholarship is
overwhelming. But since it is the present crisis in the theology of marriage which helps to raise our questions about sexual difference, it is appropriate to begin by reviewing what prior traditions of moral theology
about marriage have actually claimed.

THE EARLY PATRISTIC BACKGROUND

As is commonly known, Augustine is the key theologian and interpreter
of scripture for the dominant tradition of western theology about marriage.[1] To appreciate how Augustine has formed our tradition over against

1. Good historical introductions to this tradition include Banner, "Sexualitat" and
Woodhead, "Woman/Femininity." Professor Banner was my PhD supervisor, and Dr.
Woodhead was one of my external PhD examiners, and I am very grateful to both of
them for guiding my thoughts on this topic. Of course, neither of them are responsible

alternative possibilities, it helps to begin with a brief note about the most important Christian theorists of sex, celibacy, and marriage prior to the establishment of what we might term an Augustinian consensus.

If one reads the likes of Tatian, Tertullian, Clement of Alexandria, Gregory of Nyssa, and Jerome, one finds that they had a great deal to say about habituating sexual behaviour into forms compatible with Christian polities, yet their views on the significance of sexual difference itself are scattered, ad hoc, and contradictory. Perhaps this inchoateness is owing to the fact that they rarely entertain the topic directly; to learn what they might have thought about it, one usually has to read their treatises on marriage and virginity with an eye towards what is latent and presupposed. Did God create male and female for the sake of prelapsarian life, or is our existence as sexed creatures ineluctably associated with sin, something which God made only because he knew we were destined to be fallen, fleshly creatures? Are humans fundamentally sexual, destined to always be male or female even in the age when there is no more marriage, or is the teleological thrust of Christian life towards a certain angelic sexlessness, an eschatologically neutered identity in which humanity is synthesized into some third thing, something beyond the tangibility of male and female which we know in history? Is our sexual duality something for which we should give thanks, a vocation which somehow should evoke our gratitude and praise, or is it something which we should lament, a fleshly handicap, a consolation prize, something which we can aspire to overcome, something which is besides the point *en route* to more ultimate things? Taken as a group, and often even within the writings of a single theologian, there are no consistent answers to these questions in the early patristic theologians.[2] The early fathers both presupposed, and occasionally argued, contradictory answers to these questions.

AUGUSTINE'S ARGUMENT AND A NEW THEOLOGICAL SYNTHESIS

However, after Augustine, in at least the mainstream of moral theology in the west, one can discern relatively consistent answers to these

---

for the shortcomings of my argument and presentation. I have not, unfortunately, been able to assimilate all of their advice.

2. I examine the pre-Augustinian theologies of sexual difference in more detail in chapter 1 of my book, Roberts, *Creation and Covenant*.

questions. Again, as with the earlier theologians, it is not as if Augustine and his successors regularly had this discussion in any systematic way. It is only relatively recently in the west, arguably with the writings of Karl Barth, that the subject has become a topic for systematic investigation. But from time to time the subject does arise, usually in the service of other theological themes, as a brief exegesis of Augustine helps to demonstrate.

From around the year 400 onwards, Augustine's own evolving views begin to stabilize, and his mature arguments on this topic are relatively clear and concentrated in book 14 and a few other places in *The City of God*. Here Augustine argues that the purpose of God's creation is to raise up a people who will dwell with him eternally. From the beginning, Augustine proposes that God had in mind a society of rightly-ordered love, the heavenly city, and that this city needed to be populated with flesh and blood persons. To populate this city, the two protological humans needed to reproduce. Augustine says that "the coupling of male and female is the seedbed, as it were, of a city."[3] Thus Augustine's theorizing about sexual difference, and marriage, begins on the premise that these things were always supposed to be a cornerstone not for the human species in general, but for human social life in its primordial ecclesial form. Being in the flesh as male and female is not a curse, for it pertains to creation's original goodness: "the procreation of children pertains to the glory of marriage, not to the punishment of sin."[4] The marriage of male and female is one way in which human creatures participate in divine providence.

However, while our sin could not derail providence, life is no longer innocent on humanity's side. As fallen mortals, we live at least partially in the earthly city, which "is made up of men who live according to the flesh,"[5] as if our good creatureliness were something even better than it actually is. There can be no peace in such a city, riven and divided against the real good. In the pride-driven, absurd attempt to ground ourselves in ourselves, we are all in an inherently unstable, chaotic situation. No true freedom of action is possible in a context whose first premise is disobedience.

---

3. Augustine *City of God* §15.16 (667).

4. Ibid., §14.21 (620–21).

5. Ibid., §14.1 (581).

Given that Augustinian sexual difference is a nexus with both biological and spiritual significance, it is perhaps not surprising that Augustine finds the sexually differentiated organs a particularly apt illustration of our disordered existential situation. Before sin, Augustine speculates that man and woman could have used their sex organs for coitus under the governance of an ordered love and a rational will; as every aspect of their lives would have been ordered to the love of God, their sexuality would be no different. Sex would be used for its natural, created purposes of populating the heavenly city and thus undergirding the social life of the saints. In this hypothesis, when the time came to procreate, Adam and Eve could have employed their genitals with the same freedom of will with which we now move our other limbs: "We move our hands and feet to perform their tasks when we so will, without any conflict and with all the ease that we observe in ourselves and others. . . . Why, then, with respect to the procreation of children, should we not believe that the sexual organs could have been as obedient to the will of mankind as the other members are. . . ."[6] Sexuality could have been— should have been and would have been—an aspect of human life lived in freedom, "in tranquillity of mind" and "without any corruption."[7]

But now, post-fall and with the root of disobedience in our will, sex is different. Now the sexual organs are efficacious only in conditions of lust, i.e., when our freedom has been overcome and our appetite appears irresistible. "But the sexual organs have somehow fallen so completely under the sway of lust that they have no power of movement at all if this passion is absent, and unless it has either arisen of its own accord or been aroused by another."[8] We are in some sense alienated from ourselves, for we cannot control when we are aroused, and we cannot control when we are frigid or impotent. Augustine summarizes:

> Sometimes the urge arises unwanted; sometimes, on the other hand, it forsakes the eager lover, and desires grow cold in the body even while burning in the mind. Thus strangely, then, does lust refuse to serve not only the desire to beget, but even the lust for lewd enjoyment.[9]

6. Ibid., §14.23 (623).
7. Ibid., §14.26 (629).
8. Ibid., §14.19 (619).
9. Ibid., §14.16 (614–15).

The notion of a divided will, the notion of a person divided against him or herself, has been a feature of Augustine's anthropology at least since the *Confessions*. Here Augustine not only exegeted Romans 7:15, and speculated about his own confused motives as an adolescent stealing pears for no real reason, but he also confessed his sexual confusion, as someone with a rabid appetite who was once convinced it would be impossible to live a celibate life.[10]

Sometimes modern readers react incredulously to Augustine's speculations about protological sexuality;[11] the innuendo of penises rising and falling with obedience or disobedience to the will can sound farcical to some; we are unaccustomed to thinking about Genesis in this way. But we should not be so haughty and Augustine's point should not be so unfamiliar to us. The theme of our fickle, mysterious sexual desire has been explored in our own day by psychology; the whole idea of the subconscious mind is arguably a claim that sometimes we are mysteries to ourselves, and that our rational, willing self is not always in charge, particularly as regards sexuality. The theme of the divided will comes to the forefront in *The City of God*, for here Augustine's claim is combined with an argument about the place of sex within the human social order. His claim is that our social life is marked by chaos, and that our sexual life is a particularly apt example of this chaos at work. We ought not snicker. The fact that in addition to all that is good about sex, we also experience sex as a field of vulnerability and anxiety, that we use sex to buy and sell products, that we manipulate our desire with commercialized pharmaceuticals, and that we abuse each other and compete against each for the prizes of sexual glamour and attractiveness—all of these things are what Augustine's account of desire in the earthly city should lead us to expect.

However, this chaos and sin are not the last word—for Augustine, at least, if not for moderns. In Augustinian terms, when we marry, we ally our sexual lives with the good order which God offers to us in creation. Marriage is a way of keeping faith with the original teleology of creation, of testifying to God's goodness by subordinating our roaming desires to his original hopes for us. However, marriage is not the only way in

10. See Augustine *Confessions* §2.4.9 (29) on pears and *City of God* §6.11.20 (106) on Augustine's appetite and his inability to imagine life without an erotic partnership.

11. For example, Wallace, *For Fidelity*, whose handling of Augustine is infelicitous. She is "tempted to laugh" at him in certain respects (43).

which Augustine believes we may ally ourselves faithfully with God's designs for sexuality. In his debate with the Manichees about the goodness of creation, Augustine was led to certain anthropological conclusions which raise possibilities for celibacy and the eschatological status of sexual difference. In this debate, Augustine was led to argue that nothing "pertains more closely to a body than its sex,"[12] that bodies are "not an ornament" or a garment but "belong to the very nature of man,"[13] and that spiritual flesh is not spiritual because it is incorporeal but because it serves the spirit,[14] and so he reasons that sexual difference shall not be discarded in heaven. "He, then, who instituted two sexes will restore them both."[15] Augustine is not claiming that our restored, eschatological bodies will be the same as mortal bodies—indeed, he believes the final body will be "better then than it was here even when in perfect health; it will also be better than those bodies which the first human beings had before they sinned."[16] But because sexually differentiated embodiedness is so essential to human identity, it cannot be entirely left behind, and Augustine is lead to suggest a radically transformed eschatological body. "The sex of a woman," he writes, "is not a vice, but nature," so why should it be shed in heaven?[17] Unlike so many other ancient authorities, including Aristotle and Plato, Augustine does not believe that human nature is essentially neutral or masculine; as we have seen, he believes that there are genuinely two sexes in God's created order, and that God will always remain in solidarity with what he has made.

Celibacy arises as a testimony to the eschatological aspect of this solidarity. In addition to his various conclusions about the intimate connection between body and identity, Augustine also believes that eschatological sexual difference will not be ordered to marriage and procreation. He takes seriously Christ's claim in Luke 20 that in heaven there is no marriage; "there will be no generation there, when regeneration has led us thither."[18] In other words, sexual difference, which was significant in one way before the fall, and adapted for the situation

12. Augustine *City of God* §5.6 (195).
13. Ibid., §1.13 (22).
14. Ibid., §13.20 (566), and §22.12 (1152).
15. Ibid., §22.17 (1145).
16. Ibid., §13.20 (566), and §23 (573).
17. Ibid., §22.17 (1145).
18. Ibid., §15.17 (669).

after the fall, will be adapted yet again in the era to come. In heaven, "they [the sexual parts of a woman, but also of a man] will then be exempt from sexual intercourse and childbearing, but the female parts will nonetheless remain in being, accommodated not to the old uses, but to a new beauty, which, so far from inciting lust, which no longer exists, will move us to praise the wisdom and clemency of God. . . ."[19] Once upon a time in salvation history, sexual difference existed for marriage and procreation. But Augustine's logic and rhetoric now push him to include sexual difference amongst that which will be redeemed, making it thinkable to include it in the worship of heaven. As a consequence, we might say that Augustine has given sexual difference an inexhaustible, if shifting, *telos*. Sexual difference in heaven will no longer be an arena for competition and exploitation, and it will no longer be the occasion for marrying, and it will somehow be redesigned so that it is fully compatible with our heavenly business. Virgins, who in Augustinian thought pursue their vocation in order to be free for God, and not in flight of creation or in repudiation of marriage,[20] are thus plausibly described as being, in principle, men and women who affirm the goodness of their sex, and who patiently wait for the disclosure of how their sex will be incorporated into the heavenly city.

AUGUSTINE'S SUCCESSORS

The Augustinian tradition of moral theology about marriage is, of course, not limited to Augustine, but includes those theologians who work within his framework. In a longer essay, one could explore Augustine's major successors in the realm of moral theology about marriage—Thomas Aquinas, Martin Luther, John Calvin, Karl Barth, and John Paul II come to mind, among others. Less predictably perhaps, one might also want to include on that list theologians of erotic desire, such as Bernard of Clairvaux, who presupposed Augustine's anthropology as they ventured into commentaries on the Song of Songs.[21] But in a short essay, where one must prioritize, it is worthwhile to focus next on Barth's theology of sexual difference.

---

19. Ibid. §22.17 (1145).

20. See, for example, *De Sancta Virginitate*, especially §1 and 13.

21. I explain Bernard's views on this point in Roberts, *Creation and Covenant*, chapter 3.

Many arguments could be adduced in support of this leap. As Paul Ramsey has observed, at least until very recently, Barth and Augustine are the only two theologians who link sexuality explicitly to a Christological conception of salvation history.[22] Moreover, it is not until Barth that we find sustained, explicit, systematic discussion of sexual difference. In other words, prior to Barth, and as we saw with Augustine, theologians tend to discuss sexual difference in light of other, more primary doctrinal concerns, and, with a handful of notable exceptions, to offer their comments only in passing.[23] It seems as if the tradition after Augustine and prior to Barth was largely able to presuppose (rather than argue) the significance of sexual difference, perhaps because the Augustinian consensus was not widely disputed in the west. One might even speculate that this history of relatively implicit theology about sexual difference is one factor contributing to contemporary confusion about this topic—it is almost possible to be literate in the theological history of the west and have never read any systematic theology on this topic. In any case, with Barth one can see a new self-consciousness about the subject, and while he gives homosexuality notoriously brief and dismissive treatment, we at least begin to see some of the present era's concerns and questions explicitly brought to the fore.

BARTH'S ARGUMENT AND A NEW THEOLOGICAL EXPLICITNESS

When Barth makes his argument about sexual difference, it is dependent upon a premise which he has argued elsewhere, to the effect that Jesus Christ determines what is true about and what we can know about God, creation, and ourselves. Jesus is "the one Archimedean point given us beyond humanity" which is available for "discovering the ontological determination of man."[24] Through lengthy Christological meditations on scripture, Barth deduces that God creates for the sake of the covenant which God establishes in Christ. Barth reasons that if we are created for the sake of this relationship with God, then it is necessary that we human creatures should also be beings who engage in covenantal re-

22. Ramsey, "Human Sexuality," 84.

23. Notable exceptions include Luther's forthright statements on the theological significance of sexual difference. For discussion and references of this moment in Luther, see *Creation and Covenant*, chapter 5.

24. Barth, *Church Dogmatics* III/2, 132.

lationships amongst ourselves. The God we meet in Christ, the "Deus triunus," cannot have, as a covenant partner, a "homo solitarius,"[25] i.e., an essentially atomized creature who is not structured for sustained, committed I-Thou relations. "God is in relationship, and so too is the man created by him. This is his divine likeness."[26]

In light of this anthropological premise, a wide field of human relationships suggest themselves as ripe for theological exploration. Barth has a great deal to say about the implications of his anthropology for relations between parents and children,[27] and with our near and distant neighbours in our own culture and in distant lands.[28] However, throughout all of his anthropological discussions, Barth maintains the distinctiveness of male-female relations as the only irreversible structural human differentiation.[29] By this he means that the male-female relationship is the basic differentiation which makes humanity ontologically determined to be co-humanity; this difference is uniquely prior to the other differences and it is the one difference which is inevitably "one long reference to the relationship."[30] It is inescapable, because one cannot refer to humanity without saying "male or female" and therefore "male and female."[31] Other apparent human differences (such as race) are only based on or derived from this structure,[32] and our relations with our neighbours are fluid and provisional.[33] In and amongst the many ways in which humans are beings in relationship, sexual difference abides and has a ubiquity which other human differences do not. Barth is certainly prepared to say that there are many other types of significant human relationship in addition to sexually differentiated ones, but he insists that there is always this one too. "Man never exists as such, but always as the human male or the human female."[34]

25. Ibid., III/4, 117.
26. Ibid., III/2, 324.
27. Ibid., III/4, 240–85.
28. Ibid., III/4, 285–323.
29. Ibid., III/4, 117.
30. Ibid., III/4, 117.
31. Ibid., III/2, 286.
32. Ibid.
33. Ibid., III/4, 302.
34. Ibid., III/4, 117.

This point is made most forcefully in Barth's discussion of the *imago dei*. "By the divine likeness of man in Genesis 1:27ff. there is to be understood the fact that God created them male and female, corresponding to the fact that God Himself exists in relationship and not in isolation."[35] In the man-woman relation, a human is called to be a Thou to another human and therefore "an I in responsibility to this claim."[36] For Barth, the *imago dei* is not found by searching for some inner disposition or possession which separates humanity from other creatures. "It is not in something which distinguishes him from the beasts, but in that which formally he has in common with them, viz. that God has created him male and female, that he is this being in differentiation and relationship, and therefore in natural fellowship with God."[37] It is on the occasion of the biological difference between male and female, which is in itself not unique to humans, that God speaks to men and women and calls them into a distinctively human relationship which will model his own being as I and Thou. What humanity has in common with the animals is the prototypical site for God's inimitable summons to come and emulate his own divine way of life.

Barth reasons that if we are commanded to emulate God's being-in-relationship in and through our sexual differences, then the relationship itself—the actual encounter between male and female, i.e., the meeting, confrontation and discovery of whatever is non-interchangeable between the sexes—is the theologically significant aspect. No qualities which might be imputed to either sex are at stake. The significance of sexual difference therefore cannot and should not be expressed in terms of social roles or biological functions; sexual difference is not theologically significant because masculinity and femininity are complementary in some psychological sense, or because it is through maleness and femaleness that our species procreates. Instead, Barth says the significance of sexual difference is expressed in the "conjunction and inter-relatedness of man as male and female which cannot be defined as an existing quality or intrinsic capacity, possibility or structure of his being, but which simply occur[s]. In this relationship which is absolutely given and posited there is revealed freedom and therefore the divine likeness."[38] That the

35. Ibid.
36. III/1, 198.
37. III/1, 185.
38. III/1, 195.

relationship between male and female may occur, that the juxtaposition and encounter should and does happen, is God's gift, determination, and command to humanity, but what the content of this relationship will be, what men and women should do as they confront one another and live together, is left up to actual men and women to discover and unfold.

This rationale means that while there are certain guidelines for discerning the command of God in any particular encounter between the sexes, the actual content of sexual differences is left perhaps shockingly open-ended. Man and woman cannot repudiate their creatureliness and resent the call to engage as a man or a woman with the other sex, but beyond that, Barth is wary of prescribing or defining in advance what it means to be male in relation to female, or female in relation to male:

> Our present concern is not with the physiology and psychology of the sexes, and we shall not attempt to describe their distinctive structure. But we may perhaps be permitted to issue the following warning . . . it is much better if we avoid such generalised pronouncements as that man's interests are more outward and objective and woman's inward and subjective. . . . Statements such as these may sometimes be ventured as hypotheses, but cannot be represented as knowledge or dogma because real man and real woman are far too complex. . . . [I]n what the strength and precedence consists on the one side, and the weakness and subsequence on the other, what it means that man is the head of woman and not *vice versa*, is something which is better left unresolved in a general statement, and value-judgements must certainly be resisted. . . . What distinguishes man from woman and woman from man even in this relationship of super- and subordination is more easily discovered, perceived, respected and valued in the encounter between them than it is defined.[39]

In other words, Barth does not want to venture beyond where his theological premises entitle him to go. He is not interested in having a theory of the sexes which will answer all questions one might have about sexual life; he is interested in asking how a God whose being is relational can be analogized in a creature who is made by that God to be relational in its sexual difference. In short, whatever Barth feels able to say about the content of sexual differences will always be disciplined by his doctrine of God and that doctrine's consequences.

39. III/2, 287.

If we will follow Barth in submitting to that discipline, the logic of traditional sexual ethics can perhaps be heard with fresh ears. Because God's way of relating to humanity is by means of a covenant, it follows that human relations, and specifically male-female relations, will also turn on the question of covenant. For Barth, the question of sexual difference is bigger than marriage, and hence marriage can never be compulsory, but nevertheless the male-female relation has "its crown and centre in the question of marriage."[40] He says that the male-female encounter is only fully realized "where there is the special connexion of one man loving this woman and one woman loving this man in free choice and with a view to a full life-partnership."[41] God's covenant does not exist provisionally, in the hope or expectation that God's creatures will be other than what we are, or that God might find some more attractive or interesting partner to take our place in the covenant. To live in the arena of transient, experimental, conditional relationships means that one has not yet really begun to love on Christological grounds.[42]

However, as with Augustine, a man or a woman need not marry in order to affirm the nuptial teleology of sexual difference. Barth specifically rejects the proposition that procreative marriage is a "better state, more pleasing and possibly alone pleasing to God."[43] He insists that viable responses to sexual difference exist for the permanently unmarried. Barth says the decision to marry "is not open to each individual, and there are reasons why it is open to many not to do so."[44] The unmarried

> are still men and therefore male or female, male and female. . . . Here again we must allow ourselves to be led out into the open by the divine command, not being diverted from the special problem of marriage, but considering it together with the problem of male and female as it exists and requires to be solved even outside marriage.[45]

Even those outside marriage "share in the fellow-humanity which is implicit in the dualism of male and female and has its goal in marriage."[46]

40. III/4, 118.

41. III/2, 288.

42. III/4, 195.

43. III/4, 141.

44. III/4, 140.

45. III/4, 140–41.

46. III/4, 142.

For Barth, it is not that marriage is compulsory; rather, it is compulsory that each man and woman consider the possibility that God might be calling him or her to marriage, and that they order their lives in ways which testify towards the goodness of marriage.

As with Augustine, celibacy is the vocation which enables testimony to the goodness of marriage and the two sexes without actually marrying. Barth's account of sexual difference enables Christians to imagine faithful ways of belonging together as male and female which are neither transient nor marital. On this line of thought, continence ought to be construed as a discipline embraced in order to enable a certain type of community, a social life which is premised on solidarity between men and women and consequently repudiates sexual exploitation. In this community, men and women premise their social relations on being men and women, i.e., they do not organise themselves as if they preferred an androgynous humanity. Yet in this sexually differentiated community, sexual desire and lust are restrained and not permitted to dominate interpersonal relations. This solidarity aspires to transcend concupiscence and romantic approaches to solving the problem of aloneness. The chaste community life of unmarried Christians demonstrates that our faith rejects cultish eroticism; in chaste community life, we see that our faith denounces the false belief that salvation comes from the fulfilment of genitalized longing. Like any sensitive person in a good marriage in the fallen world, healthy celibates are alert to the possibilities of sexual tension with many potential partners, but by abstaining from conditional, temporary sexual liaisons, celibates and married Christians alike can testify that Godly eros is faithfully and fully manifested only within covenants. This should be good news for men and women who are not married, for this discipline frees their life together from the caprice and competitiveness of the sexual marketplace. It is this type of freedom which can be conceptualized when everyone lives under the call and sign of marriage, but is not necessarily compelled to marry.

If we understand this logic, then it becomes more understandable why Barth's discussion of homosexuality is notoriously brief, and occupies only one page out of the many hundreds of pages which he devotes to sexual difference. In this discussion, Barth acknowledges what he calls the potential of homosexuality to be "redolent of sanctity."[47] One could push Barth on this point, and imagine that Barth is crediting homosex-

47. III/4, 166.

ual relationships for their capacity to be dedicated, profound, and rooted in friendship. A relationship does not need sexual difference to practice these virtues. In fact, superficially, these traits might be taken to resemble the Christian idea of covenant. One can certainly imagine that, in some circumstances, a sexual minority (e.g., homosexuals who live together in life-long partnerships) might learn to practice these virtues in ways which rebuke the hypocrisy of some sexual majorities (e.g., heterosexuals who practice so-called "serial monogamy").

But Barth nevertheless condemns homosexual relationships, seeing in them at least an implicit refusal of his claim that each man or woman has a vocation with respect to the other sex. It is not, in particular, an attack on homosexuality, for Barth critiques same-sex religious orders, "ladies' circles," and any intention to permanently segregate the sexes on the same grounds.[48] For Barth, any attempt, either as a group or a couple, to create a fellowship without the other sex is a de-humanising attempt at self-sovereignty, for such attempts refuse the command of God to fulfil one's co-humanity with the opposite sex.[49] God has created humanity with a specific determination, and man "can forget it. He can misconstrue it. He can despise it. He can scorn and dishonour it. But he cannot slough it off or break free from it. Humanity is not an ideal which he can accept or discard, or a virtue which he can practice or not practice."[50] In other words, in Barth's account, homosexuality must be rejected as an impossible attempt at self-rule; self-rule, however, is not peculiar to gay people; it is a temptation to which all of us are prone. It was, we should recall, the very foundation of Augustine's earthly city. In this analysis, homosexuality is only one manifestation of a universal spiritual problem, a point that bears emphasis in situations where homophobia and hysteria create obstacles to sensitive, humane, and patient pastoral responses.

A CHRISTIAN THEOLOGY OF SEXUAL DIFFERENCE

If, then, we are thinking in the terms of this ancient Christian tradition, we might offer a general casuistry of sex by saying that in the panoply of sexual possibilities, an act is always to be assessed through questions deriving from Christological anthropology. As Barth would explain it,

48. III/4, 165.

49. cf. III/4, 166.

50. III/2, 285.

the "command of God is not concerned" with "sexual organs and needs as such but only as they exist in the order and sequence of the rest of" the human being.[51] In this reading of Christian ethics, humanity never belongs to itself and is never seen in isolation. From Augustine onwards, God's creation of the two sexes for mutual participation in God's covenant is the inevitable and inexorable background. Theologically-speaking, promiscuous heterosexual relations and monogamous homosexual relations can now be seen to point to a single problem. They may seem different in that homosexual relations fail to honor creation and promiscuous heterosexual relations fail to honor covenant, but creation and covenant are two sides of the same ontological coin.

It is important to emphasize, then, that this theology of sexual difference intends to be evangelical. The proper work of the church is to enable all humanity to render praise, thanks and obedience to God in all aspects of life. To fulfil these tasks, to be glad of being male and female, to be gracious to one another as male and female, is the *telos* implicit in Christian marriage and celibacy, at least in this tradition of moral theology in the west. It is not as if the most noteworthy theologians in the tradition, such as Augustine and Barth, agree on every detail. But they share this basic teleology, which has always been latent in this strand of Christian theology about marriage with varying degrees of explicitness. Everything which Christians say or do in the sexual sphere should be transparent to this premise. When traditional Christians say "no" to contemporary construals of homosexuality, it should only be in order to say "yes" to their own proposals for the theological significance of sexual difference. The churches should be in the business of inviting men and women to discover the exciting good news implicit in having been created as male and female; the churches should focus their attention on finding ways to render their invitation plausible and attractive. Among other things, renewed awareness of the traditional significance of sexual difference probably warrants heightened attention to the viability of celibacy (and in distinction from the question of celibacy and holy orders) as a common Christian vocation, which would, in turn, probably revolutionize most congregational assumptions about marriage, romance, courtship, and living arrangements for unmarried adults.

Perhaps the first step in this revolution should be epistemological. Just as the young Augustine, who once, reflecting on his own intense

51. III/4, 132.

appetites, was unable to imagine life without a concubine,[52] young Christians find it hard to imagine that a call to celibacy or any other type of chaste living is "good news" unless they are already convinced, as Augustine came to be, that their identity is truly disclosed only in the heavenly city. Augustine ultimately embraced a coherent sexual ethic only after accepting the premise that creation has the teleology of an eternal social life with God. Likewise, Barth did not offer prescriptions for Christian living until after establishing the Christological premise of creation for covenant. Christian dating and courtship, among other things, therefore need to take place against a similar epistemological background. Even then, the slow work of patterning our sexual lives in holy ways is usually a process that requires patience, support, prayer, confession, accountability, and a sense of humor. But the key first step is committing to the idea that one's identity is hidden in Christ (Col 3:3). For the Christian discerning whether, when, and whom to marry, these questions must be asked within the context of an overall apprenticeship in ecclesial living. To become who we are called to become, in the sexual aspect of life as in any other, cannot be a matter of private ambition and individual choice, for those horizons lack theological accountability. Sub-theological horizons and criteria suggest that one's conversion to Christianity is not yet complete. One must use a Christological perspective to judge and assess whatever other culturally-grounded techniques for sexual selection might be available. The modern individual selecting a mate on the basis of romantic appetite, or the member of a traditional clan selecting a mate on the basis of a family alliance—a Christian living in either situation would need to reconsider his or her options in ecclesial and eschatological perspective. All cultural systems of sexual selection cultivate the imagination, and provide participants with a horizon of expectations, hopes, and desires. It is this horizon of aspiration and intention which a Christian epistemology should interrogate and critique. Do my living arrangements make chastity easier or harder? Does my manner of being masculine or feminine testify to the goodness of God's creation? Do I have the kinds of friends who are interested in helping and deepening the life of prayer? Does the media which I read or watch cultivate my Christian identity or subvert it? Is my church offering opportunities for friendship, opportunities which make Christian interdependence tangible? Are my choices premised on demonstrating

---

52. See above, note 10.

thanksgiving for God's gifts? Such questions are the logical and necessary second step if one has already committed to knowing one's personal sexual vocation in Christian terms.

Such questions transform the inevitable asceticism and struggle of sexual holiness. Without a Christological perspective, one might experience chastity as a recipe for resentment. One might begrudge surrendering what our culture assumes are sexual entitlements. But the right theological perspective can transform such asceticism into growth in holiness and love, a true adventure of joy.

A BRIEF CRITIQUE OF REVISIONIST THEOLOGIES

Renewed familiarity with the traditional theology of sexual difference also helps to reveal the novelty and inadequacies of contemporary theologies which would propose something like marriages for homosexuals. Typically, these revisionists theologies emphasize the covenantal aspects of marriage while de-emphasizing the creation aspects. They propose that marriage is meant to be a covenant between two people, who, through the *ascesis* of their fidelity and dwelling-together, come to learn more and more about God's faithfulness and extravagant love for them.[53] To the extent that they root themselves in the doctrine of creation at all, it tends to be in order to associate themselves with the claim that "it is not good that humans should be alone."[54] If that is indeed the *telos* of marriage, then the evangelical thing to do is to prepare the way for homosexual marriage. The two characters in a marriage need not be sexually differentiated in order to keep one another company in ways "redolent of sanctity."

However, having studied the traditional moral theology of marriage, we can now realize that this revisionist marital teleology would appear to overlook the way in which marriage has been the fruit and consequence of a particular theological anthropology. Traditionally, male and female are theologically significant for our bodies and our identity, and so, seeking a way to render God thanks, praise, and obedience in this area of our lives, Christians discern whether they are called to marriage or celibacy. Sexual difference creates the question and pos-

---

53. Eugene Rogers's book, *Sexuality and the Christian Body*, is probably the most pre-eminent and persuasive of these theologies. I discuss Rogers's proposals in detail, as well as two other revisionist theologies, in *Creation and Covenant*, chapter 8.

54. Glossing Gen 2:18; see, for example, Warner, "Living by the Word," 18.

sibility that one might be called to marry. But in the revisionist theology of marriage, male and female can be only idiosyncratically significant; the existence of the opposite sex is, in principle, irrelevant. Whether one needs a member of the opposite sex for a spouse is entirely contingent on one's private erotic appetites. In this situation, sexual difference is no longer a theologically significant aspect of God's good creation. Sexual difference would presumably become something like eye colour or hair or muscular build, which, while being a feature of our good bodies which has aesthetic significance to some people, is not necessarily significant in the drama of salvation history.

It is, of course, possible that the revisionist theories of sexual difference are correct and that the arguments and presuppositions of the tradition are wrong. Arguments are not coherent and true merely because they are traditional. That question probably cannot be settled in an essay as brief as this one. But we can conclude with one observation: if the revisionists are correct, it creates a curious diastasis between Christian and natural epistemologies of sexual difference. Consider that evolutionary biologists seem to have concluded that if one considers the immanent and material ordering of life from an immanent and material perspective, i.e., on the basis of a natural and non-theological epistemology, sexual difference has a way of asserting its significance. The biologists say that sexual difference is a powerful and basic feature of our identity, shaping psychological and physiological factors not only at the species level, but in individuals as well. On the terms of the traditional Christian view, one is not surprised to hear biologists saying these things. Since Augustine, the theological tradition has been clear, for theological reasons, that the immanent and material world is given by God for good and significant purposes. The created order therefore has an integrity and ontological distinctness from God which renders it susceptible to immanent and material study. If, for their own reasons, Darwinian biologists also reach the conclusion that sexual difference is significant, that should not be shocking. Reality is reality, and certain aspects of creation are there to be discovered, even if the theological teleology of that reality cannot be evident in Darwinian terms.

But the biological significance of sexual difference, as deduced and explained by natural knowledge, puts the revisionist theologians of today in an awkward situation. They are, of course, free to offer theological reasons for minimizing the theological significance of sexual difference.

Their success or failure depends upon their theological coherence, and not their correlation with evolutionary biology. Nevertheless, if the revisionist case as it currently stands were to succeed, and if Christianity is to withdraw its claim that an apparently basic feature of human biology is also spiritually significant and necessary for the work of all persons in the church, then does it not seem that we have taken an implicit step towards disassociating our redemption from the tangible and material world in which we live? Scientists will tell us that strong and compelling forces, arising from the fact of sexual difference, tend to shape human behaviour and culture. Meanwhile, theologians will be in the position of saying that these same sexual differences are only personally significant on an idiosyncratic and ad hoc basis. It is perhaps conceivable that such diastases between scientific and theological accounts of reality could exist, but it would fly in the face of what the traditional theological argument has led us to expect.

It also seems odd that theologians would want to withdraw claims for the universal theological significance of sexual difference, particularly when one considers that the world which the biologists present is so often bleak and uninviting. For instance, scientists report that many primates tend to live in violent societies of intense competition between males for mates; the males form coalitions to dominate and co-opt weaker males to serve the possessiveness and territoriality of stronger males, and the females, if they have any influence at all, can only respond with strategies which adapt to this hierarchy.[55] From a purely evolutionary and genetic perspective such societies seem to be successful, and, from a Darwinian point of view, one has no grounds for complaint. Here we have a situation in which sexual difference is significant, but in which there seems to be little gospel. If one wants to object to such an order for life, and declare the gospel with regards to biology, then surely it is helpful to have an account of how real flesh and blood sexual difference somehow features and has a purchase in the Christian account of reality. The Christian tradition has had such an account, and it is this account which the revisionists appear to want to dismantle.

The Christian tradition, as explained in this essay, includes a redemptive vision for sexual difference. The Christian tradition acknowledges the power and force of sexual difference to organize a society and a person. It accounts for that power on its own theological terms,

55. Geary, Male, Female, 84–95.

explaining a creation, a fall, and a route towards redemption. But to offer this vision, it does not make fickle desire the premise of who we marry. Neither does it point to the world of biological research, selfish genes, and competitive mating strategies. The Christian tradition can account for desire, pleasure, biology, selfishness, competition, and mating, but without relying on any of those things for its premise. Instead, Christianity traditionally proclaims that God offers us a promise about sexual difference, an alternative history in which sexual difference was made for Christological purposes. It is this alternative vision, this prophetic announcement that sexual difference can, should and will mean something other than its fallen versions, which is obscured in the revisionist proposals for homosexual marriage, and which would be lost if they prevail in their current guise.

BIBLIOGRAPHY

Augustine. *The City of God against the Pagans.* Translated by R. W. Dyson. Cambridge: Cambridge University Press, 1998.

———. *Confessions.* Translated by Henry Chadwick. Oxford: Oxford University Press, 1998.

Banner, Michael. "Sexualitat." In *Theologische Realenzyklopadie,* 195–214. Berlin: Walter de Gruyter, 2000.,

Barth, Karl. *Church Dogmatics.* III/1: *The Doctrine of Creation.* Translated by J. W. Edwards et al. Edinburgh: T. & T. Clark, 1958.

———. *Church Dogmatics III/2: The Doctrine of Creation,* trans. H. Knight, et al. Edinburgh: T. & T. Clark, 1960.

———. *Church Dogmatics III/4: The Doctrine of Creation,* trans. A.T. Mackay, et al. Edinburgh: T. & T. Clark, 1961.

Geary, David C. *Male, Female: The Evolution of Human Sex Differences.* Washington, DC: American Psychological Association, 1998.

Ramsey, Paul. "Human Sexuality in the History of Redemption." *Journal of Religious Ethics* 16 (1988) 56–88.

Rogers, Eugene. *Sexuality and the Christian Body: Their Way into the Triune God.* Oxford: Blackwell, 1999.

Roberts, Christopher C. *Creation and Covenant: The Significance of Sexual Difference in the Moral Theology of Marriage.* New York: T. & T. Clark, 2007.

Wallace, Catherine. *For Fidelity: How Intimacy and Commitment Enrich our Lives.* New York: Knopf, 1998.

Warner, Andrew. "Living by the Word." *Christian Century* 123:20 (2006) 18–19.

Woodhead, Linda. "Woman/Femininity." In *The Oxford Companion to Christian Thought,* edited by Adrian Hastings et al., 755–57. Oxford: Oxford University Press, 2000.

Lightning Source UK Ltd.
Milton Keynes UK
UKOW04f1345111214

242950UK00002B/52/P